Contents

FOREWORD

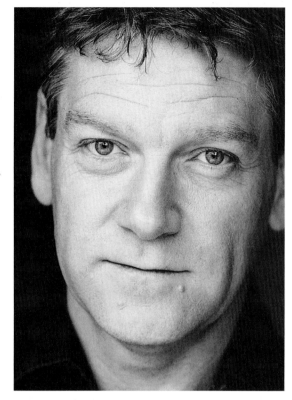

The history of dramatic art is both exciting and extraordinary, and Neil Fraser's splendid book certainly provides a vivid blend of these elements. Neil imbues the story of over two thousand years of performance with the fastidious eye of someone who has also enjoyed every moment of his own professional explorations.

Stage productions are about the vitality and truthfulness of live performances – the real re-made before our eyes. But in fact, whether the performance is conveyed to us on stage or on screen, all of us who love the imaginative quality of brilliant, unexpected and emotionally-telling drama know that, when it is superbly done, it makes for an unforgettable experience.

Dramatic work, as actor, director or writer, is an act of creativity that is quintessentially bound to the very moment in time within which it is conceived. The work should aspire to be honest, robust, and contemporary. Importantly it should talk of who we are now; and this remains true whether we are producing a new work or one by Sophocles or Shakespeare. The moment of creativity can also be enriched by a knowledge of all that has preceded it both historically and dramatically, and it is valuable to understand it well within such contexts.

Books such as this one can only add to our knowledge and to our ability to create drama from an informed position. As an introduction to a complex and wondrous story I am happy to recommend it to you.

KENNETH BRANAGH

INTRODUCTION

The instinct for imitation is inherent in man.
ARISTOTLE

This book is aimed at providing the reader with a detailed introduction to the history of theatre. In many ways it is a testament to man's long-lived imagination. For theatre as we understand it today is, if nothing else, an art form that deals with wonder, with the creation of a fragile truth that is constantly changing; that holds, as Shakespeare would have it, 'a mirror up to nature', but is yet also strangely unreal, much as the common usage of the term 'theatrical' surely tells us.

Theatre can be the very essence of excitement and, at its best, theatre engages us in a manner that film and television can never hope to. Echoing Shakespeare, the madman philosopher of the avant-garde Antonin Artaud described theatre as 'life's double'. He also bestowed on it the same savage potential to change us as he saw in the ravaging plagues of the nineteenth century.

Theatre is also often said to be a cathartic experience, and this catharsis possibly a fundamental reason for its abiding appeal. By being able to watch and experience the escapades of others from a relatively safe standpoint, we learn and grow, both emotionally and intellectually, without undue suffering.

Theatre is a collaborative art and can take many forms. Many people come together to make it, the playwright (when there is one) is merely the initiator of an often complex process. The audience plays a part in this collaboration that is unique in the arts. Each performance of every play is different from night to night, from production to production, and from generation to generation. Exploring how this works, and how this came to be is the purpose of this book.

Generally speaking this book is laid out in chronological order, and looks at the history of theatre by studying the work of the major playwrights in each generation. Of course history is never tidy and the practitioners of this often extravagant art form often resist definition by period or style. Certainly, although set out in a rough chronology, this does not mean the theatre of today is superior to that of yesterday. The Romans looked back on the Greek theatre of circa 600BC as a golden age, and we can still make a case for the great plays of that period as having never been bettered.

Ancient and modern influences often played equal roles in the reinvention of dramatic style needed to keep theatre alive through the years. In this way the early innovators of the twentieth century looked to the spirit of the, so-called, primitive performances of Bali or Mexico. Jerzy Growtovski and Peter Brook sought to pare away the inherited trappings of tradition, the latter describing the poetic simplicity of the 'empty space'.

The last one hundred years or so of human experience have seen a profound diversity of exploration in many fields, and drama is not absent from the list. It is this exploration that feeds immediately in to the theatre that we have around us today and thus roughly half of this book details this explosion of styles and discoveries. All this, and much more, is explored in the pages to come.

One of the terms discussed in what follows is that of 'naturalism'. It is illustrative to understand that when the great explorers in theatre of this period – Stanislavsky, Chekhov, Ibsen amongst them – used this term they were rebelling against a kind of theatre which even in its time had set out to establish a new reality on stage, and in doing so supplanted that which had proceeded it. For all great theatre, in one way or another, is revolutionary and looks to create change – in the individual if not in society. But theatre also seeks to relate to the audience it serves. Because only by making this most basic of connections does theatre succeed.

Greek masks of comedy and tragedy.
(From original drawings of the period.)

1 GREEK AND ROMAN THEATRE

Drama ... an imitation of action, not the thing itself.
ARISTOTLE

THE THEATRE OF ANCIENT GREECE

Standing in the shimmering brightness of a Greek hill-side, the hot sun burning down, fellow workers are busy around you. The newly harvested wheat has been brought for winnowing, and it is thrown to and fro across the sandy floor, allowing the warm wind to sep-arate chaff from grain. The area on which you stand has been designed by circumstance over centuries to aid this process, and is wide, circular and flat. It has also found a use as a central meeting place for the village, for religious ceremony, and in some places it is also where the first performances of what is to become theatre are to take place. You wipe the sweat from your brow with the back of your arm, taking a final good look around you before bending back to the work.

The Origins of Ancient Greek Theatre

Whether in Athens or Alexandria, or the towns of Bali, Mexico, China or India, drama arose from the sacrificial fires of ancient religions. Greek theatre was born of the same need to imitate life, to tell sto-ries, and to support religious ceremony, as has been the case with all early dramatic art.

It would seem that the desire to imitate and per-form is innate within the human psyche. Ancient Greek life was particularly rich in myths and leg-ends, and it is thus not surprising that it came to lend itself so well to dramatic expression – but a dramatic expression so distant in time that unfor-tunately many of its methods and details are lost to us, hidden behind the mists of the intervening cen-turies. Yet so vital was the experience it afforded, that much has been handed down or left for us to subsequently unearth.

The role of 'drama' in the ancient Greek culture was a specific one: it played a significant part in the religious rites of the period. Like many things human,

the theatre of ancient Greece would appear to have started simply, perhaps as nothing more than a sin-gle voice, one speaking in oration as part of a reli-gious ceremony.

At which point the 'drama' became clearly sep-arated from its ritualized origins is impossible to say, although it would certainly have been a grad-ual process. We can imagine its progress perhaps like this: the earliest 'prototype' dramatic works of ancient Greece would have started even before the single voice took hold, using a group of priests chanting or speaking as a chorus. It was from this group of probably choreographed performers that an individual performer was found. To begin with the solo voice is perhaps simply announcing a part of the ritual, then maybe it is explaining it. Next it may be telling the story behind the rite, and finally we find it taking on the persona of a 'character' from the religion itself, extolling the watchers to worship.

Dramatic Dinosaurs

Our knowledge of Greek theatre bears comparison to that of the dinosaur. From one perspective it appears we know a lot about these ancient beasts. From their remains, we know their shape and size, many of their habits and how they evolved. Yet again, there are huge gaps in our knowledge – even something as fundamental as what colour they were. This analogy is particularly apt because whilst we still have some texts from the ancient Greek world, precisely how ancient Greek theatre was performed, and how it looked, is mostly lost.

7

The early dramatic forms described above should not be considered naïve in any way: they simply represented the best form for the kind of ritual presentation required at the time. When eventually a second solo voice was added, this was not because a third was not thought of, but because it was simply not required at that time.

Initially the drama of this period, that told a simple narrative story or described an event, did so in the form of a highly rhythmic poem, written in verse, and involving music and dance. Of particular relevance here are the ceremonies connected with the worship of Dionysis: they involved a chorus of fifty men singing a hymn in unison – a *dithyramb* – and connect directly to the earliest known dramatic works, which also involved a chorus of fifty men.

Early forms were quite probably all sung, and developed into a mixture of spoken episodes punctuated with sung choruses or odes. Later forms added 'actors' because the need was then for greater characterization, for conflict, and thus plot. The chorus was also reduced in number, and then in importance. By the period of the first of the great Greek dramatists – Aeschylus, for example – the chorus had been reduced to twelve.

The Development of the Play Form

The stories of these plays, originating as they did in religious rites, concern themselves with myth and ancient history. As characterization and plot developed, the role given to the individual strengthened, although it still mostly dwelt in their being caught in the inexorable machinations of fate. Most of the real action of each play happens off-stage – for example Oedipus's blinding and Jocasta's suicide in *Oedipus Rex* (*see* page 17): on stage these events are described and reacted to, in themselves they were considered unseemly and not to be displayed.

The themes of ancient Greek drama are those of divine law, free will, fate, justice and retribution. In the case of many of the tragic heroes the greatest sin is that of *hubris*, which can be defined as an arrogant pride or presumption: it is this flaw in Agamemnon, in Clytemnestra, in Electra and in many more, that leads to their downfall. In many ways the epic nature of these works seems to belie the fact that they deal with the often ironic, if not

unfair way that fate plays with us as individuals, asking the question who is really master of his own fate? From a modern viewpoint it does seem unfair that the destiny handed out to Oedipus or to Heracles is such that they can be said to have blindly, and thus unknowingly, entered into it – whereas the fate meted out to Antigone or Medea for their actions seems fully justified, their sins self-inflicted. This moral 'cause and effect' view of the narrative was not, of course, how the Greeks themselves would have seen these familiar stories, it being, as we have said, much too modern a viewpoint.

The chorus remains a common factor in Greek theatre, preparing the audience for what is about to happen, and delivering exposition on what has just taken place. However, we do not know if the members of the chorus always spoke as one, in unison, or shared the words among their number.

In common with all early Western societies, a male-dominated society dictated that all actors were men, and this continued to be true throughout the history of ancient Greek theatre – indeed, throughout theatre history generally. Women on the stages of certain Eastern cultures (India and early Japan, for example) and in ancient Rome were seen as dancers rather than actors. This remained generally true until around the middle of the seventeenth century, when finally women began to represent themselves on stage.

Masks we know were used, but not always – and when, how and why is mostly lost to us, so we can only make an educated guess. We do know from their design, however, that they were over-sized in order to better express and convey the characteristics and emotions of characters in the large theatres. Of course they allowed a single performer to play many parts, and they were also often designed to help project the voice, like a megaphone loud hailer.

Costumes appear to have been versions of the normal Greek dress of the period, although they became more and more exaggerated with time. However, with the use of masks, and with formalized movement, dance and singing, it is likely that ancient Greek theatre would have appeared closer to our understanding of opera than to that of theatre.

As indicated at the beginning of this chapter, it is likely that the Greek stage developed from an already

Greek-style masks in use in a modern production.

available space – the threshing floor on a hillside that in turn had become a place for religious ceremony. The stage thus derived from a simple, flat and circular space, with an altar in the centre and spectator space around it. In time the spectator space became restricted to a smaller arc, and an 'up stage' area developed to accommodate 'off stage' storage of props, masks, costumes and stage machines; this also served as a simple unchanging backdrop to the action. These ancient sites have been found to have near-perfect acoustics, a good example being Epidaurus on the Corinthian peninsular.

Many words familiar to us in modern theatre herald from this era, including the word 'theatre' itself. The word 'scene' comes from 'skene', as applied to the tiring house behind the stage, 'orchestra' from the area in front of the skene, and so on.

Tragedy

The word 'tragedy' comes from the Greek word for goat – *tragos*. Originally it was thought that this was because the winner of the annual dramatic competition was awarded a goat! Today, however, it is thought more probable that it comes from either the fact that early dramatic performers wore goatskins, or that the forerunner of Greek dramatic song was sung on the sacrifice of a goat.

Stage machinery was used to place and remove bodies, and to lower gods and goddesses. The term *deus ex machina* comes from this period, its literal meaning of 'god from the machine' applying to the use of these simple mechanical devices – for example, the arrival of Dyonisis at the conclusion of Euripides'

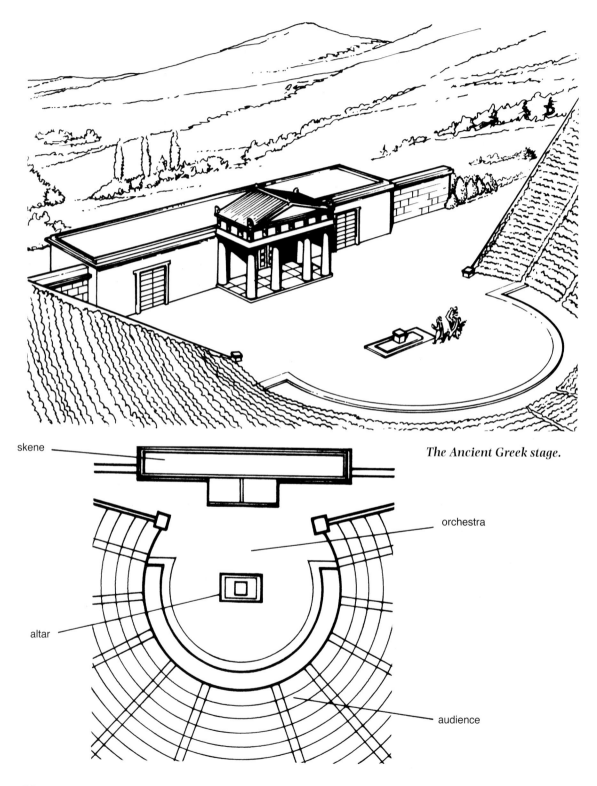

The Ancient Greek stage.

skene

orchestra

altar

audience

tragedy *The Bacchae*. In time this phrase grew to mean any resolution of a play by the intervention of an artificial outside agency, and we still use it today.

A typical Greek theatre stage would have been roughly 20m across, and the auditorium would have seated between ten to twenty thousand spectators – a huge proportion of the surrounding population. Dramatic competitions would therefore have witnessed the biggest annual gathering of humanity in the world at that time, second only to that of the four-yearly Olympic games. The event would have begun at dawn and lasted throughout the daylight hours.

Playwrights and Actors

Each annual competition was between the work of three playwrights. Many Greek playwrights are known from the competition records, including: Mestatos; Agathon who is recorded as writing plays called *Antheus* and *Women at the Thesmorphria*; Ion of Chios; Choerilus from whom only two quotations survive; and Phrynichus who wrote *Capture of Miletus* and *Phoenician Women*. Of all these artists it can be said that whilst we know of their work, unfortunately it has not survived. Of those scripts that have come down the years to us we are particularly indebted to the statesman Lycurgus who, in 330BC, established a library of the official editions of the three great Greek tragedians.

The earliest recorded theatre practitioner of ancient Greece was Thespis who, in 534BC, is mentioned as the first winner of the competition for the performance of tragic plays. This competition was instigated by the Athenian leader Peisistratus. Little else is known of Thespis – it is not even clear if he was an actor, a playwright, a priest, or all, or only some of these! His name, however, lives on in the word 'Thespian'.

Ancient Greek actor in costume (from original artwork of the period).

Ekkyklema

Alongside all the theatrical words that have come down to us from the world of ancient Greece there are some that have only caused us total confusion. Such is the term 'Ekkyklema', which has caused great consternation amongst scholars. It translates as 'wheel-out', and may have been some kind of technical device; suggestions include: a movable platform, a stage cart, a couch on wheels and even a grouping of the chorus. But literally, we simply haven't got a clue!

One aspect of ancient Greek theatre is the obvious development of the work with time. The style of the dramatic performance changed over the years, and in particular as it was handed down from practitioner to practitioner, and playwright to playwright. We know that those that followed called the heyday of Greek theatre the 'Golden Age', and that this coincided with the rise of Athens as a political and cultural centre.

The type of competitions that Thespis won can be said to define this 'Golden Age', and all extant plays, and our knowledge of the playwrights that wrote them and of the general workings of Greek theatre, come from the Athenian competitions of this period, roughly 500–400BC. Among these playwrights Aeschylus, Sophocles and Euripides seem to have been among the most revered, and clearly this is not the judgement of time alone because even as early as 405BC Aristophanes in his play *Frogs* is proclaiming their superiority (*see* page 23). From probably well over one thousand plays written in this era, only their work has survived: just over thirty plays. Consequently it is this body of work that has come to define what we know of ancient Greek theatre.

For competition, ancient Greek tragedies were written in threes, plus an additional single comic play; the three plays had a connecting theme or storyline, and the comic piece was called a satyr play, and was played after the trilogy. Only one such

An Ancient Greek Satyr (from original art work of the period).

trilogy, although not its satyr, has survived: it comprises the last of Aeschylus' surviving plays – *Agamemnon*, *The Libation Bearers* and *The Eumenides*. These plays have as their central character Orestes, and are thus usually known as the Oresteian Trilogy, or the Oresteia (*see* page 14).

The only complete satyr play that posterity has left us is *Cyclops* by Euripides (*see* page 20), although two other notable extracts have survived from *Net Drawers* by Aeschylus and *Trackers* by Sophocles. These dramas dealt with the more sensual and basic elements of human existence – namely food, drink and lust – and must have acted to 'sugar the pill' of a tragic trilogy, coming as they did at the end, and thus sending the audience away in a generally less downhearted mood. Satyrs were mythical followers of Dionysus, again strengthening the link with drama and the rites of this God – and as the illustration shows, satyrs were of a rather base nature!

Satyr plays would often take up the story and themes of the trilogy that came before them (they were of course written by the same playwright), and burlesque them. They contained vigorous dancing, vulgar expressions, and on occasion quite possibly featured incidents that the puritanical would have no hesitation in describing as quite indecent!

Aeschylus (525–456BC)

Born at Eleusis outside Athens, Aeschylus fought at the Battle of Marathon against Persia. He is credited with the introduction of the second actor, where before there had been only a solo performer and the chorus, and because of this he is often described as the 'father' of Greek tragedy. Although none of Aeschylus' satyr plays remains, he was acknowledged as a master of this idiom as well as of the tragic.

The Plays of Aeschylus

About ninety plays have been attributed to Aeschylus: seventy-nine have been named, and thirteen of these won him the coveted first prize in the Athenian drama contest. However, only seven texts actually survive, and these are listed below in probable chronological order.

The first of Aeschylus' plays are often described as typical of simpler forms of ancient Greek theatre, and

Aeschylus.

Death by Tortoise

Aeschylus has one of the strangest claims to fame – death by tortoise! Aeschylus was bald, and the story goes that a passing eagle, looking for a rock on which to drop and crack open a tortoise in order to eat it, dropped it on him by mistake, killing him outright! The fate of the tortoise was not recorded!

the developments in his later works as defining the beginnings of the 'Golden Age'. These early works, the order of which is disputed, are described as 'lyric' or 'old' tragedies. Their focus is predominantly choric and they have only one separated 'actor', and this emphasis on the chorus leads naturally to the opinion

Encore?

Before 456BC plays were only performed once, but after this date the people of Athens voted to allow the works of Aeschylus to be re-staged. The revival of the works of others, however, continued to be banned until 386BC.

that all of Aeschylus' tragedies retain a certain quasi-religious structure.

PLAYS

The Supplicants (*c*.492BC)
The chorus forms the main character in this work, which is the first of a trilogy, the other texts being *The Egyptians* and *The Danaids*. Its plot deals with the marriage of the fifty daughters of Danaus. Its choral songs are considered amongst the most beautiful ever written.

The Persians (*c*.472BC)
Once again the chorus dominates in this piece. This is a historical tragedy set in the court of the mother of King Xerxes I of Persia. The play deals with the return to the court of the defeated Persian army after the victory of Athens over Persia at the naval battle of Salamis.

Seven against Thebes (*c*.467BC)
The surviving last play of a trilogy, the other two being *Laius* and *Oedipus*. In *The Septem*, as it is also known, the main actor is clearly dominant. The play deals with part of the Theban legend, describing the rivalry for the throne between Eteocles and Polyneices, the sons of Oedipus.

Prometheus Bound (undated)
Less clearly dated, but probably lying between *The Septem* and *The Oresteia*. The first of a set of three, the others being *Prometheus Unbound* and *Prometheus the Fire Bringer*. The play deals with the punishment meted out to Prometheus by the God Zeus, and is controversially thought not to be by Aeschylus, but by an acolyte.

13

The Oresteia (c.458BC)

The only remaining complete trilogy, comprising *Agamemnon, The Libation Bearers* and *The Eumenides.* This trilogy deals with the return from Troy of King Agamemnon. The first play concerns itself with his murder at the hands of his wife Clytemnestra and her lover Aegisthus. The second play concerns Clytemnestra's murder, in revenge, by her son Orestes. The final play deals with the need to stop this potentially endless revengeful pursuit with the expunging of Orestes' guilt by the courts, and the intervention of the Goddess Athena.

Agamemnon is rightly considered one of the greatest works of dramatic literature. The trilogy as a whole deals fascinatingly with the shifting of responsibility for crime from the individual to the state, and as such displays well the connecting of theme, as well as storyline, throughout a trilogy.

Extract from *Agamemnon* by Aeschylus

The final fateful words of the first play of the Oresteian Trilogy give an idea of the timbre of this drama, and also show us how the chorus is now working as another character in the piece, albeit still a commentator.

CLYTEMNESTRA:
Stop, stop, Aegisthus, dearest! No more violence!
When this first harvest ripens we'll reap grief enough.
Crime and despair are fed to bursting; let us not
Plunge deeper still in blood. Elders, I beg of you,
Yield in good time to Destiny; go home, before
You come to harm; what we have done was
     foreordained.
If our long agony finds here fulfilment, we,
Twice gored by Fate's long talons, welcome it. I speak
With woman's wisdom, if you choose to understand.

AEGISTHUS:
Then are these gross-tongued men to aim their
     pointed gibes
At random, and bluff out the fate they've richly
     earned?

CHORUS:
You'll find no Argive grovel at a blackguard's feet.

AEGISTHUS:
Enough! Some later day I'll settle scores with you.

CHORUS:
Not if Fate sets Orestes on the Argos road.

AEGISTHUS:
For men in exile hopes are meat and drink; I know.

CHORUS:
Rule on, grow fat defiling Justice – while you can.

AEGISTHUS:
You are a fool; in time you'll pay me for those words.

CHORUS:
Brag blindly on – a cock that struts before his hen!
(The chorus leave)

CLYTEMNESTRA:
Pay no heed to this currish howling. You and I,
Joint rulers, will enforce due reverence for our throne.

Sophocles (496–406BC)

Born in Colonus Hippius, which now forms part of Athens, Sophocles initially took part in dramatic art as a choric performer, being chosen as chorus leader in 480BC. As a playwright it is known that he first defeated Aeschylus, the long-reigning champion, in dramatic competition in 468BC. He was twenty-eight. It is recorded that he subsequently won first prize a further twenty or so times.

Sophocles is credited with the introduction of the third actor – although it should be noted that, as the

Sophocles and Athens

Sophocles lived for ninety years and his life is said to have more or less coincided with the rise and fall of the Athenian state. He died just before the final Athenian defeat by Sparta in the Peloponnesian War. Notable acquaintances were Herodotus the historian and Pericles the statesman. He was twice elected to high military office.

Sophocles.

The Plays of Sophocles

Sophocles is credited with over 100 plays, yet sadly only the seven texts listed below survive, all tragedies. He was a powerful writer of tragedy, and the dark climax of many of his plays has rarely been surpassed. As already stated, the introduction of a third actor allows for more complex characterization. It can perhaps be said that, whereas in Aeschylus the nature of any given character is understood from the outset, in Sophocles a character becomes known from their actions and the comments and behaviour of those around them. In this case the drama is something more familiar to us and becomes, for the audience, more of a journey.

Although not written as a triptych, three of Sophocles' plays concern the Theban Legend, and all three are considered masterpieces within his art. *Antigone* represents the final part of the Theban story, with *Oedipus Rex* and *Oedipus at Colonus* forming two early parts of the history. All three are often published together as the 'Theban plays'. Notably, however, they

working lives of the three great ancient Greek playwrights overlap, they all produced plays with three protagonists at some time. Certainly in *Agamemnon*, one of Aeschylus' later plays, there are, for example, scenes with Agamemnon, Clytemnestra and Cassandra all on stage at the same time. However, it is still the case that no three-way dialogue actually takes place.

It is thus still possible to think of Sophocles not only as the originator of this form, but also as the first great exponent of it. He would appear to have added the third protagonist to allow for more than one viewpoint to exist in any dialogue. This also allows for greater character exposition. Consequently, and certainly compared to the works of Aeschylus, Sophocles' works become more actor led than choric: the tempo and much of the exposition have been taken from the chorus and given to the individual characters, and indeed in his hands the chorus speaks more as a character than ever before, and in his later works plays an increasingly small role.

As well as introducing the third actor, Sophocles is said to have increased the chorus to fifteen, although in this case it is thought he did this for technical rather than artistic reasons, probably to allow for certain groupings in the choric movement.

The Theban Legend

This legend tells of the curse placed on its ruler King Laius: he is told that his son will be his nemesis, and so he has his infant son, Oedipus, left on a hillside to die. But Oedipus survives and is adopted by the king of Corinth, Polybus. On growing up, Oedipus is also told that he is doomed to kill his father: thinking this to be Polybus, he leaves Corinth and travels to Thebes where, sure enough, he (unknowingly) kills his father. Thebes at this time is prey to the monstrous Sphinx, but Oedipus takes on this creature and proves the only one who can answer its fiendish riddle, thereby destroying it. Now a hero in Thebes, Oedipus marries his mother, the widowed queen Jocasta. But Thebes still fails to prosper, and Oedipus determines to discover why it remains cursed – only to realize finally that he is the reason. With this revelation Jocasta hangs herself and Oedipus blinds himself and leaves Thebes, to wander forever in exile. The story and curse continue in the acts of his sons Polyneices and Eteocles, and his daughter Antigone. (*See* the various plays listed overleaf.)

do not work philosophically as a whole, primarily because Sophocles' position on the rights and wrongs of the arguments contained within the Theban legend differ from play to play, and make more sense when viewed in the order in which he wrote them, rather than in story order.

PLAYS

Ajax (c.450BC)

The first of Sophocles' extant works, but notably some eighteen years after his initial victory over Aeschylus, so not the work of a novice by any means. Ajax is a typical Sophoclean central character, one that chooses to defy circumstance or convention, and in so doing suffers the consequences of his actions. In this case, divine retribution is wrought by the goddess Athena for Ajax's arrogant and misguidedly proud behaviour.

As with many of the other works of Sophocles, the title character, whilst most important, does not necessarily have total dominance. Ajax dies several verses before the play ends, and Athena certainly rivals him in importance – indeed the piece is notable for the beauty of the passage given to Athena concerning the transience of existence: 'One single day can overthrow or raise up anything human,' she says.

Antigone (c.442BC)

This lyrical work deals once more with an individual defying the dictates of the gods and refusing to yield to custom or tradition. In this case Oedipus' daughter Antigone allows the traditional rites of burial to proceed for her brother Polyneices, despite him being ruled outside the law (he stormed the city of Thebes and killed his brother Eteocles who was defending it).

Antigone – *a modern production, directed by Nona Shepphard.*

The Trachiniae (441–430BC)

Considered less structurally sound than his other works, this play concerns the trials of Heracles, whose hubristic actions eventually bring about his demise. The same subject is also dealt with in two plays of Euripides: *Heracles* and *The Children of Heracles*.

Oedipus Rex (429–420BC)

The first of the so-called Theban plays and sometimes translated as Oedipus Tyrannus or Oedipus the Tyrant, this is perhaps the most powerful of the three. It is also arguably the most archetypal of all ancient Greek dramas. It is said to be most pure in form, having enormous dramatic power, with an intense use of dramatic irony.

The story deals with attempts by King Oedipus to save his adopted country from plague, only to find his insistent inquiries lead forever back to him. The revelation that the ill fortune of the city has been caused by Oedipus having unknowingly broken two of the most human of taboos, murdering his father and fathering children by his mother, still reverberates powerfully down through the centuries.

Understanding Oedipus

The epic nature of these plays is potently evident in *Oedipus Rex*, where the basic nature of our very being is exposed. Not surprising, then, that even several thousand years later Sigmund Freud turns to such dramas to describe his understanding of the working of the subconscious. The concept of the 'Oedipus complex' was thus born.

Electra (430–415BC)

A play of almost unrelenting darkness and gloom. Electra goads Orestes into the murder of their mother Clytemnestra, in revenge for her murder of their father, Agamemnon. Interestingly, of course, the same subject is central to part of the Orestian trilogy by Aeschylus, and is also treated by Euripides in his play *Electra*.

Philoctetes (409BC)

This play deals with part of the story of the fall of Troy, in this case the struggle between Odysseus and Philoctetes. The role of the chorus is notably reduced, and the character of Neoptolemus is arguably the most rounded in all Greek drama.

For in this play, Neoptolemus starts believing one thing to be true and is thus on one side of an argument, but by the end of the play has completely changed his position. This complete U-turn is unprecedented in the Greek dramatic literature that remains for us to study, and thus makes this play a very interesting project.

This play links thematically with *Ajax*, and Euripides' play *Andromache*.

Oedipus at Colonus (401BC)

This play is said to have been produced posthumously, and thus would seem to come from the later part of Sophocles' life. It forms the middle part of the Theban legend and concerns the arrival of the outcast Oedipus in Athens, and his subsequent death. Antigone, who has accompanied him in exile, features, as do his sons Polyneices and Eteocles. Their rivalry, that is to end in their death, as related in *Antigone*, starts here over the custody of their father's remains.

Sophocles at Colonus

Like Oedipus, Sophocles also met his end in Colonus, dying there a greatly respected old man, in 406BC.

Extract from *Oedipus Rex* by Sophocles

The dreadful and bloody deeds of this play take place, in traditional style, off stage. At its climax an attendant is given the task of describing them to the chorus of the citizens of Thebes, and thus to us. (Note that Laius is the name of Oedipus' father.)

ATTENDANT:

O you most honourable lords of the city of Thebes,

Weep for the things you shall hear, the things you shall see,

If you are true sons and loyal to the house of Labdacus.
Not all the waters of Ister, the waters of Phasis,
Can wash this dwelling clean of the foulness within,
Clean of the deliberate acts that soon shall be known,
Of all horrible acts most horrible, wilfully chosen.

CHORUS:
Already we have wept enough for things we have
    known,
The things we have seen. What more will your story
    add?

ATTENDANT:
First, and in brief – Her Majesty is dead.

CHORUS:
Alas poor soul: what brought her to this end?

ATTENDANT:
Her own hand did it. You that have not seen,

And shall not see, this worst, shall suffer the less.
But I that saw, will remember, and will tell what I
    remember
Of her last agony.

You saw her cross the threshold
In desperate passion. Straight to her bridal-bed
She hurried, fastening her fingers in her hair.
There in her chamber, the doors flung sharply to,
She cried aloud to Laius long since dead,
Remembering the son she bore long since, the son
By whom the sire was slain, the son to whom
The mother bore yet other children, fruit
Of luckless misbegetting. There she bewailed
The twice-confounded issue of her wifehood –
Husband begotten of husband, child of child.
So much we heard. Her death was hidden from us.
Before we could see out her tragedy,
The King broke in with piercing cries, and all
Had eyes only for him. This way and that

Oedipus Rex – *a modern production, directed by Anthony Clarke.*

He strode among us. 'A sword, a sword!' he cried;
'Where is that wife, no wife of mine – that soil
Where I was sown, and whence I reaped my
    harvest!'
While thus he raved, some demon guided him –
For none of us dared speak – to where she was.
As if in answer to some leader's call
With wild hallooing cries he hurled himself
Upon the locked doors, bending by main force
The bolts out of their sockets – stumbling in.

We saw a knotted pendulum, a noose,
A strangled woman swinging before our eyes.

The King saw too, with heart-rending groans
Untied the rope, and laid her on the ground.
But worse was yet to see. Her dress was pinned
With golden brooches, which the King snatched out
And thrust, from full arm's length, into his eyes –
Eyes that should see no longer his shame, his guilt,
No longer see those he had longed to see,
Henceforth seeing nothing but night ... To this wild
    tune
He pierced his eyeballs time and time again,
Till bloody tears ran down his beard – not drops
But in full spate a whole cascade descending
In drenching cataracts of scarlet rain.

Euripides.

Euripides (480–406BC)

Born on the island of Salamis, Euripides did not start to write plays until over thirty years of age, previously being trained in painting and philosophy. So although in age almost a contemporary of Sophocles, his works only came to prominence after the success of those of Sophocles. Euripides' 'late start' saw to it that he did not win his first dramatic prize until he was forty; his controversial style also meant he did not win a second prize until he was fifty-four. In later life Euripides was often presenting new plays at the same time as Sophocles, and in fact they both died in the same year, 406BC. Euripides is nevertheless seen as a successor to Sophocles, this in no small part because the works of Euripides continue the progress in Greek drama towards greater complexity of character, greater exposition and stronger plot.

And the Winner is ...

Euripides is the last of the three great poet-tragedians of Greek drama. It would, of course, be pointless to say which is the greater. But here are the known results from the Ancient Records:

	No. of Surviving Plays	No. of Prizes Won
Aeschylus	7	13
Sophocles	7	18
Euripides	18	5

Interestingly, in the period immediately following the end of the great Athenian state, it is the works of Euripides that stay in favour, which may account for why so many have survived.

His emphasis on the personal rather than the public dilemmas of his principal characters, and the political stance within his works, made Euripides an *enfant terrible* even in his own time. It also made him an easy target for parody (*see* Aristophanes below). In particular, he was criticized for putting the mundane into the formal lyrics and diction of classical theatre, thereby offending against the strict etiquette of the genre.

The Plays of Euripides

Euripides is said to have written around ninety plays, of which only the eighteen listed below survive; another play, *Rheus*, is sometimes attributed to him, but is probably a fourth-century work. In his works the chorus is less important, and as a result the characters become more so. The plight of the individual often carries the day, and Euripides' female characters are in particular worth serious study.

Aristotle described Euripides as 'the most tragic of the tragic poets', although interestingly some of his plays can be described as tragi-comedies (*Alcestis, Ion* and *Iphigenia in Tauris*) and one a high comedy (*Helen*). *The Phoenician Women* is more of a pageant play, and Euripides is author of the only surviving Satyr play in *Cyclops*. Euripides also developed the concept of a prologue. Earliest Greek drama had begun with a choric song, and even the works of Sophocles have a distinct opening scene, called a prologus. However, in Euripides it becomes a formal device, used to convey the background to the story about to be told. In his works the prologue is usually put into the mouth of a character in the play or an external deity.

Reputation

Euripides' reputation rose so high that Plutarch reported (in his *Life of Nicias*) that Athenian prisoners, held captive during the Peloponnesian War, could escape death and even be set free if they could recite passages from his works.

PLAYS

Cyclops (undated)
This play deals with the story of Odysseus and his meeting with, and eventual victory over, the one-eyed giant Polyphemus. It is the only complete satyr play that posterity has left us (*see* page 12).

Alcestis (438BC)

Medea (431BC)
His first real tragedy.

Hippolytus (428BC)

Children of Heracles (c.428BC)
Tells of the persecution of the children of Heracles by Eurystheus.

Andromache (c.420BC)
Concerns part of the Trojan mythology – as do also *The Trojan Women* and *Hecuba* by Euripides, and *Agamemnon* by Aeschylus.

Hecuba (425BC)
Often translated as *Hecabe*.

Heracles (420BC)
Often called *Heracles Furens* or *The Fury of Heracles* to distinguish it from *The Children of Heracles*.

The Supplicants (undated)
Tells of the refusal of Creon of Thebes to bury the Argive warriors.

Ion (undated)
This play tells the story of Ion, the founder of the Ionian race.

Electra (415BC)
A brutal study in madness. Interesting to compare this with the play of the same name by Sophocles, and indeed the part of *The Oresteia* of Aeschylus that deals with the same story.

The Trojan Women (415BC)
Also known as *The Troades*.

Iphigenia in Tauris (c.414BC)

Helen (412BC)
Based on the famous story from the Trojan War.

The Trojan Women – *a modern production, directed by Deborah Paige.*

The Phoenician Women (411BC)
This play tells of the story of Eteocles and Polyne-
ices, with a chorus made up of Phoenician maidens.
It deals with the same story cycle as Aeschylus'
Seven against Thebes, and Sophocles' *Antigone* and
his two *Oedipus* plays.

Orestes (408BC)
Many Greek plays deal with same potent mythology. The curse of the ancient house of Atreus thus
forms the backdrop to nine surviving texts: Aeschylus' *Oresteia*, Sophocles' *Electra*, and Euripides'
plays *Electra*, *Orestes*, the two *Iphigenia* dramas, and
Helen. It may also have been the case that plays in
competition were more likely to be judged good if
they seemed to deal in a superior manner with the
same material as a rival.

The Bacchae (407BC)
Written in self-imposed exile in Macedonia, and
telling of the destruction of King Pentheus at the
hand of his mother, a Bacchanite. Produced
posthumously, and won a prize thus.

Iphigenia in Aulis (undated)
Also produced posthumously.

Extract from *The Bacchae* by Euripides
The chorus at first tries to draw attention away
from the unhappy events of the story, but cannot
help but return to the subject of vengeance and
punishment by the Gods.

CHORUS:
Dirce, sweet and holy maid,
Ancheloüs Theban daughter,
Once the child of Zeus was made
Welcome in your welling water,
When the lord of earth and sky
Snatched him from the undying flame,
Laid him safe within his thigh,
Calling loud the infants name:
'Twice-born Dithyrambus! Come,
Enter here your father's womb;
Bacchic child, I now proclaim
This is Thebes shall be your name.'

Now, divine Dirce, when my head is crowned
And my feet dance in Bacchus' revelry –
Now you reject me from your holy ground.
Why should you fear me? By the purple fruit
That glows in glory on Dionysus' tree,
His dread name yet shall haunt your memory!

Aristophanes (*c.*448–380BC)

Aristophanes was born in the Athenian town of
Cydathenaeum, and became known politically as a
conservative who favoured the aristocracy rather
than too broad a democracy. This in some way must
have fuelled his desire to poke fun at Euripides, who
was by inclination much more of a rebel. Aristophanes first plays were performed in 427BC, under
the pseudonym 'Kallistratos'.

Comedy Tonight ...

Other Comedic dramatists are known from this
period, but as was the case with many tragedians, none of their work has survived. These
include Cratinus and his plays *Pytine* (*Wine-
flask*), a comedy on the over-indulgence of
alchohol, and *Dionysalexandros* that pokes fun
at Dionysus and the Helen of Troy myth.

The Plays of Aristophanes
Aristophanes is said to have written over forty comedies, of which eleven survive.

PLAYS
The Acharnians (425BC)
Although the oldest to survive, this was in fact the
third of Aristophanes' plays to be produced, and it
is known to have won first prize. The play is set during the Peloponnesian War. After experiencing the
results of six years of war, a farmer called
Dikaiopolois decides that he has had enough. The
play takes the form of his attempts to convince the
chorus that war is pointless, which he does in ever-
more humorous and politically satirical ways. The
play is also notable for the first appearance of

Euripides as a character for Aristophanes to poke fun at.

Knights (424BC)

Also winner of first prize, this play was the first that Aristophanes presented under his real name. Tradition has it that he took the role of the main character, Paphlagon, himself. Full of caricature and robust humour, this play's theme is overtly political, and although its topicality is lost on us today, the basic portrayal of bullying tyrants and attempts to overthrow them still holds the stage magnificently.

Clouds (423BC)

This play won third prize in competition, and is a satire on the teachings and methods of Socrates. Socrates was about forty at the time; he was a friend of Aristophanes, and story has it that he was more flattered than insulted by its cutting ridicule.

Wasps (422BC)

A second-prize winner, this play was Aristophanes' seventh, and is a satire on the law.

Peace (421BC)

Another second-prize winner, this play was written during the cessation of hostilities in the Peloponnesian War known as the Peace of Nikias. It combines a genuine yearning for a real peace with very broad slapstick, and concerns an attempt to rescue the goddess Peace, who has become trapped in Heaven.

Birds (414BC)

Once again a second-prize winner, this play is a fast paced, satirical allegory on the nature of the state and those that govern. It concerns the creation of a new state of birds by those who are tired of the old governing ways and want a simpler life. However, even a new Utopian state leaves the governing class open to all the temptations they have previously despised.

Lysistrata (411BC)

In recent years this has undoubtedly become the most often performed of all Aristophanes' works, if for no other reason perhaps than the fact that its central theme is sex and equality. Tired of the seemingly endless war, the women of Athens, led by Lysistrata,

go on strike. They withhold their favours from their men in order to make them see sense and sue for peace. The humour in this play, like those others that feature women as central protagonists, was only enhanced by the fact that, as was the tradition, all the parts would have been played by men.

Women at the Festival (Thesmophoriazousae) (411BC)

Set at the festival of Demeter and Persephone, this is one of Aristophanes' broadest farces, and is less political than most of his other works. Once again Euripides turns up as a character – here a misogynist who smuggles a relative into the women-only festival, gets found out, and then attempts to rescue him by using plots from his own plays.

Frogs (404/5BC)

A first-prize winner, and another play that has Euripides as a character. However, unlike previous plays, this one reflects the fact that Euripides had recently died. The piece involves a competition in Heaven between Aeschylus and Euripides to decide who shall come back to Athens. Whilst it is still a comic piece, it also includes a certain feeling of yearning for the old Athenian days.

Women in Parliament/Power (Ecclesiazousae) (392BC)

The last two surviving works of Aristophanes are closer to the New Comedy that Menander will personify than his earlier works (see below). The subject matter moves away from the God-ruled world, and is given a more secular and personal treatment. As a result the role of the chorus dwindles in importance in both these two last works, in this one working more as a group of individuals.

The broad farce of this play concerns women disguising themselves as men to be able to enter the Assembly and thus vote for power for the women. Once again the fact that men would have played these parts shows how far this comedy seeks to go, and is added to by the fact that eventually, because their clothes have been taken, some of the men have to dress as women to be able to return to the Assembly.

Ploutos or Wealth (388BC)

A play about whether honesty or dishonesty is the best policy, and in which the chorus has an increasingly negligible role to play as the play proceeds. The plot revolves around the fact that the God Wealth has been blinded by the God Zeus out of pure spite for Mankind. Unsighted, Wealth bestows good fortune on all the wrong people.

Extract from *Lysistrata* by Aristophanes

Late in the play the pressure is increased as Myrrhine, one of the women, makes matters worse by pretending that she will consort with her husband Kinesias, whilst in fact all she is doing is leading him on. The text is one thing, but in performance the physical humour can be superbly funny. The extract starts mid scene ...

KINESIAS: Don't you remember? The plans we made? Just you and I? Our own little Olympic Games?

MYRRHINE: There'll be no Olympic Games, till you get that treaty signed.

KINESIAS: Treaty? Oh, treaty. Anything!

MYRRHINE: Sign that, and I'll come right home. Till then, excuse me.

KINESIAS: Don't go: I'll sign. Could you ...? Can't we ...? Just a little ...?

MYRRHINE: Sorry. Though I must say I'm tempted.

KINESIAS: You are? You must? Oh darling, now.

MYRRHINE: You filthy beast! In front of baby?

KINESIAS: Oh my God, Baby. (to the slave) Here, man, here. Get him out of here. (Exit slave with baby) He's gone, darling, gone. Now, come to bed.

MYRRHINE: Bed? Where?

KINESIAS: Where? Um... in the Grotto!

MYRRHINE: It's dusty, darling. Where can I wash?

KINESIAS: In the fountain. Do come on.

MYRRHINE: But what about my oath? I swore an oath.

KINESIAS: Blame me. I broke it. Hurry up.

MYRRHINE: I'll just fetch a bed.

KINESIAS: What? On the ground, the ground.

MYRRHINE: No darling. You may be a pig. But I won't let you wallow on the ground. (She goes in.)

KINESIAS: She loves me. She loves me. You can always tell.

MYRRHINE: (Returning with a folding bed) You set it up. I'll get undressed. No, silly me. I forgot the mattress.

KINESIAS: Forget the mattress.

MYRRHINE: I can't have you having me on the sacking.

KINESIAS: Give me a kiss before you go.

MYRRHINE: Mmmmmmmmmmmmmm. (She goes in.)

KINESIAS: Hoo-hoo-hoo. For God's sake, hurry. (Myrrhine returns with a mattress.)

MYRRHINE: There. You lie down. I'll get undressed. Oh no. No pillow now.

KINESIAS: I don't want a pillow!

MYRRHINE: But I do. (She goes)

... and so on, with increasing cunning on the one hand, and frustration, linked with almost physical pain, on the other.

Menander (342–292 BC)

The comic writings that are known from the later period of ancient Greek history are characterized as being gentler, less politically satirical and less slapstick than those of the 'old' period. The works of Menander represent the only existing examples of what is known as 'New Comedy', and his first works date from around seventy years after the death of

Aristophanes. Although foreshadowed in the comic elements contained in the lighter works of Euripides, Menander's style represents a clear departure from the earlier comic style typified by the broader works of Aristophanes. Menander's plays contain complicated love stories, with perspicacious social and human commentaries based on tales of everyday folk.

Little is known of Menander. From his writings and his reputation we know he was an Athenian and a philosopher. He had a friendship with the governor of Athens from 317–307BC, Demetrius of Phalerum, who was later disgraced and removed from office. Menander may have suffered for this association, although we do not know for sure. Even after Menander died, aged fifty, in 292BC, his works continued to be highly thought of and were often performed.

Dramatic Remains

Many of the texts that were eventually found containing the writings of Menander were papyri wrapped as coverings around the bodies of ancient Egyptian mummies! So there may be still more to be discovered.

The Plays of Menander
Although believed to have written over a hundred comedies, only fragments of Menander's work and his reputation were thought to have survived, until quite substantial portions of certain texts were discovered in Egypt in the last hundred years. Parts of the first four plays listed below were discovered in 1905–07, with more of *Samia* discovered in 1955 alongside a fifth text, *Duskolos*. In 1963 a sixth play turned up, *The Man from Sicyon*, and in 1965 a seventh, *Misoumenos*. The plays remain undated.

PLAYS
Heros

Dyskolos (or *The Ill-Tempered Man*)
The first of Menander's plays to be published in the modern world in 1959, and also variously translated

as *The Curmudgeon*, *The Malcontent* and *The Misanthrope*. Probably an early work dating from 317BC. An indication of the lesser role given to the gods in his works is the fact that Menander uses the far-from-mainstream god Pan to deliver the prologue of this play. The play tells the story of a young girl's attempt to persuade her father to allow her to marry (the father, Knemon, being the title character). It shows a clear insight into the human condition, in that Knemon changes his mind as a result of practical considerations, and certainly does not undergo a God-influenced conversion.

Samia (or *The Woman from Samos*)
The full text of this play was not available to be published until 1969. On reading the text it became clear that in this play Menander had abandoned any attempt at giving the gods a serious role in the drama. The play deals exclusively with aspects of social and family life. The 'old comedy' interest in political context is completely absent, and the play deals with love, intrigue and misunderstandings.

Perikeiromene
Translated and used as a source for the 1941 play *The Rape of Locks* by Gilbert Murray.

Epitrepontes
Translated in 1945 and similarly used as a source for *The Arbitration*, also by Gilbert Murray.

The Man from Sicyon

Misoumenos (or *The Man She Hated*)

Aristotle (384–322BC)

Aristotle was a philosopher and scientist who counted among his interests the theatre of his day. He wrote many pieces of philosophy, among them the 'Poetics' or 'On the Art of Poetry', which dates from *c.*330BC, and from which his thoughts on the theatre are taken. Indeed, Aristotle is known to have written on both comedy and tragedy; however, only his writings concerning the latter have survived. His analyses of the works of the great Greek tragedians, Sophocles in particular, were held in particularly

Aristotle.

high regard when rediscovered during the explosion of interest in the classical period of the Renaissance.

Aristotle held Sophocles' *Oedipus* to be the ultimate model for Greek theatre. He considered the earlier works of Aeschylus to be immature in comparison to those of Sophocles, and those of Euripides to be weaker.

Aristotle's writings have been greatly misunderstood by many who have sought to find in them a formula to criticize the writers of their own period, or to simplify teaching of theatre. For example, Aristotle famously discusses the concepts of time, place and action in plays. His thoughts on these basic constituents of any play are based on a description of what he has seen to work, again mostly in the plays of Sophocles. What he does not do, but has often had claimed for him, is to express the opinion that these 'unities' can only work in a set way. It was thus often claimed, incorrectly, that Aristotle said that drama only worked if the action took place during the passing of one day, in a single location, and with the action following a logical sequence (in other words, no flashbacks or suchlike).

In fact he does say that the action of a play should be consistent, and he comments that the time-period used should try 'as hard as possible to fall within a single revolution of the sun' – although he is far from dogmatic about it. Regarding the setting of a play, he says nothing.

As the quotes below show, a lot of information has come down to us about the great playwrights from the writings of Aristotle. Likewise so also have many basic concepts concerning tragic drama. Notable amongst these is the idea that tragedy, and perhaps any theatre, has a cathartic effect upon the viewer – that to watch, at one remove, emotions, personal disasters and any strongly effecting events, allows the viewer to experience them without becoming too involved. The third person of the actor carries the burden of the disaster, the tragedy, for us, and we have the freedom to choose how much involvement we wish to have, and finally leave the feelings behind us in the theatre if we wish. This is one of the most persuasive arguments as to why theatre is so attractive to us, indeed how it has continued to hold its spell over us for well over two thousand years.

Extracts from the *Poetics* of Aristotle

The following extracts from the *Poetics* may help give the reader a further insight into Aristotle's teachings and his writing style:

> Comedy aims at representing men as worse than they are nowadays, tragedy as better.

> The instinct for imitation is inherent in man from his earliest days ... he learns his earliest lessons by imitation.

> Inborn in all of us is the instinct to enjoy works of imitation.

> It is not known who introduced masks, or prologues, or the plurality of actors.

Aeschylus was the first to increase the number of actors from one to two, cut down the role of the chorus, and give the first place to the dialogue. Sophocles introduced three actors and painted scenery.

The chorus must be regarded as one of the actors.

The grandeur of tragedy: it was not until late that it acquired stateliness, when progressing beyond the methods of satyric drama.

Tragedy is a representation of an action that is worth serious attention ... (its) language is enriched by a variety of artistic devices ... and by means of pity and fear, brings about the purgation of such emotions.

Spectacle is an essential part of tragedy.

Thought and character are two natural causes of action.

The ordered representation of action is the plot of the tragedy.

Tragedy has six constituents ... these are plot, character, diction, thought, spectacle and song. ... of these the most important is plot.

THE THEATRE OF ANCIENT ROME

The dramatic work that derives from ancient Rome is thought to be generally inferior to that of the ancient Greeks – even the Romans considered Greek theatre to be superior, looking back on a 'Golden Age'. Much Roman drama was thus based on, or derived from, the ancient Greek, and adaptations and revivals

The Ancient Roman stage.

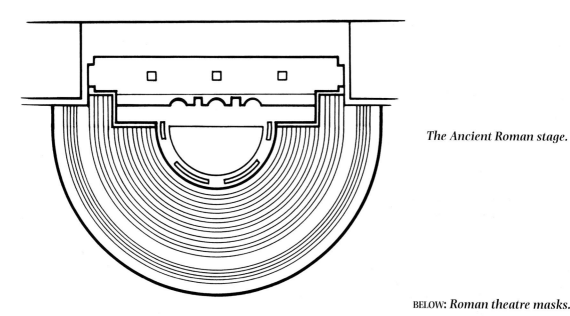

The Ancient Roman stage.

BELOW: *Roman theatre masks.*

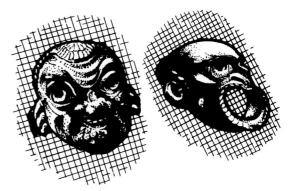

abounded. The theatre space did continue to develop, however. As the illustrations (*see* below and p.28) show, the Roman stage halved the original Greek circle, and further developed the skene, or backdrop.

Performers still wore masks in ancient Rome, although these were now more exaggerated than their Greek predecessors. Examples would include masks that depicted the following: the handsome youth, the father, the prostitute, the parasite, the miser, the mother, the clever slave and the braggart soldier. Many of these types create the archytypes for characters that we can easily recognize, even in the dramatic art of today. For example, from the work of Plautus in particular, the character type of the 'Miles Gloriosus' (the braggart soldier) sees its counterpart in Commedia dell'Arte (*see* page 51), in Shakespeare and his contemporaries (*see* page 77), and so on.

Terence (*c.*190–*c.*159BC)

Six plays have survived from the works of Terence, a freed slave of African origin, whose adopted name on being freed was Publius Terentius Afer. These plays are all re-workings of Greek comedies, four of them after Menander; these include *Andria* or *The Woman of Andros*, his first play, which was an immediate success. It is said that Terence's warm personality made him a particular favourite of the

Rome literary élite. His two other extant works derive from originals by Apollodorus of Carystus (300–269BC). Terence died whilst returning from a trip to Greece in search of more plays by Menander.

The Plays of Terence

Terence's writing is characterized as being light and witty. He satirizes the life of his fellow citizens, and his farce is less broad than that of Plautus. He uses far less singing and dancing generally, and his characterization and use of plot is far more sophisticated than that of his predecessor. In story terms he foreshadows many a later plot in his use of pairs of lovers, mistaken identity, and gentle wistful humour. His surviving plays are *Andria* (166BC), *Hecyra* (165BC), *Heauton*

Timorumenos (163BC), *Eunuchus* (161BC), *Phormio* (161BC) and *Adelphi* (160BC).

Famous Quotes from the Works of Terence

'A lover's quarrel is the renewal of love.' *Andria*

'Fortune favours the brave.' *Phormio*

'As many opinions exist as there are men, each a law unto himself.' *Phormio*

Plautus (*c*.254–184BC)

Titus Maccius Plautus came from Umbria to Rome to work as a comic actor, and went on to write over 130 plays, of which twenty still survive today . As with Terence, they are all based on Greek works from the era of New Comedy and thus deal with bold characters and complex plots. Much debauchery occurs, along with songs, jokes and topical allusions. Although said to be a rougher exponent of the craft of the playwright, certainly than Terence or Menander, nevertheless the verve and vigour of Plautus' work cannot be denied.

20th-Century Plautus

The successful Broadway musical *A Funny Thing Happened on the Way to the Forum* (1962) was based, in part, on material from several plays by Plautus, as was the concept of the seventies British television series *Up Pompeii* starring Frankie Howard.

The Plays of Plautus

PLAYS
Stichus (200BC)
One of only two dated plays by Plautus. This piece involves the return of long-absent relatives in the aftermath of the war against Hannibal.

Bacchides
One of many of Plautus' plays set around the life of a brothel.

Pseudolus (191BC)
This play again has a brothel as its setting, although this time it also includes the appearance of an archetypical figure in much of Plautus' work and in Roman comedy generally: the trickster slave or servant.

Truculentis
Once more set around the working of a brothel.

Casina
A play within which Plautus takes farce to outrageous lengths.

Menaechmi (The Brothers)
To a large extent this play can be regarded as the source of Shakespeare's play *The Comedy of Errors.*

Captivi (The Captives)
A play that boasts a higher moral tone than many of Plautus' works – or does so in the prologue and epilogue, at least! It deals with the honour of a noble woman, and a brave and devoted slave saving his master from captivity, then discovering he was his master's long-lost son!

Amphitryo
As the play above, this piece deals with the complications involved with mistaken identity, and can also be seen as an influence on *The Comedy of Errors.*

Aulularia
This piece involves a poor old man made crazy with the discovery of a buried treasure.

Mostellaria
A ghost story that involves the plotting of a slave, who is caught unexpectedly by his young master's father when the latter returns from travel.

Rudens
This play involves a storm, a shipwreck, a treasure, and a long-lost daughter returned to her parents.

29

Fragments of one other play, *Vidularia*, have survived; two other plays, *Mercator* and *Asinaria*, that were originally ascribed to Plautus, are now thought unlikely to be his.

Seneca (*c.*4BC–AD65)

Lucius Annaeus Seneca left nine tragedies to posterity, the only examples of ancient Roman tragic drama to survive. Seneca was born in Cordoba in Spain into a noble Roman family. His father, a famous rhetorician, was also named Seneca, and so the playwright was referred to as 'Seneca the Younger' during his lifetime.

In AD49 Seneca was appointed tutor to the young Nero, who on the death of Claudius in AD54 became emperor. Initially a civilizing influence, Seneca slowly lost power over the emperor; indeed in AD62, after he had retired, Nero unsuccessfully tried to have Seneca poisoned, jealous of his success and consequent wealth. In AD65, however, Seneca was implicated in a plot to assassinate the emperor, and a imperial 'suicide' was ordered. Seneca thus took his own life.

Nero

The Emperor Nero loved the theatre and would often take a solo part – thinly masked. Like this he played such roles as Hercules, Oedipus and Orestes. In 66AD he undertook a tour of Greek theatres, returning to Rome with 1,808 triumphal crowns!

Seneca was widely respected as a philosopher and statesman as well as a dramatist. Although few of his plays survive, many more of his other writings have: these include *The Pumpkinification of the Divine Claudius* (*c.*AD54), a satire on the former Emperor's divinity, seven books of scientific inquiry combined with moralizing, called *Natural Questions* (AD63–64), 124 letters, and many stoic treatises.

The Plays of Seneca

All of Seneca's extant tragedies are based on ancient Greek works: the first four, as listed below, are based on works by Euripides; the *Agamemnon* is taken from Aeschylus; the next three derive from the works of Sophocles; and finally the *Thyestes* is based on an unknown Greek original – although a fragment of another *Thyestes* by Sophocles does exist and may well have been its model. Another extant play of the period, *Octavia*, once credited to Seneca, is now thought unlikely to be his. The surviving works (dates unknown) are as follows: *Hercules Furens*, *Medea*, *Phaedra* (also known as *Hippolytus*), *Troades* (also known as *The Trojan Women*), *Agamemnon*, *Oedipus*, *Phoenissae* (or *Thebais*), *Hercules Oetaeus* and *Thyestes*.

Seneca's work was highly rhetorical, and seems more likely to have been written for declamation and study, rather than for acting or performance. His adaptations tended to emphasize the gory and the melodramatic, and yet his words can also be highly captivating and very engaging. In his work Seneca takes up the prologue of Euripides, and generally it seems to have been the latter's plays that Seneca chose to translate and adapt for the Roman audiences.

Horace (65–8BC)

The poet and philosopher known as Horace was born Quintus Horatius Flaccus in Venusia in Apulia. He was ultimately educated in Athens. Horace was present on the losing side at the battle of Philippi, but was pardoned and allowed to return to Rome. In Rome Horace came under the patronage of nobleman Gaius Cilnius Maecenas, as did the poet Virgil (70–19BC). Horace gained renown for his many writings, amongst them the *Satires*, *Odes*, *Epodes* and the *Ars Poetica*. It is in this latter book that Horace's thoughts on drama are found.

In the *Ars Poetica* Horace expounds on the theories of Aristotle, interpreting the latter's ideas and adding some of his own. It is through his work in Latin that the thoughts of Aristotle initially came to be known during the resurgence of interest in things classical that was the Renaissance (*see* page 47). It is also through Horace that many assumptions concerning the staging and performing of ancient Greek theatre came to be made, including the notion that the major three Greek dramatists, as we known them, came in some neat, dramatically developing chronological order.

Extracts from the *Poetics* of Horace

The following extracts from the *Poetics* may help give the reader a broad understanding of Horace's teachings:

An episode is either acted on the stage, or reported as having taken place. However, the mind is less actively stimulated by what it takes in through the ear than what is presented to the eye.

... however, you will not bring on stage a thing that should rightly be occurring off stage ... and can be described later through the words of an eloquent narrator ... also Medea must not butcher her children in the presence of the audience, nor monstrous Atreus cook his dish of human flesh within public view ... these things I will not look upon.

If you wish for a success a play will be no shorter nor longer than five acts.

A *deus ex machina* will not be called for unless absolutely unavoidable.

There should not be more than three speaking characters on stage at any one time.

The chorus should hold the stage as an actor, and like an actor, make only contribution that will contribute to the plot and action ... it may also assist and advise the characters on stage.

A satire must be seemly, it must not show the high born in lowly action or speaking in crude tongue ... tragedy scorns the trivial.

To the Greeks the muses gave native wit and the ability to turn phrases.

Poets aim at giving either profit or delight, or at combining the giving of pleasure with some useful precepts for life.

CONCLUSION

Classical theatre remains one of the most vivid and exciting forms of dramatic art. Unlike anything that follows, Greek tragedy in particular remains unique in its power to enthral and move us. I hope some of this has been communicated on the preceding pages, but whatever the case, and as with all dramatic art, nothing can replace the experience of actually seeing the drama in performance. I would thus urge any student of dramatic literature to take every opportunity to see good productions of these works, whether in classical or modern dress: they are not to be missed.

2 MEDIEVAL THEATRE

Explaining the ways of God to man.
GLYNNE WICKHAM [1]

Within the weathered city walls we stand amongst friends and family awaiting the approach of the next pageant cart. We have seen much already, and the sunny spring day wears on. The next decorated stage rumbles into place, and we cheer the familiar faces in strange and colourful costumes that appear before us. Broad accented voices tell us of the nativity and the coming of our saviour, acting out the many roles. There is much humour; the antics of one of the shepherds makes us roar with laughter. Yet despite the familiarity of much, our hearts are in our mouths and tears are in our eyes when we behold the mother of Jesus finally able to present her baby to the world. It is a moment of vivid confirmation of all we believe in, and one we will never forget. The play over, the wagon pushes off to its next audience, and we settle down to await the next. We know what is to follow, but wait with bated breath nevertheless.

THE ORIGINS OF MEDIEVAL THEATRE

Classical theatre had all but died out by what is generally known as the 'Dark Ages', the period in Western history that leads into the medieval. The dramatic art of ancient Greece and Rome was rediscovered and very influential in later periods, but initially, and in the Western world at least, theatre had to be reinvented. This reinvention found its source in a dramatic art both religious and secular. It seems more than likely that in secular terms, a broadly comic tradition, the performing of comic pieces to a village gathering for example, derived from remaining Roman texts, and meandered its

OPPOSITE PAGE: *A modern mystery play,* **The Son of Man** *by Dennis Potter, directed by Robin Midgley.*

way through to a point where a strong liturgical drama helped to redefine it.

The moral nature of early medieval dramatic works can be traced, not unlike the dramatic art of the classical period, directly to religious ceremony. St Augustine prescribed the use of music in churches, and even as early as the sixth century AD, Pope Gregory the Great was encouraging the use of painting to tell the biblical stories to the generally illiterate masses. The development of religious drama followed this trend, the stories of the Bible moving from the voices of the clerics to the voices of the people in a quite logical, but nonetheless extraordinary way and making, as they did so, a journey from a medium of clerically spoken Latin to one of performance acted out in the common speech of the day.

The starting point for the development of liturgical drama is evident in the development of the music that accompanied the religious Roman Catholic ceremonies of the period. Originally this music was simple in form, the plain song or Gregorian chant of pre-AD1200 being of an uncomplicated and deliberately pure style. Around this date, however, it began to develop an increasingly sophisticated form, and as the music became more difficult, the need became apparent for ways to remember the ever-convoluted tunes being created. Whereas previously a single note had perhaps been given to a single word – for instance, 'amen' – now this one word could encompass pages of notation. Thus a kind of sub-text was invented, as a mnemonic, to make the tunes easier to remember, and what may initially have been half spoken under one's breath, grew to become a natural part of the music. The name for such a literary or musical addition to an authorized text is a 'trope'.

The words chosen for tropes were ones suitable for the subject being sung, usually an extension or elaboration of a biblical story. And as these tropes developed, they eventually incorporated reported speech, and then direct speech; it is from these that medieval drama mostly derives. Probably the best example of an early trope is the tenth-century *Easter Trope* from the Swiss monastery of St Gall. In this manuscript the following dialogue occurs:

> Quem quaritis?
> Responderunt ei:
> Jesum Nazarenum.
>
> Quem quaeritis?
> Illi autem dixerunt:
> Jesus Nazarenum.

This passage concerns a simple question and answer made at the visit of the three Marys to the tomb of Christ. One set of singers asks, 'Whom seek you?'; and antiphonally another set replies 'Jesus of Nazareth'. Even in this straightforward form the use of two sets of singers would have encouraged the congregation to begin to identify roles with each group, and the drama is evident.

Later tropes include those in the *Regularis Concordia*, or *Harmony of Rule*, written *c.*970 under the aegis of Aethelwold, the Bishop of Winchester. As well as text it included 'stage directions', as in this example of the setting for the women approaching the tomb to confront the angel sitting outside:

> Let four brothers vest themselves, one of whom, vested in alb [i.e. white], enters as if to do something, and, in an inconspicuous way, approaches the sepulchre, and there, holding a palm in his hands, sits quiet. ... Let three others approach, all alike vested in copes, bearing thuribles [incense burners] with incense in their hands, and, with hesitating steps, in semblance of persons seeking something, let them come before the sepulchre.

Obviously it was just a small step to take the reported speeches and stories within any trope, and begin to act them out as part of a church ceremony. There followed therefore the *ordo* – several scenes 'acted' out as part of a church ceremony – and then the *ludus* – a group of scenes (a play?) with a Latin text. The ludus were also for church use and performed by clerics.

The most quoted ordo is the *Ordo Propetarum*, a thirteenth-century version of which sees a succession of prophets, costumed and with identifying props, walking in procession and speaking in a liturgical setting.

Ludus and Pleg

'Ludus' is the Latin word for 'play' or 'game'. Ludo and Lego, both children's games, come from the same route. The Anglo-Saxon equivalent was the word 'pleg', from which the words 'play' and 'playwright' (a maker of plays) derive.

The best example we have of a ludus is the *Ludus Danielis* of *c.*1180. This was written as an expansion of an original trope by students of the Choir School of Beauvais in France, to be performed on Christmas Eve. It concerns the biblical story of Daniel and his dealings with King Nebuchadnezzar of Babylon and King Darius of Persia, and includes his famous confinement within a lion's den. It shows an exciting dramatic content despite the fact that it was sung rather than spoken. It was written mostly in Latin but with some passages in the vernacular French, scored for fifteen solo voices and a chorus, and an intricate musical accompaniment. Glynne Wickham, one of the world's experts on this period of drama, says of the *Ludus Danielis* that it 'stands at the gateway between two worlds'[ii], a perfect example of drama moving from ceremony to performance, and from the formal to the vernacular.

Professor Wickham's words are perhaps even truer for another ludus, the *Mystère d'Adam* (*c.*1130), notable for being written completely in the vernacular, in this case Anglo-Norman, with stage directions in Latin. The piece has three sections: the first deals with the story of Adam and Eve's fall from grace; the second with the Cain and Abel story; and interestingly the third section returns us to the liturgical style of an ordo, and features the prophets Abraham, Moses, Aaron, David, Solomon, Balaam, Daniel, Habakkuk, Jeremiah, Isaiah and Nebuchadnezzar.

At some point the telling of stories from the Bible left the church and became the property of the people, and comprised the mainstay religious festival throughout much of Europe, and particularly in the British Isles. They grew to take the form of a pageant, in which a cycle of short plays would tell the biblical stories from Creation to the Last Judgement. These collections of plays are known as 'mystery' or 'miracle' cycles, the later title being more commonly used when the plays expand to include the lives of the saints.

MYSTERY CYCLES

Although they may have started out as related more to the church than the people, eventually it would seem that the size and length of each pageant meant that the organization and responsibility for each performance devolved to the populace. Certainly by the time they had reached their peak, the mystery cycles had become the responsibility of the trade guilds of a town or city. A particular guild would often take an appropriate story – the shipwrights acting out the story of Noah, and the butchers the last supper, and so on.

Dramatic Costs

A document left by the Guild of Smiths in Coventry tells us of these costs for presenting a play and providing a pageant wagon:

Cost of first rehearsal	2s. 2d.
For bread, ale and cooking during second rehearsal	2s. 4d.
Cost of a quart of wine to hire dress for Pilate's wife	2½d.
Repairs to pageant wagon	1s. 2d.

As they were based on the Bible, each cycle took a similar format; this is the generic form of the English mystery play cycle:

The Fall of Lucifer
The Creation
Adam and Eve and the Temptation
Cain and Abel
Noah and the Flood
Abraham and Isaac
Moses and the Ten Commandments
Mary and Joseph and the Annunciation
The Birth of Christ, including the shepherds, the three kings, and the Nativity
Stories from the Life of Jesus
The Passion
The Crucifixion
The Resurrection
Christ appears amongst his disciples
The Ascension
The End of the World
The Last Judgement

The episode of 'Abraham and Isaac', which appears in all surviving cycles and some of the remnants, is most often used by scholars in comparing the qualities of the different cycles.

Within each area above, different guilds would have acted out different parts of the story, and because within a cycle each play was quite short, a pageant could have up to something in the region of forty individual plays. The main climaxes of each cycle were the Nativity and the Passion.

The writing within these long pieces varies enormously, from easily memorized doggerel to verse of some maturity. Despite their religious content the plays were written and performed in a vigorous, lively and entertaining manner, although not without due reverence. Historical accuracy and dramatic logic were often dispensed with in order that the entertainment might proceed at a good and hearty pace. Local references and in-jokes would have been common, and the staging ranged from very basic to very imaginative. Gruesome stories seemed to have been given particular attention – realistic crucifixions, and fiery harrowings in hell. Symbolism, much borrowed from the church, would probably have featured greatly; for example, coloured cloths may well have been used to represent the parting of the Red Sea. The performers, all men, were of course also all amateurs, and no doubt their skills varied greatly.

Amateur Theatre

It is perhaps apposite to remember that the word 'amateur' derives from the Latin word for 'to love'. As such we should never forget that some of the greatest theatrical enjoyment comes from watching the work of talented amateurs – and it started here, in the medieval period.

With so many scenes to get through it is likely that a pageant would have taken typically between one to three days to complete. No doubt single playlets may well have been performed alone or in lesser sequences away from the main festivals of Whitsun and Corpus Christi.

The mystery plays of England were contemporary with the French *mystères*, the Italian *sacre rappresentazioni*, the German *Geistspiele* and the *autos sacramentales* of Spain. Mystery cycles are recorded as having taken place in Borges, Florence, Frankfurt, Lucerne, Mons, Perranzabuloe, St Just and Valenciens, and there is even a record of a pageant – to impress the natives with religious fervour – in Cuzco, Peru; indeed a Passion play is still famously performed regularly in Oberammergau (in modern Germany), and has been since 1634.

In Britain, records exist that tell us of mystery pageants in Aberdeen, Bath, Beverley, Bristol, Brome (in Suffolk), Canterbury, Chester, Coventry, Dublin, Ipswich, Kendal, Lancaster, Leicester, Lincoln, London, Louth, Newcastle-upon-Tyne, Northampton, Norwich, Preston, Towneley (aka Wakefield), Worcester and York. Undoubtedly there were more than this, but even this list shows their profusion.

Of the cycles listed above, only four texts or lengthy parts of texts have survived, from Chester, York, Towneley and Coventry. There are also a few surviving single pieces from other cycles.

The Chester Mystery Cycle

This cycle dates from *c.*1375, and exists in five different manuscripts. A lot of recorded evidence remains, much in the form of civic documents that show the development of this cycle. As would seem to be the case with all cycles, this one grew from simple beginnings, with the cycle being added to and expanded over the years.

Dating in some form from *c.*1375, this cycle was certainly performed by guilds from at least 1422, and by 1467 eight separate guilds were known to have been involved. By 1500 this number had risen to twenty-four, whilst records of 1540 show twenty-six. Records of 1575 show twenty-four plays in the cycle, and the first of the surviving manuscripts contain these scenes and date from 1607. The full list was preceded with banns and with those guilds that performed each play; it looks like this:

PLAY	GUILD RESPONSIBLE
Fall of Lucifer	Tanners
Creation and Fall; Death of Abel	Drapers
Noah's Flood	Water-leaders and drawers in the Dee
Lot; Abraham and Isaac	Barbers and wax chandlers
Balaam and his Ass	Cappers and linen drapers
Salutation and Nativity	Wrights and slaters
Shepherds	Painters and glaziers
Coming of the Three Kings	Vitners
Offering; Return of the Kings	Mercers
Slaughter of the Innocents	Goldsmiths
Purification	Blacksmiths
Temptation; Woman Taken in Adultery	Butchers
Lazarus	Glovers
Christ's Entry into Jerusalem	Corvisors
Betrayal of Christ	Bakers
Passion	Fletchers, bowyers, coopers and stringers
Crucifixion	Ironmongers
Harrowing of Hell	Cooks and innkeepers
Resurrection	Skinners
Pilgrims to Emmaus	Saddlers
Ascension	Tailors
Descent of the Holy Spirit	Fishmongers
Ezechiel	Cloth-workers
Antichrist	Dyers
Judgement	Websters

The York Mystery Cycle

Records date this cycle, in an early form, from before 1378, but it is mostly known from a single manuscript of forty-eight scenes, dated 1430–40. Interestingly, it was recorded as having fifty scenes in 1415, but then contraction and editing must also have played a part in the development of such cycles. Certainly this work was contemporaneous with the Chester cycle, but comparison of the two shows York to have been more detailed, and longer. Written in fifteenth-century Yorkshire dialect, the crucifixion scene in this cycle is noted in particular for its use of vivid realism. The full cycle was as follows:

PLAY	GUILD RESPONSIBLE
Creation; Fall of Lucifer	Barkers
Creation, to the Fifth Day	Plasterers
Creation of Adam and Eve	Cardmakers
Adam and Eve in Eden	Fullers
The Fall of Man	Coopers
Expulsion from Eden	Armourers
Sacrifice of Cain and Abel	Glovers
Building of the Ark	Shipwrights
Noah and his Wife; the Flood	Fishers and mariners
Abraham and Isaac	Parchmenters and bookbinders
Exodus of the Israelites from Egypt; Ten Plagues; Crossing of the Red Sea	Hosiers
Annunciation and Visitation	Spicers
Joseph and Mary	Pewterers and founders
Journey to Bethlehem; Birth of Jesus	Tile-thatchers
Shepherds	Chandlers
Coming of the Three Kings to Herod	Masons
Coming of the Kings; Adoration	Goldsmiths
Flight into Egypt	Marshals
Slaughter of the Innocents	Girdlers and nailers
Christ with the Doctors	Spurriers and loriners
Baptism of Jesus	Barbers
Temptation	Smiths
Transfiguration	Curriers
Woman Taken in Adultery; Lazarus	Capmakers
Christ's Entry into Jerusalem	Skinners
Conspiracy	Cutlers
Last Supper	Bakers
Agony and Betrayal	Cordwainers
Peter's Denial; Jesus before Caiaphas	Bowyers and fletchers
Dream of Pilate's Wife; Jesus before Pilate	Tapiters and couchers
Trial before Herod	Litsters
Second Accusation before Pilate; Remorse of Judas; Purchase of the Field of Blood	Cooks and water-leaders
Second Trial before Pilate	Tilemakers
Christ lead to Calvary	Shearmen
Crucifixion	Pinners and painters
Mortification of Christ; Burial	Butchers
Harrowing of Hell	Saddlers
Resurrection	Carpenters
Christ's Appearance to Mary Magdalene	Winedrawers
Travellers to Emmaus	Sledmen
Purification of Mary; Simeon and Anna	Hatmakers, masons and labourers
Incredulity of Thomas	Scriveners
Ascension	Tailors
Descent of the Holy Spirit	Potters
Death of Mary	Drapers
Appearance of Mary to Thomas	Weavers
Assumption and Coronation of the Virgin	Hostlers
Judgement	Mercers

The Towneley Mystery Cycle

This cycle was originally known as the Wakefield cycle. It has thirty-two scenes dating from a single manuscript of 1450, and was named after the Towneley family of Burnley, Lancashire, who held the manuscript for many years. Although there are two records of performances in Wakefield, in 1554 and 1556, and Wakefield is mentioned twice in the text, it is nevertheless possible that, although closely related, the Wakefield cycle may well have been of a different text entirely.

On the other hand, there was no clear sense of copyright for these pieces, and many borrowings and importations may well have taken place. Indeed there are close similarities between the Towneley and the York cycle, for both are written in the same vernacular and contain six scenes that are virtually identical: the Pharaoh, Christ before the doctors, Christ led to Calvary, the Harrowing of Hell, the Resurrection, and the Last Judgement.

The Towneley Cycle is noted for its particularly broad humour in parts, and it contains the unique and very farcical second *Shepherd's Play*, featuring Mak the sheep stealer. This play is credited to an individual writer known as the Wakefield Master, thought to have been responsible for revising the Towneley cycle at the beginning of the fifteenth century; in particular he is credited as having been the author of six plays within the cycle: *The Murder of Abel, Noah and his Sons*, the two *Shepherds' Plays, King Herod*, and *Conspiracy*. These plays are noted for their sense of humour and pathos. The full list follows, although in this case the guilds responsible for each section are generally unknown. Plays marked * are those considered to be by the Wakefield Master.

PLAY	GUILD RESPONSIBLE
Creation	Barkers of Wakefield
Murder of Abel*	Glovers
Noah and his Sons*	Merchants of Wakefield
Abraham and Isaac	
Isaac	
Jacob	
Prophets	
Pharaoh	Litsters
Caesar Augustus	
Annunciation	
Salutation of Elizabeth	
First Shepherds' Pageant*	
Second Shepherds' Pageant*	
Offering of the Magi	
Flight of Joseph and Mary into Egypt	
Herod the Great*	
Purification of Mary	
Pageant of the Doctors	
John the Baptist	
Conspiracy*	
Buffeting	
Scourging	
Crucifixion	
Talents	
Harrowing of Hell	
Resurrection	
Pilgrims to Emmaus	Fishers
Thomas of India	
Ascension	
Judgement	
Lazarus	
Hanging of Judas	

The Coventry Mystery Cycle

This cycle was more often known as the *Ludus Coventriae*, and had forty-two scenes dating from a single manuscript of 1468. However, it is more likely to have come from Lincoln than Coventry, and it has also been known as the Hegge Plays and the N-town cycle. It is worthy of another title because it differs from the other cycles in certain ways: it is the only cycle where no evidence exists of its having been performed by guilds; and its actual town of origin is still unclear.

Acting Costs

The following information is also taken from the document left by the Guild of Smiths in Coventry, whose play dealt with Christ before Pilate and the dream of Pilate's wife. Performers were paid, the amount being according to the length of their part(s).

to God/Jesus	2s.
to Herod	3s. 4d.
to Pilate's wife	3s. 4d.
to the devil and Judas	18d.
Costs of costumes and other workmanship:	15s.

Although broadly similar to the other cycles, it has a more scholarly structure and complex staging requirements, the latter suggesting it may have been staged on a single stage (see below). The cycle unusually contains two passion plays, which may have been used on alternate years, and two plays that stand out as possible imports from other occasions: a Saint Anne's Day play, and a play dealing with the Assumption of the Blessed Virgin Mary.

Other Remnants

Apart from these four cycles other remnants survive; these include two plays from the real Coventry cycle, and a single text from each of the Brome, Norwich, Northampton and Newcastle cycles.

Staging

Mystery plays were probably staged in one of three different ways: in England, the pageant wagon would seem to have been the norm, although the *Ludus Coventriae* seems to indicate a stationary single stage, or series of fixed stages. In mainland Europe a circular staging often seems to have been used. Men would have played all the parts. (*See* illustrations p.40.)

Extract from *The Creation*, and *Adam and Eve*, Chester Mystery Cycle

This is from the second part of the pageant, traditionally performed by the drapers' guild – probably because it is the part in the story where Adam and Eve realize the need to clothe themselves!

SERPENS:
Take of this fruite and assaie.
It is good meate, I dare laye.
And but thou fynde yt to thy paye [advantage],
Say that I am false.
Eate thou on apple and no moe,
And yow shall knew both wayle and woe,
And be lyke to goddess, both twoo,
Thou and thy housband also.

EVA:
Ah, lord, this tree is fayre and bright,
Greene and semelye [beautiful] in my sighte,
The fruyte swete and much of mighte,
That goddes it may us make.
An apple of it I will eate,
To assaye which is the meate;
And my housband I will get
One morsell for to take.

Adam, husband, life and deere,
Eate some of this apple here –
It is fayre, my leeif fere,
It may thou not forsake.

ADAM:
That is sooth, Eve, without weere [doubt].
The fruit is sweete and fayre in feere;
Therfor I will doe thy prayer,
One morsell I will take.

Tunc Adem comedit et statim nudi sunt, et lamentando dicat. [Then Adam eats and at once they are naked, and weeping he shall say]
Out! Alas! What eales me?
I am naked, well I see;
Woman, cursed must thou be
For bothe now we be shente [destroyed].
I wotte not shame whether to flee,
For this fruite was forbydden me;
Now have I broken, through red [advice] of thee,
My Lordes commaundement.

EVA:
Alas! This adder hath done me nye.
Alas! Her red why did I?
Naked we bene bothe for-thye,
And of our shape ashamed.

ADAM:
Yea, soothe said I in prophesie,
When thou wast taken of my body,
Man woe thou woldest be witlie;
Therefore thou wast so named.

EVA:
Adam, husband, I red we take
Thes figg-leaves, for shame sake,
And to our members a hillinge [covering] make
Of them for thee and me.

ADAM:
Therewith my members I will hyde,
And under this tre I will abyde;
For sickerlie [certainly] come God us beside
Owt of this place shall we.

Tunc Adam et Eva cooperiant gentalia sue cum foliis et stabunt sub abore, et venit Deus clamans cum alta voce. [Then Adam and Eve shall cover their genitals with leaves and hide beneath the tree, and God comes, calling with a loud voice.]

*Medieval staging: 1) pageant wagon;
2) single stage – multi-stage, booth
or mansion; 3) circular setting.*

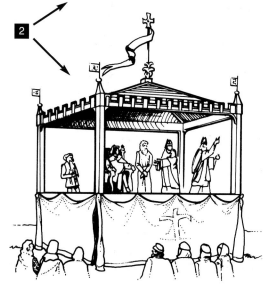

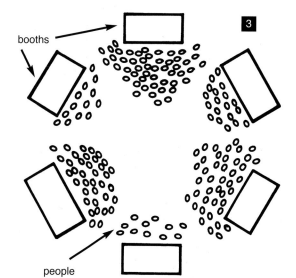

booths

people

A pageant wagon.

Whilst the morality play is the next important development in dramatic art, it must also be remembered that the tournament and adjacent festival were also of this period. Mumming, which had been around for several centuries, was still also a popular event: it is perhaps best defined as a transitional entertainment where performers 'disguised' themselves to recreate famous scenes from history or myth. The pieces were often set to music with specific choreography, although they nevertheless remained fairly static and unscripted. The mummers therefore took their place amongst the troubadours and other common purveyors of amusement of this period.

MORALITY PLAYS

The tendency towards secularization saw the morality play develop from the traditions of the mystery cycle; indeed, morality plays were very similar in structure and content to the mystery plays that preceded them. And although no longer based on stories from the bible, morality plays nevertheless still sought to instruct and educate their audience. Written in the vernacular, they were often long and rambling, like the mystery plays; however, performances were no longer restricted to particular religious festivals. Most notably, morality plays featured performers playing the roles of abstracted concepts, for example Old Vice, Virtue, World, Riches, Luxury and Holy Church, as well as characters such as the Devil and, famously, Mankind and Everyman.

Early morality plays from the thirteenth century include *The Marriage of Faith and Loyalty* and *The Seven Deadly Sins and the Virtues*, both from France, and *The Pride of Life* and *Dux Moraud*, both from England. One of the earliest recorded and well documented morality plays is *The Castell of Perseverance* (*c.*1410). Staged much like a mystery play (*see* illustration, p.42), this work involves the character of Mankind being taken through their life and, despite meeting such negative characters as Backbiter, Folly and Lust, finding, through Perseverance and Mercy, a generally good end.

Evidence of the staging of this piece, with a castle surrounded by scaffolds named Flesh, World, Belial, Covetousness and God, combines with some wonderful stage directions and costume details, to indicate a spectacular and visually stunning entertainment.

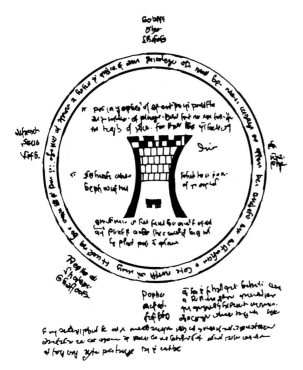

The Castell of Perseverance *staging diagram.*

The following is an extract from *The Castell of Perseverance*'s directions within the text:

> The four daughters shall be clad in mantles, Mercy in white, Righteousness in red
> altogether, Truth in sad green and Peace in black, and they shall play in the place all together till they bring up the soul.
> He that shall play Belial, look that he have gunpowder burning in pipes in his hands and in his ears and in his arse when he goeth to battle.[iii]

Later morality plays include, in England, *Wisdom* (*c.*1460) and *Mankind* (*c.*1470), and several works by Henry Medwall, such as *Nature* and *Fulgens and Lucres* (*c.*1496). Interestingly the latter includes a tournament and a dumb-show, as well as a long morality play concerning the wooing of Lucretia, and a 'moral interlude'.

Moral interludes were shorter than morality plays, and usually more humorous. Medwall was known for his satires, and certainly alongside the moral message that was self-evidently contained within these plays, was placed a good amount of vigorous humour. In both interludes and plays, and alongside bold characters such as the seven deadly sins, would have appeared the Devil and his agents. In fact they appear in a number of pieces, and in bold physical settings such as Hell's Mouth; they would have been extravagantly dressed, and have played to an enthusiastic crowd, with much appropriate booing and hissing. These early moral interludes lead to the genre of interlude proper, discussed below. Other examples include the anonymous pair *Hickscorner* (*c.*1513) and *Youth* (*c.*1515).

Other morality plays include *Maitre Pierre Pathelin* and *La Condamnacion de Bancquet* from France, and *Fastenachtspiele* from Germany.

Of all extant morality plays perhaps *Everyman* has been most performed in recent times, and it remains a remarkably powerful piece. It was originally written in Dutch ('Elkerlijk') and dates from around 1495. Once more it tells of the journey made by the title character through life, and his meetings with various abstracted personae. The full cast list below is in order of appearance, and thus starts with the messenger, who reads a prologue, and ends with the doctor, who reads an epilogue.

Cast of *Everyman*

Messenger	Knowledge
God	Confession
Death	Beauty
Everyman	Strength
Fellowship	Discretion
Kindred	Five Wits
Cousin	Angel
Goods	Doctor
Good Deeds	

The following is an extract from *Everyman*, the opening of this piece allowing us a clear understanding of what is to follow:

HERE BEGINNETH A TREATISE HOW THE HIGH
FATHER OF HEAVEN SENDETH DEATH
TO SUMMON EVERY CREATURE TO COME AND
GIVE ACCOUNT OF THEIR LIVES IN THIS WORLD,
AND IS IN MANNER OF A MORAL PLAY.

MESSENGER:
I pray you all give your audience,
And hear this matter with reverence,
By figure a moral play:
The Summoning of Everyman called it is,
That of our lives and ending shows
How transitory we be all day.
This matter is wondrous precious,
But the intent of it is more gracious,
And sweet to bear away.
The story saith: Man, in the beginning
Look well, and take good heed to the ending,
Be you never so Gay!
Ye think sin in the beginning full sweet,
Which in the end causeth the souls to weep,
When the body lieth in clay.
Here shall you see how Fellowship and Jollity,
Both Strength, Pleasure, and Beauty,
Will fade from thee as flower in May;
For ye shall hear how our Heaven King
Calleth Everyman to general reckoning:
Give audience, and hear what he doth say. [Exit]

INTERLUDES

An interlude was a short dramatic sketch that took its name from the Latin *interludium*. As the name suggests, these sketches were often performed as part of a bigger entertainment, a festival or banquet, in private homes or at court. The people who performed them were usually individuals dedicated to this form of performance, and thus could be said to be the first professional 'actors'. For example, a group of players known as the 'King's Interludes' (*Lusores Regis*) was recorded as early as 1493 in the reign of Henry VII, and played at the wedding of his daughter Margaret to the King of Scotland, James IV, in 1503.

Notable Interludes

Amongst significant interludes of the time was *Magnyfycence* (*c.*1515), written by John Skelton (*c.*1460–1529; Skelton was tutor to Henry, the son of Henry VII, later crowned Henry VIII). In this play Prince Magnyfycence is a kindly ruler who becomes corrupted by characters such as Folly and Mischief. Luckily other personas, such as Hope and Perseverance, are there to aid him and bring him back to his senses. This is the only work of Skelton's to have survived, although he is recorded as the author of three morality plays and other interludes.

Then there is the play called *The Satyre of the Thrie Estaites* (*c.*1530) by David Lindsay (*c.*1490–1554), the first recorded dramatic work to include a discussion directly dealing with the world of politics, and possibly too long to properly be described as an interlude.

John Heywood (*c.*1497–1580) was also noted for plays in this genre, and is often quoted as the first dramatist to make good use of the form. As the titles of his work show, they remained close in intent to the moralities that preceded them. His most famous play is called *The Playe called the foure P.P.; a newe and a very merry enterlude of a palmer, a pardoner, a potycary, a pedler* (*c.*1530), in which each participant tries to out-lie each other in a battle of wits. He also wrote *The Play of the Wether* and *The Play of Love* (both 1533), and *The Dialogue of Wit and Folly* (*c.*1533).

Thomas More

John Heywood was married to Elizabeth Rastell, a niece of Sir Thomas More, who himself took a great interest in the theatre of the day. He refers to the group known as the King's Interludes in his writings of 1595.

These works preceded the great flourishing of drama of the Elizabethan age, though as always, it is difficult to categorize and define any actual moments and changes of style. Many scholars have in fact attached different names to them – for example, there are many superb studies in a collection compiled and edited by Peter Happé [iv]. His book is entitled *Tudor Interludes* and contains *Fulgens and Lucres*, which I have called a morality, alongside Heywood's *The Play of the Wether*.

Also included in Happé's book are *Wit and Science* (*c*.1535) by John Redford, described by some as an ethnic morality; and the anonymous *Respublica*, which I have also seen defined as a moral interlude. All this can be rather overwhelming, so it is perhaps better that the plays speak for themselves; they certainly make fascinating reading, and many are readily available.

Other interludes include: *Wealth and Health* and *The World and the Child*, both anonymous; *The Four Elements* (*c*.1517) by John Rastell; *Lusty Juventus* (*c*.1550) by R. Wever; *Apius and Virginia* [v] (*c*.1567), by an author only known as R.B.; *Like Will To Like* [vi] (*c*.1568) by Ulpian Fulwell, a cleric; and *Sir Thomas More* [vii] (*c*.1590), by Anthony Munday.

LATE MEDIEVAL PLAYS: THE FIRST REAL PLAYS?

Interludes saw a transition from the abstract moral works that preceded them, to the first plays of a length and shape similar to what we now think of as a play. These were authored works, they contain characters and events, and they seek to tell a story rather than just make moral points. They are followed therefore by what we may choose to call the first real plays in dramatic literature, written by the first 'real' playwrights. Such men as Roger Ascham, William Cornish, Sir John Dee, Richard Edwards, Nicholas Grimald, John Heywood, William Hunis, Ralph Radcliffe, John Rastell, John Redford, John Rightwise and Nicholas Udall. Generally these were educated men who took for their models the classical Roman plays known at that time. Some adapted or translated them (Dee and Ascham), others attempted to write new works in the same style, for example Grimald and Udall.

Nicholas Udall (1505–56) was a scholar, and the headmaster of Eton and Westminster schools. His only surviving work was written for the boys of Eton to perform alongside their usual Roman dramas, and was called *Ralph Roister Doister*, *c*.1532/3. This play is often dubbed the first comedy written in the English language – although of course this is to ignore much of the comic content of the mystery plays. Modelled on the work of Plautus more than Terence, *Ralph Roister Doister* is set in London and tells of Ralph, the conceited central character's attempts to win the hand of a wealthy widow, Dame Custance. It includes real stage dialogue of a contemporary nature, particularly between Ralph and his unctuous side-kick Merrygreek. Other, wonderfully named characters include the nurse Madge Mumblecrust, and maids Tibet Talkapace and Annot Alyface.

Gammer Gurton's Needle (*c*.1550) is an anonymous piece written by a 'Master of Arts' of Cambridge, and shows a far greater complexity than *Ralph Roister Doister*. It follows a classical pattern that adheres to the Aristotelian unities – there is no change of scene, for example. It concerns the hunt for the needle of the title: Dame Chat is blamed for stealing Gurton's needle by scandal-monger Diccon, but all comes to a happy ending when the needle is found in servant Hodge's breeches. Although the plot is too simplistic to entertain a modern audience, it is cleverly woven, and the dialogue and repartee show a remarkable maturity for the period. In addition this play probably sees the beginnings of the long English tradition of the country bumpkin.

Gorboduc (*c*.1561) by Thomas Norton (1532–84) and Thomas Sackville (1536–1608) is a play modelled fully on the Senecan tradition. In five acts it uses blank verse to great effect in direct speech. As with the classical model, a chorus and a messenger are used. However, the play derives much of its power from the fact that the plot revolves around the moral dilemmas of the very human characters – thus moving further and further from the abstract personifications that have otherwise so far occupied us. The storyline is that Gorboduc, King of Britain, divides his kingdom between his two sons Ferrex and Porrex, and they quarrel. Porrex kills Ferrex, and is then killed in turn by his vengeful mother, Queen Videna. The population, aroused to great anger by these acts, then kill both the king and the queen. *Gorboduc* was known to have been first performed before Elizabeth I on New Year's Day in 1562 in Inner Temple Hall, London.

The source for this story is certainly the idiosyncratic *History of Britain*, written by Geoffrey of Monmouth, and it is not difficult to see how the play, alongside the history, may well have acted also as a model for Shakespeare's *King Lear*.

The following is an extract from *Gorboduc* by Thomas Norton and Thomas Sackville.

Queen Videna's soliloquy, taken from the opening to Act Four, shows just how far dramatic writing had come in the period covered in this chapter – indeed, there are distinct echoes of the work of William Shakespeare, who was perhaps being conceived even as it was being written!

Act IV, Scene I, Videna sola.

Why should I live, and linger forth my time
In longer life to double my distress?
O me, most woeful wight [a], whom no mishap
Long ere this day could have bereavèd hence.
Might not these hands, by fortune or by fate,
Have pierc'd this breast, and life with iron reft?
Or in this palace here, where I so long
Have spent my days, could not that happy hour
Once, once have happ'd, in which these huge
   frames
With death by fall might have oppressèd me?
Or should not this most hard and cruel soil,
So oft where I have press'd my wretched steps,
Sometime had ruth of mine accursèd life
To rend in twain, and swallow me therein?
So had my bones possessèd now in peace
Their happy grave within the closèd ground,
And greedy worms had gnawn this pinèd heart
Without my feeling pain: so should not now
This living breast remain the ruthful tomb,
Wherein my heart yielden to death is grav'd;
Nor dreary thoughts, with pangs of pining grief,
My doleful mind had not afflicted thus.

O my belovèd son! O my sweet child!
My dear Ferrex, my joy, my life's delight!
Is my belovèd son, is my sweet child,
My dear Ferrex, my joy, my life's delight,
Murder'd with cruel death? O hateful wretch!
O heinous trator both to heaven and earth!
Thou, Porrex, thou this damnèd deed hast
   wrought;
Thou, Porrex, thou shalt dearly bye the same.
Traitor to kin and kind, to sire and me,
To thine own flesh, and traitor to thyself:
The gods on thee in hell shall wreak their revenge
On thee, Porrex, thou false and caitiff [b] wight.

a Wight = a person
b Caitiff = a captive, a mean and despicable person

CONCLUSION

The flow of ideas in this chapter is perhaps somewhat misleading. It must be understood that, as with all human events, nothing quite as neat as a sequence of events actually occurred. Tropes, ludus, ordo, mystery and morality plays all probably co-existed, and continued to do so alongside the newer developments of moral interludes, interludes and so called 'real plays'. What is true is that eventually all such genres became outmoded – or rather, grew and developed into new ones.

The extraordinary drama of the medieval period, with its colourful and often very human face, concludes in this chapter with work of some fine maturity. Not surprisingly, then, that these works lead us to a veritable explosion in the field of dramatic art. Indeed, what followed was an era of many such great explorations, in the arts, the sciences and indeed in the world itself, and it is to this, the theatre of the Elizabethan Age, that we now turn.

3 THE RENAISSANCE AND EUROPEAN THEATRE

Ah, la belle chose que de savoir quelquechose.
Oh, how fine it is to know a thing or two.
MOLIÈRE

Gasping for breath, you grip fiercely on to your friend next to you for support. You cannot believe that anything could possibly be so funny, and so painful. You are watching the antics of your hero Tristano Martinelli playing the rascally character of Arlechino for the company of players called 'Confidenti'. His comic timing is superb, his physical and verbal humour are, in your opinion, unmatched. From the moment his masked figure enters the stage a smile cracks your face, a smile only too willing to transform into a hearty belly-laugh. And you are not alone – seemingly the whole audience cheer and jeer him on. The man behind the cunning mask is much loved. You have heard that as a performer Martinelli can be very exacting, and is not so adored by his company; nevertheless, as far as you are concerned, he can do no wrong: the man is simply a comic genius! You sigh with exhaustion at the sheer joy of the comedy being played out before you.

THE RENAISSANCE AND THEATRE IN ITALY

As indicated at the close of the previous chapter, secular drama became increasingly influenced by classical models. Throughout Europe, and in Italy in particular, a reinterpretation of all things classical took serious hold, and began to influence fine art, literature and drama; the interest in the classical was the spur for what we call the Renaissance.

OPPOSITE PAGE: *The use of masks, in Classical style, was often adopted in the theatre of the Renaissance*

The way in which the classics influenced theatre was related to both the manner in which certain texts were available, and how they were interpreted. Certainly, although Roman works by Plautus, Terence and Seneca had never been completely lost, they took on a new importance at this time. Knowledge of Roman plays in particular spread as they became available for the first time in print. Printed editions of Terence's plays date from 1471 in Italy, and they appeared in England between 1495 and 1497. Seneca's works appeared between 1480 and 1490.

The understanding of ancient Greek took a little longer for scholars of this period, and thus the works from that culture appeared in print later. Some works of Aristophanes had appeared in Venice as early as 1498, but more importantly those of Sophocles appeared in Italy in 1502, followed by those of Euripides in 1503. More works by Aristophanes appeared in 1516, and finally the works of Aeschylus in 1518. Starting with the Roman comedies and the tragedies of Seneca, these works were seized upon as the perfect models for the writing of drama – as was an overly structured understanding of the theoretical works of Horace and Aristotle.

In his splendid book *A History of the Theatre*, Glynne Wickham describes the explosion in interest in the classical texts and their influence as having two stages: revivalism and innovation.[i] As would be expected, he dates the former from 1471, the date of the first printed edition of the comedies of Terence. The point he makes is that initially the Italians sought to copy the classical works as they understood them; only later did more original work appear. Thus a period of revivals and adaptations

47

can be charted, the first notable revival being of Plautus' play *Menaechmi* (*see* page 29) in the theatre at Ferrara (*see* below) in 1486. In 1509, Seneca's *Phaedra* (*see* page 30) was first performed in Rome, and then again in Ferrara.

New works in this period, mostly adaptations, are collected together under the title 'Commedia Erudita', which translates as 'serious or learned drama', and generally suggests the rather turgid nature of the pieces. Examples are *La Cassaria* (*The Chest*) (1508) and *I Suppositi* (1509), both by Lodovico Ariosto (1474–1533), written in prose, and also for the theatre in Ferrara. Ariosto also wrote a later play, this time in verse: *Il Negromante* (1520).

Commedia Erudita

Italian scholar K.M. Lea comments that to enjoy and understand 'Commedia Erudita' you need to 'acquire a taste for Plautus and Terence, a good working knowledge of the *Decameron* ... a relish for realism in the close representation of men and manners, and a callous, quick enjoyment of human folly.'

Commedia Erudita

Examples of Commedia Erudita include *La Calandria* (1506), first performed in Urbino and later in Rome, and freely adapted from the works of Plautus, by Bernado Bibbiena (1470–1520); and also the works of Pietro Aretino (1492–1556). Aretino was often quoted by those that followed him as a great wit: Thomas Nash (1567–1601) described him as 'one of the wittiest knaves God ever made'[ii], and Milton called him 'that notorious ribald of Arezzo'[iii] (Aretino was born in Arezzo in Italy). His plays are as follows: *La Cortigiana* (1526); *Il Marescalco* (1533), based on *Casina* by Plautus (*see* page 29); *La Talanta* (1541); *Lo Ipocrito* (1542); *Il Filosofo* (1546); and *Orazio* (1546), his only tragedy.

Another example of this genre is Niccolò Machiavelli's play *La Mandradora* (*The Mandrake*), *c.*1515; it is really the only play from this period that has held its

interest down the years. Machiavelli's dates are 1469–1527, and his play rises above the usual narrow formula typical of these comedies and delivers a piece that works on a number of levels. The plot is both ingenious and complex: an impotent old man married to a young girl is fooled by the girl's scheming mother, amongst others, into allowing her to sleep with a young man. He does this for profit and on the understanding that a drug, derived from the root of a mandrake, is taken by the girl, and that this will have the effect of killing the young man directly he has had his way! The lover in turn naturally proves just as cunning in his scheming, and the whole plot is aided by a corrupt priest called Father Timoteo. The play works as a comedy, a thriller, and as a brutal critique of contemporary Florentine society. It is the only piece of this period to be regularly revived.

Machiavelli

Niccolò Machiavelli is known in history for works other than his plays. In casual conversation he seems often to be cast as a villain – we call devious and underhand trickery 'Machiavellian'. This derives from his political treatise *Il Principe* (1513), which deals very frankly with the political machinations of the period in which he wrote. However, although he described these wicked ways, he did not necessarily advocate them!

The following is an extract from *Mandradora* by Niccolò Machiavelli, taken from Act One, Scene Four, in which Nicia has been sent to fetch a sample of his wife's urine to convince him that the trickster Ligurio and Callimaco are capable of helping him get her with child. The latter's servant Siro has been a witness to events, and now addresses the audience.

SIRO: And they say judges are brainy men! Well, if the others are like this one, the rest of us must be as thick as bricks. One thing's for sure, that Lurgio and that crazy master of mine have got him by the nose, and they will wind him up as tight as a drum in making a fool of him. It suits me, just as long as it's not found out – 'cos if it was, my life would be in danger, and so would my master's ... and his property. And would you believe that now, my master's setting himself up as a quack! Well, I can't begin to guess what they are up to, or where this trick is leading to. But here comes Mr Nicia, and clutching a chamber pot. Who wouldn't laugh at such a buffoon?

Renaissance Staging in Italy

The theatre building in Ferrara was typical of the day. It was built for the court of the Count d'Este, the Count being patron to a number of artists, including playwright Lodovico Ariosto. The theatre was built in the classical style as understood from the works of the Roman architect Vitruvius (70–15BC), whose manuscript *De Architectura* had been discovered in 1414 and printed in 1484.

Theatres built in this period were not, however, the outdoor amphitheatres of ancient Greece or Rome that were described in Chapter one: instead the classical architecture of columns and friezes was placed indoors. Thus the forestage, or 'pro skene', of ancient Greece became the wide opening of an internalized stage, defined by the framing of a 'proscenium' arch.

The continuing embellishment of these ideas, irresistible to the artists and craftsmen of the burgeoning Renaissance, produced the beautifully detailed and highly perspectivized settings synonymous with the theatre of this period. Indeed, much of the scenery at Ferrara is said to have been painted by the artist Raphael.

Just as the theatres echoed the interest that Renaissance artists had in exploring perspective, so also were the decorative styles of the period incorporated

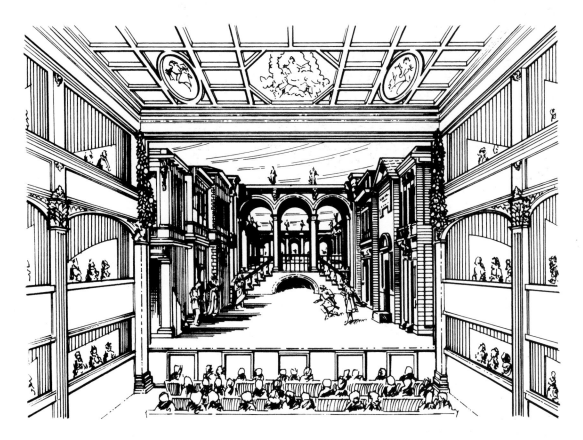

The Italian Renaissance stage.

A stage setting

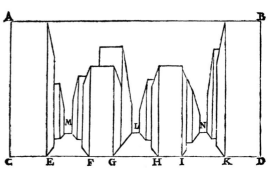

Renaissance stage devices; diagrams from the work of Nicola Sabbattini.

The technical drawing to realize a perspectivized set

The specifications for a stage ship

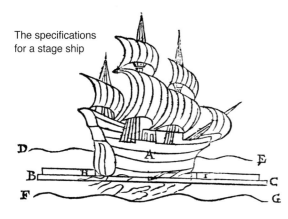

How to realize stage waves …

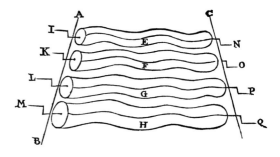

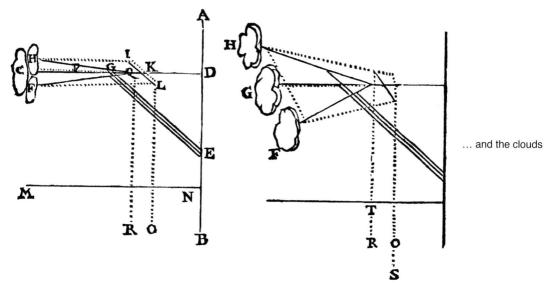

… and the clouds

to make lavish backdrops, scenery and stage machinery. Eventually treatises were written on the subject, notably by Sebastino Serlio (1475–1554), Leone Ebreo Di Somi (1527–92) and Nicola Sabbattini (1574–1654), the illustrations from these works serving to display the breadth and attention given to this field at this time.

The Development of Dramatic Art

At around this time three other notable styles of dramatic art appeared in Italy: intermezzi, opera seria and Commedia dell'Arte. **Intermezzi** were entertainments combining music, great spectacle and scenic invention. Originating as short pieces to be played between the acts of a Commedia Erudita (or later an opera) or the courses of a banquet, they developed in length to stand alone as court entertainments. They were similar to mystery plays in their inventive quality, and often used pageant wagons, and were also like the English interludes described in Chapter 2 (page 43). They usually portrayed mythological events, often in tableau form, and were often highly pastoral in nature. Typical examples of intermezzi were those of the Camerata in Florence.

Opera seria saw the beginnings of what became opera. The spectacular entertainments of intermezzi were brought into the theatres and used as a backdrop for a story told with increased contributions from the musical talents of the day. For example, as early as 1597 the composer Jacopo Peri and the poet Ottario Rinuccini set the story of Daphne on stage for the court of Tuscany; the piece included songs, recitative and spoken dialogue. In 1607 Claudio Monteverdi took up the challenge of writing music drama, and thus the first operas began to appear: dramatic works combining in equal measure song and story-telling. Such pieces led eventually to the construction of theatres that included space for musicians on a suitable scale (opera houses), and which appeared from around 1630 onwards; the musicians were placed in the area before the stage that was called by the Greeks the 'orchestra' (*see* page 10).

Commedia dell'Arte

Commedia dell'Arte comes as an almost direct development from Commedia Erudita, the term translating as 'theatre of the professional artist' – that is, not of the amateur or untrained. It was nevertheless a lighter, less scholarly theatre style than Commedia Erudita, one more likely to encourage inventiveness and lightness of touch, and was therefore generally more fun.

Commedia dell'Arte dates from around 1570, and involved a team of highly seasoned professional performers who improvised around a basic plot synopsis. There was no fixed script or dialogue. The performers, many of whom gained great renown for their skills, took the same character in each piece, their life's work thus being to perfect the idiosyncracies of their chosen role. And as they became totally identified with their roles, so they also developed and redefined them.

Although much of the substance of these performances is now lost to us, the names of many of the performers are not. For example one of the earliest originators of the character 'Pedrolino' (*see* below) was Giovanni Pellesini (*c*.1526–1612), and the character of 'Scapino' became forever associated with the performer Francesco Gabrielli (d.1654). In this form of dramatic art it is easy to see how the influence of the classics is still very prevalent. Masks were worn, and the characters identified by them display a mixture of the classical stereotyping of Plautus and Terence, combining with an abstracted quality that we may perhaps associate with the morality play.

The plays' stock characters became well known to their audiences, and were easily identified by their clothing, often even the prevailing colours that they wore, and the masks that they used. The typical Commedia cast list was as shown in the box (pp.52–55).

Many Commedia dell'Arte companies became famous touring Italy, France and the rest of Europe, companies such as the 'Accesi', the 'Confidenti', the 'Fedeli', the 'Ganassa' and the 'Gelosi'. The pleasure and joy that the Commedia dell'Arte obviously created meant that it survived in Italy for over 200 years. Many later dramatic characters and other comic elements derive from this powerful theatrical form; examples include the English harlequinade, from which in turn came the uniquely English dramatic form of the pantomime, and even the great British seaside favourite, the 'Punch and Judy' show.

When Commedia dell'Arte did go out of fashion, the very nature of its improvisational style, the

Commedia dell'Arte Stock Characters

Name	*Characteristics/Type*	*French & English Variations & Derivative Characters, etc.*
Pantalone	Old man. Columbine's father or husband	Pantaloon (Eng) See *As You Like It* (Act II vii) 'the lean slipper'd pantaloon. With spectacles on nose and pouch at side'
Il Dottore	Pedant. Know-all	
Il Capitano	Swash-buckling soldier. A braggart	Derived from the Plautus character of *Miles Gloriosus* (*see* page 28). *See* Armado in *Loves Labour's Lost* and Pistoll in *Henry IV, Part 2*
Arlecchino	Comic servant, often principal comic figure. Lover of Columbine	Arlequin (Fr), Harlequin (Eng)
Pulcinella	Comic servant, and a ready wit. With humped back and a hooked nose	Polichinelle (Fr), Punchinello (Eng) Leading to the character of Punch in Punch and Judy.

THIS PAGE:
1) Pantalone;
2) Il Dottore;

OPPOSITE PAGE:
3) Il Capitano;
4) Arlecchino;
5) Pulcinella;

(continued overleaf)

Commedia dell'Arte Stock Characters *(continued)*

THIS PAGE:
6) Columbine;
7) Pedrolino;
8) Mezzetino;

OPPOSITE PAGE:
9) Scapino;
10) Scaramuccia.

Name	Characteristics/Type	French & English Variations & Derivative Characters, etc.
Columbine	Female maid servant Lover of Arlecchino	Columbina (Fr), Columbine (Eng)
Pedrolino	Comic servant, a clown	Pierrot (Fr & Eng). Compare with Leoncavallo's character Pagliacci from the tragic opera of the same name
Mezzetino	Male comic servant	Mezzetin (Fr), no English derivative
Scapino	Male comic servant, crafty and fleet of foot	Scapin (Fr), no English derivative. *See* Molière's *Les Fourbières de Scapin* (page 61)
Scaramuccia	Male comic servant	Scaramouche (Fr), no English derivative

A typical commedia *mask.*

BELOW: *In commedia style, a modern production of* A Servant of Two Masters *by Goldoni, directed by Peter Fieldson.*

Zany

The word 'zany' comes from this period. It was a term used to describe the male comic servants of the Commedia.

style that had made it so lively a comic form in the first place, meant that it also disappeared for ever. So much of the nature and content of these pieces relied on the contribution and skills of the individual performers that this wonderful style of theatre died with the last of them. The chain of tradition was broken, and now it is no longer possible to create the great theatrical magic that once prevailed. Equally, no scripts for Commedia dell'Arte exist, only outlines. The techniques of performance were also not committed to paper (even had this been possible), and so all that can be done is to try and glimpse how this work might have been, by looking to those it directly influenced. It is thus relevant here to jump slightly ahead in time to the work of Carlo Goldoni (1709–93), who adapted the traditions of Commedia dell'Arte for his own ends.

Goldoni's work from the early part of the eighteenth century carries the distinct echo of these pieces, and it is in this form that we are most likely to experience them today. Goldoni's most notable and still produced work is *A Servant of Two Masters*. This joyous play, with all its potential for slapstick and the broadest of farce, is well worth studying or, better still, seeing. A good production can certainly get us close to some idea of what the glories of Commedia dell'Arte may have been.

THE RENAISSANCE IN FRANCE

The Renaissance did not occur in Italy alone and, even if it can be said to have originated there to a greater degree than anywhere else, it certainly was not contained there. In France the work of Corneille and Racine can clearly be seen to follow similar trends.

Pierre Corneille

Corneille (1606–84) was born in Rouen, and was employed initially as a minor public official. He wrote his first plays, all comedies, for the theatres of Paris. However, in 1633 he had a serious falling out with Cardinal Richelieu and returned to work in the place of his birth. There he had his first great success with the tragedy *Médée*, a play that displays obvious classical roots. However, his most famous work, *El Cid*, is based on a figure from more recent history, in this case Spanish history. Returning to Paris in 1647 Corneille became increasingly fêted, and was finally elected to the Académie Française in 1647.

Cardinal Richelieu

Cardinal Richelieu (1558–1642) wielded extreme power in France as prime minister for Louis XIII. He also took a great interest in the theatre, co-writing a number of plays himself. He founded the French Academy and built the Palais-Royal theatre. He is also famously portrayed as a great villain in Dumas' novel *The Three Musketeers*.

Many of Corneille's great tragedies show good traditional Aristotelian structure, and many are based on stories from the classics or set in that world, including *Horace*, *Cinna*, *Polyeucte* and *La Morte de Pompée*, all of which are set in ancient Rome. However, the particular success of *El Cid* may well be due to the fact that it is structured in a more relaxed manner, doing away with a strict adherence to the so-called classical unities (*see* page 26).

Corneille is also known for his comedies, perhaps most notable amongst them *Le Mentuer*.

Although his later work was slightly overshadowed by the success of Racine, Corneille died in 1684 a greatly respected man of the French theatre.

PLAYS
Mélite (1630)
A comedy of manners.

Clitandre (1631)
A tragi-comedy.

Médée (1635)
A tragedy.

El Cid (1637)
Based on *Las Mocedades del Cid* by minor Spanish playwright Guillén de Castro y Bellvis.

Le Menteur (1637)
A comedy of manners, translated as *The Liar*.

La Suite du Menteur (1638)
The sequel to *Le Menteur* and, as often seems to be the case, not as successful as the original.

Horace (1640)
A classical tragedy.

Cinna (1641)
A classical tragedy.

Polyeucte (1642/3)
A classical tragedy.

La Morte de Pompée (1643)
A classical tragedy.

Rodogune (1645)

Theodore (1645)

Héraclius (1646)

Don Sanche d'Aragon (1649)
Thought to be one of Corneille's least successful pieces.

Andromède (1650)
A 'spectacle play', said to have been written to show off the state-of-the-art machinery of the Petit-Bourbon theatre.

Nicomède (1651)
A great and popular success. Revived, less successfully, in 1658 by Molière's company for Louis XIV.

Pertharite (1652)
A disaster for Corneille, that saw him take an eight-year break from writing.

Oedipe (1659)
A classical tragedy.

La Toison d'or (1660)
Another 'spectacle play', written for the marriage of Louis XIV.

Sertorius (1661)

Sophonishe (1663)

Othon (1664)

Agésilas (1666)

Attila (1667)
Produced by Molière for his company.

Tite et Bérénice (1670)
Produced by Molière for his company.

Psyché (1671)
A tragédie-ballet written in collaboration with Molière.

Pulchérie (1672)

Suréna (1674)

Jean Baptiste Racine

Racine (1639–99) was born in La Ferté-Milon, the son of a tax official. He was educated at a strict Jansenist convent, and his rigorous moral upbringing can be seen as a major influence in his work. Racine was also a fluent reader and translator of the ancient classics, in particular of Euripides and Sophocles. He originally studied to be a priest, but forsook this calling for that of the theatre around 1662/3. His first play, *La Thébaïde*, was performed by Molière's company at the famed Palais-Royal, as was his second play; but they subsequently had a serious disagreement, and all subsequent pieces by Racine were given to the rival company at the Hôtel de Bourgogne.

Racine's play *Andromache* can generally be said to have really confirmed his reputation as a great writer of drama. He then went on to write a number of highly successful pieces, and continued writing until he retired in 1677, on being appointed Royal Historiographer to Louis XIV. Racine died in 1699.

The Plays of Racine

The majority of Racine's output came from three basic sources: the writing of Euripides, tales from the Bible, and stories from more recent history. His works show perhaps a more natural humanist turn than those of Corneille. His Greek tragedies include *Andromaque*, *Iphigénie* and *Phèdre*. His tales from scripture include *Esther* and *Athalie*. His historical works include *Britannicus*, *Bérénice* and *Mithridate*. Racine is also known for a single comedy, *Les Plaideurs*.

PLAYS
La Thébaïde (1664)

Alexandre (1665)

Andromaque (1667)

Les Plaideurs (1668)
Vaguely based on Aristophanes' play *Wasps*.

Britannicus (1669)
This piece contains much fine poetic writing, although it is not as dramatically secure as many of his other works.

Bérénice (1670)
Much compared at the time (favourably) with Corneille's play on the same subject, and produced in the same year (*see* above).

Bajazet (1672)
An adaptation of a story from oriental history.

Mithridate (1673)
As above, also an adaptation from oriental history.

Iphigénie en Aulide (1674)
This play helped confirm Racine's growing reputation.

Phèdre (1677)
Whilst finishing this play Racine's enemies persuaded a lesser playwright to compose one on the same theme. Pradon's *Phèdre et Hippolyte* acted as a successful spoiler to Racine's work, and in disgust he stopped writing. His two remaining works follow much later.

Esther (1689)
Written as a favour for a performance at a school for young ladies in Saint-Cyr. Not performed in public elsewhere until 1721, it was, however, a delicate poetic work.

Athalie (1691)
Likewise written for Saint-Cyr, and a piece that finally found a public audience and success in 1716, seventeen years after Racine's death.

Molière (Jean Baptiste Poquelin)

Contemporary with both Corneille and Racine was Molière – indeed, he has already been mentioned a number of times as the producer of a number of their works. If Racine is to be considered the greatest writer of French classical tragedy, then there is no doubt that Molière wears the crown for comedy.

Molière (1622–73) was the pen name of Jean Baptiste Poquelin, and he differs from Corneille and Racine in that he soon abandoned the traditions of classical theatre, of Plautus and Terence in particular, to create a unique French style of comedy, perhaps over simplistically described as 'French farce'. He was a dramatist, an actor, a producer and a director, and he dedicated his life to comic theatre.

Molière was born in Paris, and from an early age loved the theatre. At the age of twenty-one he joined a company of professional actors, eventually marrying one of the troupe in 1662. Molière eventually came to manage the group himself, renaming it the 'Illustre Théâtre'. Having performed in Paris until 1645, the group then set out to tour the provinces, which it did until 1658. On returning in triumph to Paris, the Illustre Théâtre was then given permission by Louis XIV to perform in the Petit-Bourbon and then also, in 1661, the Palais-Royal.

Molière's future was thus secure, and in his remaining years he continued to develop his company who, in a style similar to that of the Commedia dell'Arte, concentrated on their individual comic skills and performance. In addition he was able to refine his own work, and write and produce ever-ambitious and successful comedies.

The Plays of Molière
Molière wrote about thirty-three plays, and his style supersedes those that came before him. Although deriving many of his ideas and characters seemingly from the classics, notably Aristophanes, Terence and Plautus, and from the Italian Commedia stage, Molière nevertheless writes with a greater psychological depth and insight than the mere word 'comedy' suggests. A master of comic invention and satire, Molière manages to combine this with the telling ability to reveal deeper truths, a thing we might be mistaken for thinking more likely to happen in tragic theatre. In the following complete list of his works the more notable of Molière's works are those more fully described.

PLAYS
La Jalousié du Barbouillé
Translated as *A Jealous Husband*.

Le Médicin Volant
Translated as *The Fleet-Footed Doctor*.

L'Étourdi (1653)
Translated as *The Scatterbrain*.

Dépit Amoureux (1656)
Translated as *A Lover's Quarrel*.

Les Précieuses Ridicules (1659)
Translated as *The Affected Young Ladies*.

Sganarelle (1660)
Translated as *The Imaginary Cuckold*.

Dom Garcie de Navarre (1661)
Translated as *The Jealous Prince*.

L'École des Maris (1661)
Translated as *The School for Husbands*.

Les Fâcheux (1661)
Translated as *The Nuisances*.

L'École des Femmes (1662)
Translated as *The School for Wives*, and the first really successful work in France to combine the serious and the comic. The play deals with the role of women in society, and takes a satirical swipe at the coarse and cynical manner in which women are prepared for their roles in life.

Critique de L'École des Femmes (1663)
Translated as *The School for Wives Criticized*.

L'Impromptu de Versailles (1663)
Translated as *A Versailles Improvisation*.

Le Mariage Forcé (1664)
Translated as *The Forced Wedding*.

La Princess d'Élide (1664)
Translated as *The Princess of Elida*.

Tartuffe (1664)
Partially based on Aretino's play *Lo Ipocrito* (*see* page 48), this play is considered one of Molière's masterpieces, and contains one of his great creations in the title character. In part it is a satire on the hypocrisy of the church, and although Louis XIV was said to have found it highly enjoyable, because of its delicate subject matter he banned it for five years. After its initial production, Molière rewrote *Tartuffe* at least twice, the final version dated 1669. (*See* extract on page 61.)

Dom Juan (1665)
Translated as *Don Juan*.

L'Amour Médecin (1665)
Translated as *Love's Cure-All*.

Le Misanthrope (1666)
If this is a comedy, it is an unusual one, as it ends in unhappiness for the main character, Alceste.

Le Médecin Malgré Lui (1666)
Translated as *A Physician Despite Himself*; as its title suggests, it is a satire on the medical fraternity.

Mélicerte (1666)

Pastorale Comique
Thought to be *c*.1666/7, translated as *A Pastoral Comedy.*

Le Sicilien (1667)
Translated as *The Sicilian.*

Amphitryon (1668)

Georges Dandin (1668)
Translated as *The Confounded Husband.*

L'Avare (1668)
Translated as *The Miser*; another rather 'brutal' comedy, in this case based on a work by Plautus (*see* page 29).

Monsieur de Pourceaugnac (1669)

Les Amants Magnifiques (1670)
Translated as *The Magnificent Suitors.*

Le Bourgeois Gentilhomme (1670)
Translated as *The Would-Be Gentleman*; a comedy-ballet with music provided by Jean Baptiste Lully, who was Louis XIV's favourite composer. This piece concerns the efforts of Monsieur Jourdain to transform himself into a gentleman and secure a place at court. It is thought to contain some of Molière's funniest moments.

Psyché (1671)

Les Fourberies de Scapin (1671)

La Comtesse d'Escarbagnas (1671)
Translated as *A Prententious Countess.*

Les Femmes Savantes (1672)
Translated as *The Learned Ladies.*

Le Malade Imaginaire (1673)
Translated as *The Imaginary Invalid* and Molière's last comedy. It concerns the ravings and machinations of a hypochondriac who is afraid of doctors!

Sadly, although not without comic irony in its own right, Molière, who was playing the title role, fell ill himself during a performance of this last piece, and died a few hours after being taken from the stage.

The following is an extract from *Tartuffe* by Molière. The eponymous hero uses words as constructs to bewilder those around him: here are a couple of examples from a translation by Christopher Hampton (qv):

TARTUFFE:
Those who know me would never dream of thinking
that this is a result of my self-seeking.
The riches of this world have very little
appeal to me, I'm not one to be dazzled
by their illusory glow; and if Orgon
wants me to have this gift and I decide
to take it, it will only be because
otherwise, to be honest, I'd be worried
in case all of that money were to fall
into the wrong hands; and end up with people
who'd use their share for evil purposes,
rather than keeping it, as I intend to,
for God's glory and the welfare of my neighbour.

TARTUFFE:
No, let him speak; it's wrong of you to blame him,
you'd do better to believe what he says.
Why should you favour me in this dispute?
After all, how do you know what I might
be capable of? Do you trust mere show?
You think I'm better just because I seem so?
No, no, you're letting yourself be tricked by
appearances and, I'm sorry to say,
I'm not at all the man I'm thought to be.
Everyone takes me for a good man, but
the simple truth is I'm entirely worthless.
(*He turns to Damis*)
Come on, my boy, speak up: call me a traitor,
a lost soul, a degenerate, a thief,
a murderer; crush me with viler names;
I won't deny them, I've deserved them all,

and on my knees I welcome this disgrace
in expiation of my life of crime.

ORGON:
(*To Tartuffe*) You go too far.
(*To Damis*) Aren't you ashamed, you wretch?

DAMIS:
You mean you're taken in by this ... ?

ORGON:
Be quiet, you gallows bird!

SPANISH THEATRE IN THE SEVENTEENTH CENTURY

To continue our exploration we should now turn to the end of the 1600s and to another area of the Western world: Spain. The traditions of medieval Spain were similar to those expressed elsewhere, and they changed along similar lines with the coming of the Renaissance and influence from Italy. It is to be remembered that Corneille's *El Cid* (1637) was based on *Las Mocedades del Cid* by the minor Spanish playwright Guillén de Castro y Bellvis. Thus it was that Spain also came to a period that saw a flowering of dramatic art and the production of some of Spain's greatest writers.

Lope De Vega
De Vega (1562–1635) was the first, and possibly is still, the greatest Spanish dramatist. His full name was Lope Felix De Vega Carpio, and he was a most prolific playwright, claiming to have written over 1,500 plays, of which something in the region of 450 manuscripts have survived. They covered broad comedy, tragi-comedy, the lives of saints, and generally upheld the honour system and the belief in the monarchic system that prevailed at the time. He wrote initially for the open-air theatres of Madrid – not unlike the Roman models on which they were based (qv) – and for them he wrote pastorals, and stories based on classical mythology. He later provided the same alongside more straightforward plays for the Spanish Court. He also wrote a number of *autos sacramentales* –

pieces that were performed on a succession of carts, not unlike the English mystery cycle plays (qv). He was ordained as a priest in 1614.

As the first and most prolific practitioner in the Spanish theatre, de Vega can be thought of as more or less its founder. His influence there, in France, and throughout Europe was most profound. In *c*.1609 he wrote a treatise on dramatic art called *Arte neuvo de hacer comedias* (*The New Art of Writing Plays*).

PLAYS
Castelvines y Monteses (*c*.1608)

Fuenteovejuna (*c*.1612)
Translated as *The Sheep-Well*.

Peribáñez y el comedador de Ocaña (1614)

El perro del hortelano (*c*.1615)

La dama boba (1617)

El villano en su rincón (1617)

La selva sin amor (1629)
Translated as *The Loveless Forest*.

El mejor alcalde, el rey (1635)
Translated as *The King and the Best Magistrate*.

Por la puente, Juana (1635)

El caballero de Olmedo (1641)

Alarcón
Juan Ruiz Alarcón Y Mendoza (1581–1639) was born in Mexico, and can be considered a minor playwright by comparison with de Vega. Nevertheless he was a writer who created well structured, often satirical plays that contained some fine characterization. He was himself a hunchback and suffered a degree of ridicule for this, not least of all in some of de Vega's plays. His answer to this was to make a hunchback hero in his play *Las paredes oyen*. The majority of his works are set in Madrid.

PLAYS
La verdad sospechosa
Translated as *Truth itself suspect*, and the basis for Corneille's play *Le Menteur* of 1643.

La prueba

Las paredes oyen
Translated as *Walls have Ears*.

Calderón (1600–81)

Pedro Calderón de la Barca was the first major playwright to follow de Vega. He was born in Madrid and wrote a wide range of plays – tragedies, comedies, histories and works of philosophy. He is known to have written around 120 pieces in all. In 1651 he was ordained as a priest, and in 1663 he became chaplain of honour to King Philip IV, after which he wrote only *autos sacramentales* (qv).

PLAYS
El segreto a voces (1626)

Casa con dos puertos mal es de guarda (1629)
Translated as *It is difficult to guard a house with two doors*.

El príncipe constante (1629)

La dama duende (c.1629)
Translated as *The Parson's Wedding*.

La devocion de la cruz (c.1633)

El mayor monstruo, los celos (c.1634)
Translated as *No Monster like Jealousy*.

La cena de Baltasar (c.1634)
Translated as *Belshazzar's Feast*.

A secreto agravio, secreta venganza (1635)
Translated as *Secret Vengeance for Secret Insult*.

El medico de su honra (1635)
Translated as *The Surgeon of His Honour*.

El mágico prodigioso (1637)
Translated as *The Wonder-Working Magician*.

El pintor de su deshonra (1637)
Translated as *The Painter of His Dishonour*.

La vida es sueño (c.1638)
Translated as *Life's a Dream*.

El alcalde de Zalamea (1640)
Translated as *The Major of Zalamea*.

El gran teatro del mundo (c.1645)
Translated as *The Great World Theatre*.

La hija del aire (1653)

El Maestro de Danzar (undated)
Used as a basis for his play *The Gentle Dancing Master* of 1672 by William Wycherley (*see* page 107).

CONCLUSION

In Europe the Renaissance, which saw the rise of academic interest in the ancient world, indeed in the exploration of all aspects of the world around us, connects our sophisticated world with the much simpler eras that preceded it. The Renaissance influenced every period that followed it, and is still a powerful inspiration today. However, there is yet one country we have not visited to see how the Renaissance's immediate effect altered the course of dramatic art: that country is England, and the effects were profound, as the next chapter will endeavour to show.

The Elizabethan playhouse.
The modern re-construction of Shakespeare's Globe Theatre
on the South bank of the River Thames in London.

4 THE ELIZABETHAN STAGE

*... but mark the flocking and running to Theaters and Curtains, daily,
hourly, night and day, time and tide, to see plays and interludes, where
such wanton gestures, such bawdy speeches, such laughing and fleering,
such kissing and bussing, such clipping and culling, such winking and
glancing of wanton eyes, and the like is used, as is wonderful to behold.*
PHILIP STUBBES [1] 1583

Standing in the Tower of London, on the White Tower, the royal guard watches down across the river. He is checking for any unwanted visitors by land or by water to the king's fortified keep. From his elevated height he can also see upriver across to the south bank where the strange-shaped new buildings are rising above the cottages and fields. Much activity seems to be occupying that part of the capital at this time for, amongst the bear-pits and lodgings of Cheapside, the first purpose-built buildings in London for the performing of entertainments are being erected. One is now being finished: workmen are busy thatching its roof even as he watches. Yet the high building already flies a marker to announce its name – the flag declares that it is simply called 'The Theatre'. Further along the bank another building is in the earlier stages of being constructed: people say it is to be called 'The Rose'. The guard wonders with excitement what pleasures these two may hold for him to enjoy in his well-earned leisure time: will they compete with the bear-baiting, the bull pits, and the cock-fighting that he already knows and enjoys? He certainly hopes it will not be too expensive – there is a rumour that as much as tuppence may be needed to secure entrance to The Theatre, and this occupies his mind as he paces the cold ramparts of the tower.

THE RENAISSANCE AND THEATRE IN ENGLAND

Theatre in England could well have followed the Italian model – it certainly started along similar lines; an academic interest in the plays of ancient Rome, as we have already seen, led to such dramas as *Ralph Roister Doister* and *Gammer Gurton's Needle* (see page 44). However, with the Reformation, things Italian, whether ancient or contemporary, went rapidly out of style. King Henry VIII's split with Rome did not, after all, rest simply with matters religious or matrimonial: it affected every aspect of English life, and the development of theatre simply followed the trend.

In 1543 a further movement away from religious theatre towards the secular continued as Henry VIII introduced an Act of Parliament forbidding performances of plays attempting religious doctrination. Indeed the act of 1543 specifically banned religious interludes, and a further act, in 1548, sought to suppress the feast of Corpus Christi and the mystery plays associated with it.

Censorship as a fact of theatre life starts here. Further restrictions, imposed by an ever-strengthening government in Whitehall, saw to it that strict regulations were applied to the performing of dramatic material. As early as 1530, censoring of plays had been in operation: initially to control potential mob violence, these rules were increasingly used to suppress outspoken religious views. By 1590 a licensing commission was in place to control all plays and performances: it comprised the Archbishop of Canterbury, the Lord Mayor of London and the Lord Chamberlain, and thereafter the Lord Chamberlain continued to be the official British censor of new plays until the practice ceased nearly four hundred years later in 1968 (*see* page 199). In addition, in 1572 an Act of Parliament confirmed the status of any performer who was without the patronage of a baron, or higher, as being numbered along with the 'rogues and vagabonds and sturdie beggars'.

Alongside the banning of religious material, these regulations, and the prohibition they implied, also had the effect of moving the developing dramatic art in England from its hitherto amateur status to a more professional one. As 'necessity is the mother of invention', so it is perhaps not surprising that, even within the atmosphere of turmoil that all these changes involved, the theatre in England began to flourish as never before.

PATRONS AND PLAYHOUSES

Licensed performing companies confirmed the status of the professional (strictly male) actor. Plays were no longer devised by townsfolk along religious story lines, but were actually *written* for these men, and playhouses built to cater for their work. This meant that the educated men of the Renaissance movement in England now had an outlet for their own writings, and that these writings had to differ largely from what had come before. The playmaker had therefore given way to the author or dramatist. (*See also* Plays and Playwrights on page 71.)

Early performances were given outside on temporary structures, or inside in the halls of the wealthy, or in a combination of both, the inn yard.

What's in a Name?

In England the word *dramatist* was not coined until the seventeenth century, when it is credited to John Dryden. The word *drama* was credited to Ben Jonson.

As 'professional' companies grew, the need became apparent for more permanent buildings.

One of the earliest patrons to form an acting troupe was the Earl of Leicester, who, in 1574, applied for 'letters patent' to Elizabeth I to create a company of twelve male household servants as actors. As well as perform in his household, these 'actors' were also allowed to travel to play in other places. This they did, performing regularly in London. The leader of Leicester's company was James Burbage (1531–97). Just two years later, in 1576, Burbage, with financial help from a wealthy merchant John Brayne, leased part of an old priory in London's Shoreditch and within it built London's first purpose-built theatre; he called

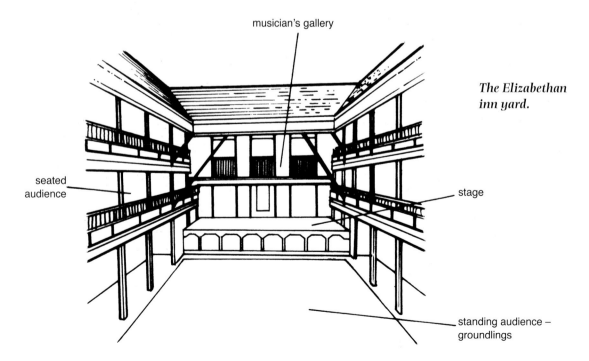

musician's gallery

seated audience

stage

standing audience – groundlings

The Elizabethan inn yard.

it, appropriately, 'The Theatre'. (Before becoming an actor James Burbage was a carpenter by trade, and thus probably had a hand in the actual building of The Theatre.)

Also in 1576, but in another part of the city, Richard Farrant, a scholar, thought to do the same thing. He erected his theatre in the former refectory of Blackfriars Priory, and called it 'Blackfriars' (*see* diagram *below*). Other theatres soon followed, mostly along the lines of The Theatre; they were The Curtain, The Rose, The Swan and, in 1598/9, The Globe. They were soon followed by two others, known as The Fortune and The Hope. The most famous of these buildings, The Globe, was erected

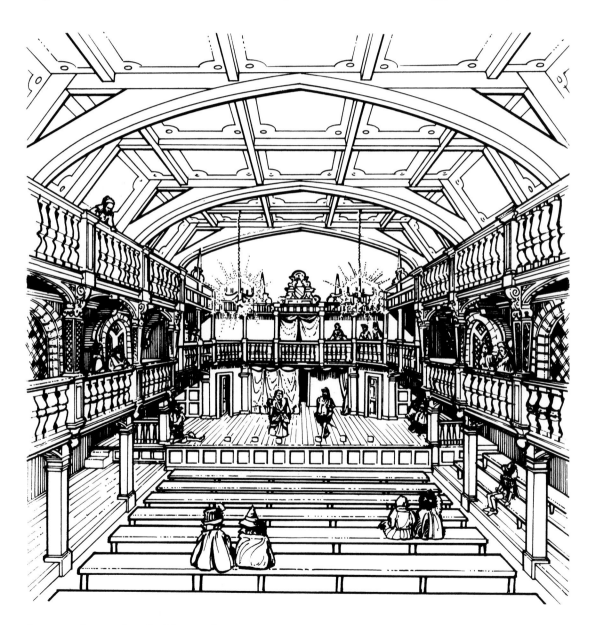

Theatre indoors – the Blackfriars Theatre.

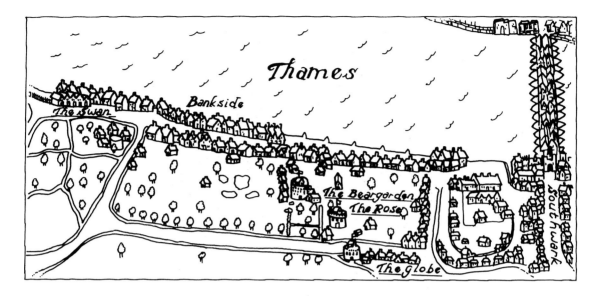

The proliferation of playhouses along the River Thames.

by James Burbage's sons Richard and Cuthbert. This came about after a dispute concerning the lease of The Theatre: unable to come to a new arrangement, the Burbages dismantled the original playhouse and, carrying many of the old timbers with them, moved across the River Thames to build a new theatre, 'The Globe'. They took with them one of their leading actors, a certain William Shakepeare.

The Elizabethan Playhouse

We know what the purpose-built English theatres of this period were like from contemporary sources and archaeological exploration. Of the former there are a number of written accounts and a few vital drawings, including the famous De Witt diagram of The Swan theatre (*right*).

The inn yard seems to have been one of the strongest influences on the shape of the Elizabethan playhouse. Similar in layout to an inn yard, these theatres were unroofed, with high sides that allowed the audience to view the performance from above. The theatres were circular or octagonal rather than rectangular, presumably because this allowed for a more even distribution of the audience; and they were usually thatched. A number of controversies

From the De Witt sketch of **The Swan.**

arise from this information, including the exact nature of the apparent pillars; whether the understage was enclosed, curtained or open; and whether the rear stage area could be revealed, by drawing

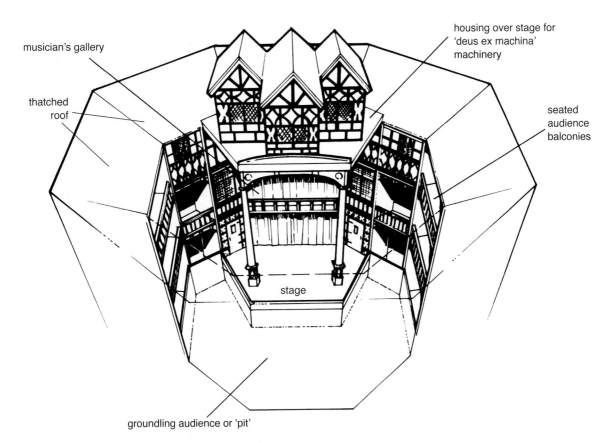

musician's gallery

thatched roof

housing over stage for 'deus ex machina' machinery

seated audience balconies

stage

groundling audience or 'pit'

The Elizabethan playhouse.

back a curtain or screen, or if it was merely used as an off-stage area (*see* illustration).

The Companies

The early theatre companies had to have a licence and a patron. Notable patrons of the period included Elizabeth I and later James I, also Queen Anne of Denmark, and the earls of Derby, Hereford, Lincoln, Leicester, Oxford, Pembroke, Sussex, Warwick and Worcester. The names of the companies themselves often tell of these sponsors, and included the following typical examples: the (Lord) Chamberlain's Men; Children of the Chapel Royal; Lord Strange's Men; the Admiral's Men (*see* Chistopher Marlowe, page 73); the Earl of Leicester's Men (*see* James Burbage, page 66); the Earl of Worcester's Men (including Edward Alleyn, *see* page 70); and the Queen's Men, later the King's Men.

ACTORS AND ACTING

The theatre of this period was a much more robust and noisy spectacle than the generally rather more sedentary theatre experience of today. Firstly, the mostly open-air productions took part during the day, so the audience was thus less separated from the performers as, with no artificial illumination, no 'house lighting' dimmed. Also, although the stages were raised, the audience stood right up to the front edge, and were often encouraged to join in. Shouting, caterwauling, joking and arguing from auditorium to stage, and vice versa, would have occurred, and certainly not only in comedies.

Within the auditorium food and drink were sold and consumed, and even more physical bodily functions expressed: fortunately the pit or groundlings had drains running from it! The smell of the pit area, where up to *two thousand* of the 'great unwashed' crammed in to watch the performance, would have seemed unbearably rank to our modern, perhaps over-protected noses! In the enclosed seated areas around the arena other dubious professions, including the so-called world's oldest profession, also traded.

Acting in this period must likewise have been a very different art from today, primarily because a company of men and boys played all the parts. Thus 'men' companies, such as 'The Chamberlain's Men', used their younger members to play the younger women, whilst 'boy' companies, such as the 'Children of the Chapel Royal', consisted of all young players and would have to choose plays that would suit their young cast. The rivalry between the men and boy companies led at one time to the so-called 'war of theatre' (*see* page 84).

It must be stressed that all the female roles were covered by the male performers, whilst this must have affected the way such roles were viewed, the parts were nevertheless played convincingly – otherwise serious roles such as Juliet, Lady Macbeth and Desdemona would not have been worth writing, or indeed have held the stage.

Individual actors of the Elizabethan and later Jacobean period were often known for their skill in portraying certain character types (*see* list below), many becoming the local equivalent of 'household names'. The cult of the actor as a 'star' can almost be said to have dated from this period. We know of various performers from play lists, legal documents and other such material, and from this evidence the following actors, in alphabetical order, are good examples of the genre.

Famous Actors of the Elizabethan Stage

EDWARD ALLEYN (1566–1626)
Tragedian performing with the Earl of Worcester's, and then the Admiral's Men combined with Lord Strange's companies. Principal roles included Tamburlaine, and the Jew of Malta, Faustus (Marlowe), Orlando (Greene), and Heironimo (Kyd). A tragedian and musician.

ROBERT ARMIN (c.1570–1615)
Writer and comic actor. Performed at The Globe with Lord Chandos's Men, then with the Chamberlain's Men. He took over from Kempe as the leading comic actor. Created the roles of Feste, Autolycus and the fool in 'Lear'. His works include *The Two Maids of Moreclake*.

CHRISTOPHER BEESTON (d.1638)
Actor and theatre manager. Companies include Worcester's and Queen Anne's Men; he then managed the Phoenix theatre, which presented work from Lady Elizabeth's and Queen Henrietta's Men. He later formed his own children's company, 'Beeston's Boys'.

RICHARD BURBAGE (c.1571–1619)
Son of James Burbage, *see* page 66. His roles included Malvolio, Richard III, Hamlet, Othello, Lear and Hieronimo (in Kyd's *Spanish Tragedy*).

HENRY CONDELL (c.1562–1627)
Comic and tragic actor, and a good friend of Shakespeare. Worked with Lord Chamberlain's Company. A joint editor of the first folio of Shakespeare's work (with Heminges). Took roles in Jonson's comedies, and played the Cardinal in *The Duchess of Malfi* (Webster).

NATHAN FIELD (1587–c.1620)
Actor and dramatist. Performed with the King's Men, with roles in Jonson's plays, Bussy in *The Revenge of Bussy D'Amboise* (Chapman), and wrote *A Woman is a Weathercock* (1609), *Amends for Ladies* (c.1611), and with Massinger *The Fatal Dowry*. Described by Jonson as 'best actor' alongside Burbage.

JOHN HEMINGES (d.1630)
Played with Strange's and Chamberlain's Men. Co-editor of *The First Folio* (with Condell).

WILLIAM KEMPE (d.c.1608)
Comic actor with Leicester's and then Strange's Men. Famous for his stage repartee, as well as his singing and dancing, known as Kempe's Jigs, and often rather obscene. He is also known to have played Peter in *Romeo and Juliet* and Dogberry in *Much Ado about Nothing*. Thomas Nashe said of Kempe that he was

'most comicall and conceited'. Kempe morris-danced from Norwich to London, and wrote a book of his exploits called *Kempe's Nine Daies Wonder.*

Other notable actors of the period include Edmund Shakespeare (1580–1607), who was Shakespeare's brother, but whose career as a performer is largely undocumented; also Robert Reynolds, who as a comic actor used the stage name 'Pickleherring' – he had a rival in John 'Hans Stockfisch' Spencer. Other renowned actors of the period include William Knell, John Lowin, William Ostler, Robert Pallant Senior, Solomon Pavy, Augustine Phillips, Richard Robinson, Thomas Sackville, Richard Sharpe, Elliard Swanston, Richard Tarlton, Jack Wilson and Robert Wilson. In addition, several people better known as playwrights also performed: these included William Rowley, Ben Jonson, Thomas Heywood and, of course, William Shakespeare.

PLAYS AND PLAYWRIGHTS

From around 1560, as plays became more and more secular, the playwright began to hold sway over the material seen on stage. This trend meant that genres of theatre also became more clearly defined, with comedy, history and tragedy becoming more easily identifiable as specific types of drama.

The growing interest in classical antecedents made sure that educated men – and by the nature of the period, it was mostly men – began to write for the stage; one such group of writers was known as the 'University Wits', amongst their members being Greene, Lyly, Marlowe, Peele and Jonson (*see* page 99).

Classical mythology also continued to play its part; in particular the plays of Seneca, Terence and Plautus influenced new writers, as did the writings of, amongst other ancients, Pliny and Plutarch. Indeed the latter's *Bioi Paralleloi* (*Parallel Lives*), with its forty-six biographical portraits, was translated by Sir Thomas North in 1579 and is said to be a major source for Shakespeare's Roman plays. Other more contemporary writers also played their part in influencing the English writers of this period: notable amongst these was Machiavelli (*see* page 48); Baidassore Castiglione (1478–1529), an Italian writer and

courtier who in 1505 was sent by the Duke of Urbino as envoy to the court of Henry VIII; and Michel de Montaigne (1533–92), a French essayist.

Naturally the inquiries that the Renaissance provoked in other areas of the arts and sciences also had their influence on the writings of this period. Publications such as Harvey's *Circulation and the Blood*, Browne's *Religio Medici*, and Burton's *Anatomy of Melancholy* can all be seen to have exerted an influence, in particular on Marlowe's *Doctor Faustus*, Jonson's *Volpone*, Marston's *The Malcontent* and Ford's *The Broken Heart*.

A review of the most notable playwrights and plays of this period follows, and it is to be noted that often in the commentary the idea of more than one playwright having authored a single play is mentioned. This is perhaps not very common today, but was much more the case in this period. We should not therefore discount the number of cross-references made below – especially to the co-authoring of Shakespeare's work – as pure jealousy on the part of the champions of the lesser playwrights. In most cases we will probably never know the truth, but certainly we should not overlook the fact that shared authorship was very common in this period.

John Lyly (*c.*1554–1606)

Lyly wrote exclusively for a courtly audience, and his works are notable for their attention to courtly detail and manners. He was highly regarded in his day and much fêted, being also a member of parliament from 1589–1601. His plays contained many veiled allusions to scandals and intrigues of the day. Alongside his more serious works he wrote pastoral comedies. Many of his pieces feature mythological characters and stories. His work is important as possibly the first example of 'high comedy' – meaning comedy of manners – and for his use of prose.

PLAYS
Sapho and Phao (*c.*1570)
First performed in 1584 at Blackfriars.

Alexander and Compaspe (*c.*1575)
Includes characters – Plato, Aristotle and Diogenes – and was also first performed in 1584 at Blackfriars.

Euphues: The Anatomy of Wit (*c.*1578)
The adventures of a young Athenian, written in an involved, elegant and courtly style, with much use of allusion. It is from this play and its sequel that the term 'euphuism' derives. To be euphuistic is to write in a pompous and affected style!

Euphues and his England (1580)
A sequel to the play of similar name above.

Endimion (*c.*1588)
Subtitled *The Man in the Moon.* Probably Lyly's most admired work, and one said to have been performed at court.

Midas
A comedy based on the mythological story of King Midas, whose touch turned everything to gold.

Mother Bombie
A comedy (*c.*1590) heavily influenced and written in the style of Terence (*see* page 28).

The Woman in the Moone (*c.*1591)
A prose play combining aspects of Utopian fantasy with Greek mythology, the central character being Pandora, who is provided by the gods to bring harmony to the idealized world of the shepherds.

Mother Bumbie (*c.*1594)
A farcical story concerning the dealings of the title character, a fortune-teller, and a popular figure in Elizabethan life. The play bears some comparison with *A Comedy of Errors*.

Thomas Kyd (1558–94)

Born in London, Kyd started work as a translator before finally making his name as a playwright with *The Spanish Tragedy* in 1589.

Kyd was a very close acquaintance of Christopher Marlowe (*see* page 75), and was implicated in the same scurrilous activities as his friend. For example, in May 1593 Kyd was arrested for, and then acquitted of, perpetuating various libels against foreigners. A few months later, and under the severe interrogation of the period, Kyd implicated Marlowe in this action, adding blasphemy and heresy; however, Marlowe's

early death meant he did not live long enough to answer to these accusations. Whilst Kyd himself was never charged, his reputation was much damaged, and he never really regained his previous position, dying in disgrace shortly after in 1594.

Kyd's work was in high contrast to the courtly elegance of Lyly, being a much more robust style of storytelling. He is credited with two early versions of plays said to have influenced Shakespeare, but which are now sadly lost: a possibly apocryphal early version of *Hamlet*; and *The Taming of the Shrew*, dated 1589. Kyd's influence has also been ascribed to *Titus Andronicus* and *The Arden of Faversham*. Very few of Kyd's plays have survived, but he is thought of as one whose work displays high ability in plot construction and in the greater development of character.

PLAYS
The Spanish Tragedy (1589)
Often compared with *Hamlet*, this play is also seen as the prototype for 'revenge tragedy' (*see* page 92), and contains all the devices to be associated with the genre of tragedy generally: soliloquy, dumb-show, supernatural appearances and discovery scenes, and in Hieronymo, a great central character.

Pompey the Great, his fair Cornelia's Tragedy (1595)
A work in blank verse, after Seneca; it concerns the lamentations of Cornelia, Pompey's wife.

Two plays, once thought to be by Kyd, have since been re-assigned: *The First Part of Ieronimo* (1605), now by author unknown; and *Soliman and Perseda*, now thought to have been written by Peele – *see* below.

Robert Greene (*c.*1558–92)

Born in Norwich, Greene is famous for having lived a lascivious and wanton life, but finally repenting his ways in *A Groat's worth of Wit bought with a Million Repentance*. Greene was also a great pamphleteer, and famed for his extremely unfavourable opinion of fellow playwright William Shakespeare, of whom he said many things, amongst them that Shakespeare was 'an upstart crow beautified with our feathers'. He is reported to have come to a sad end, having fallen ill from 'a surfeit of pickled herring and Rhenish wine'.

Greene wrote prose romances before he wrote plays proper, the most famous being *Pandosto* (1588) and *Menaphon* (1589). The first of these is said to have been the source for Shakespeare's *A Winter's Tale*. It is also thought that he may well have had a hand in the original writing of Shakespeare's *Henry VI* plays before the author rewrote them. He left thirty-eight literary works, the following plays amongst them.

PLAYS
Orlando Furioso (1591)
An adaptation of a poem of 1532 by the Italian Ludovico Ariosto.

James IV of Scotland (c.1591)
A romantic comedy comparable with *A Midsummer Night's Dream* and *Cymbeline*.

The Honourable History of
Friar Bacon and Friar Bungay (c.1594)
A tale of white magic and a possible attempt to counter the effect of Marlowe's *Doctor Faustus*.

George Peele (*c.*1558–*c.*1597)

Poet and dramatist, Peele was born in London and wrote for the Children of the Chapel Royal and for the Admiral's Men. He wrote pastoral and historical plays, and satires. It is almost certain that he was an actor as well as a writer.

For a time, Peele was also the producer of pageants for the Lord Mayors of London, notably *The Pageant before Woolstone Dixie* (1585) and *Descensus Astraeae* (1591), which were the first of their kind to emphasize classical mythology rather than local folktale. This interest in pageants means that in Peele's plays spectacle is never far away: for example, the coronation in *Edward I*, and the eponymous events of *The Battle of Alcazar*.

PLAYS
The Arraignment of Paris (c.1581)
Possibly the best romantic comedy written up to this date, and given at court before Queen Elizabeth, who is written into the play as the nymph to whom Diana gives the golden apple. The splendidly contrived pastoral nature of this play is often compared with the fifth act of Shakespeare's *As You Like It*.

David and Bethsabe (c.1587)
A biblical romance story, most successfully dramatized, and rising above the simple story to combine a patriotic contemporary relevance with high romance.

The Battle of Alcazar (c.1589)
A historical drama written in verse, and dealing with the culmination of a war between King Sebastian of Portugal and King Abdelmelec of Morocco. The battle had been fought in 1578.

The Old Wifes' Tale (c.1591)
Probably the first satire on romantic comedy, a mixture of high romance, folk tale and comedy, a subtle blend of the rustic and the literary.

Edward I (c.1592)
A patriotic historical drama with scope for much spectacle.

Soliman and Perseda
Originally thought to have been written by Thomas Kyd, but now ascribed to Peele.

Christopher Marlowe (1564–93)

Christopher 'Kit' Marlowe was born in the same year as William Shakespeare, in Canterbury. After studying at Cambridge, he became a playwright, finding success almost immediately with one of his first works, *Tamburlaine the Great*. Such is the impact of Marlowe's writing that his greatest work compares well with that of Shakespeare; in fact it has been suggested that he had a hand in the writing of both *Titus Andronicus* and *Henry VI*. Marlowe was highly thought of by his contemporaries; indeed, Shakespeare quotes from, and mentions him in *As You Like It*.

It is probable that Marlowe was also employed by the government as a spy; certainly there are enough contemporary allusions to his work for 'her majesty' among the Jesuits to reach this conclusion. Marlowe's connections with espionage and the minister responsible for security at this time, Francis Walsingham, is one of many reasons put forward as a possible motive for his assassination. His murder in 1593, whether motiveless or not – it may have been simply a drunken brawl or robbery – brought to an end a tragically short career in play writing, second only in this period to that of Shakespeare.

PLAYS

Tamburlaine the Great, Part One (1587)
First performed by the Admiral's Men with the lead taken by Edward Alleyn (*see* page 70). The only play to have been published within Marlowe's lifetime. Marlowe's *Tamburlaine* was another play highly influenced by the secular writings of the period. It took a lead in the use of blank verse, and its larger-than-life central character equals and foreshadows many of Shakespeare's great tragic heroes and villains.

Tamburlaine the Great, Part Two (1588)
Following on quickly from the success of *Part One*, both parts were seen by Shakespeare, and thought to have influenced his work.

The Tragical History of Doctor Faustus (1589)
This work has something in common with the earlier morality plays (*see* page 41): it makes superb use of a chorus, and can be seen as a dialogue between science (or knowledge) and religion. It was probably also the first dramatization of the medieval legend of the man who sells his soul to the Devil, in this case via the Devil's agent Mephistopheles. Marlowe, however, makes use of the story to tell his own tale, and his complex central title character differs greatly from other versions of the story.

Faustus sells his soul for twenty-four years of life with Mephistopheles as his slave. In this time he gets whatever he wants, including the pleasure of Helen of Troy. It is from this play that Helen is famously described as 'the face that launched a thousand ships' (*see* quote below).

The Jew of Malta (c.1590)
A somewhat brutal tragedy, but a fascinating character study nonetheless, and the complex central character, Barabas, may well have influenced Shakespeare's later depiction of Shylock in *The Merchant of Venice*.

Edward the Second (c.1591–92)
Often considered Marlowe's masterpiece, this play takes a historical subject and explores the personalities behind the politics of the time; with its allusions to the homosexual relationship between the king and his favourite, Gaveston, it often comes across with a more than contemporary feel. Charles Lamb described the brutal and violent assassination of Edward as a scene that 'moves pity and terror beyond any scene, ancient or modern, with which I am acquainted'.

Dido, Queen of Carthage (pub. 1594)
Probably a joint work with Thomas Nashe (*see* below), and written for private rather than public performance. Rather lacking in action, it can be considered a lesser tragedy.

The Massacre of Paris
Another lesser work.

The Reign of Edward III (pub. 1596)
A minor history play, thought to have been part-authored by Marlowe and Shakespeare, amongst others.

Hero and Leander (1593)
Unfinished at Marlowe's death.

The following is an extract from *The Tragical History of Doctor Faustus*, by Christopher Marlowe.

Reaching the end of his twenty-four year indulgence, Faustus contemplates his fate:

FAUSTUS:
Ah Faustus,
Now hast thou but one hour to live,
And then thou must be damned perpetually.
Stand still, you ever-moving spheres of heaven,
That time may cease and midnight never come.
Fair nature's eye, rise, rise again, and make
Perpetual day. Or let this hour be but
A year, a month, a week, a natural day,
That Faustus may repent and save his soul.
O lente, lente, currite nostis equi.*
The stars move still, time runs, the clock will strike.
The devil will come, and Faustus must be damned.

Oh, I'll leap up to my God: who pulls me down?
See, see, where Christ's blood streams in the firmament.
One drop would save my soul, half a drop. Ah, my Christ!
Ah, rend not my heart for naming of my Christ!
Yet will I call on him. Oh, spare me, Lucifer!
Where is it now? 'Tis gone:
And see where God stretched out his arm,
And bends his ireful brows.
Mountains and hills, come, come, and fall on me,
And hide me from the heavy wrath of God.
No, no. Then will I headlong run into the earth.
Earth, gape! Oh no, it will not harbour me.
You stars that reigned at my nativity,
Whose influence hath allotted death and hell,
Now draw up Faustus like a foggy mist
Into the entrails of yon labouring cloud,
That when you vomit forth into the air
My limbs may issue from your smoky mouths,
So that my soul may but ascend to heaven.
The watch strikes.
Ah! Half the hour is past,
'Twill all be past anon.

*'oh slowly, slowly run, ye horses of night'

Thomas Nashe (1567–1601)

Nashe lived by his writing, and has been described as 'the greatest of Elizabethan journalists'[ii]. His many writings, and the controversy that often surrounded them, made him a very central figure in the politics and literature of the time. His first published work was the preface to Robert Greene's novel *Menaphon* in 1589. In this preface he criticizes the work of Thomas Kyd, but praises that of George Peele. Nashe wrote satirical pamphlets, many in association with John Lyly.

Nashe argued with critic and university lecturer Gabriel Harvey, answering his accusations of plagiarism in a famous pamphlet called *Have with you*

to Saffron Waldon in 1596. He was eventually banned from the writing of polemics. His other much quoted work is *Pierce Pennilesse his Supplication to the Divell* (1592), in which he writes, amongst other things, about the revelation of historical characters as seen in works of dramatic art.

His prose works include the first real adventure novel *The Unfortunate Traveller* (1594). Only one play has survived (*see* below), although he is thought to have co-written Marlowe's *Dido, Queen of Cathage* (*c.*1593) and Jonson's *Isle of Dogs* (*c.*1596).

PLAYS
Summer's Last Will and Testament (1592)
His only surviving play.

Lenten Style (1599)
A parody in praise of eating red herring, which has not survived.

Isle of Dogs (1596) (*see* page 85)

CONCLUSION

The flowering of English literature in the Elizabethan era has at its centre – as is only too obvious from the numerous references already made to him and his work – William Shakespeare. This is not to demean in any way the skilled writers that we have discussed in this chapter, and who in many aspects lead the way. However, no other playwright in the history of literature in the English language (probably in any language) has had such a profound effect on, or given so much to, this particular art form. To say that he is the greatest playwright that has ever lived is an understatement of his achievement. It is thus to Shakespeare and those that followed him that we must now turn.

William Shakespeare.

5 SHAKESPEARE AND HIS CONTEMPORARIES

*I have heard Sir William Davenport and Thomas Shadwell (who is counted the
best comoedian we have now) say that he [Shakespeare] had a most prodigious
Witt, and did admire his naturell parts beyond all Dramaticall writers. His
comoedies will remain witt as long as the English tongue is understood.*
JOHN AUBREY [1]

Jostling for a good view, you are in The Globe for a performance of a new play by that great master of the theatre William Shakespeare. You know his work well enough to know that you will not be disappointed. In any case, his new comedy As You Like It has come highly recommended. It has cost you a penny to get in and stand in the groundlings, and you are wondering whether to go mad and shell out another penny for entrance to the seated area around you. It's not the smell (which is rank on this sunny afternoon) or the noise (which with over 8,000 people in the packed building is quite something), or even the usual elbowing for position around you that is making you think of moving; oh no, it is simply that your tired old legs could do with the rest. However, in the end you decide to see the play out amongst your fellow Londoners, standing with what you consider the best view and the best company to enjoy a raucous comedy – it should be a loud but fulfilling afternoon. In any case, you fancy spending a farthing or two on ale to help the thing along. A trumpet sounds, it is about to begin, the crowd roars its approval, and an actor takes the stage.

INTRODUCTION

Whilst one must always put Shakespeare's achievement into the context of his life and times (and the Elizabethan period seems to have been a remarkable time indeed), it is also right to try and correctly proportion this achievement. After all, it is perhaps too easy, in our cynical times, for us to denigrate the worthy or talented. From the same period the works of Christopher Marlowe or, later, Ben Jonson are very

well thought of; and in later times again, those of Ibsen and Chekhov likewise give them the position of great men of the theatre. There are many who could claim a role at the highest level of achievement in the dramatic art, but all of them would have vied with each other in our affections to be called the greatest. However, none of these even gets close to the achievement of William Shakespeare. George Bernard Shaw found it so infuriating that he wanted to 'dig him up and throw stones at his corpse'.

How can we begin to describe, let alone quantify, this achievement? Certainly the circumstances were loaded in favour of such a possibility. The richness of the English language, combined with the journey that the drama had taken, and what it had gathered to it by his time in terms of the breadth of styles, subjects and performance techniques, saw theatre well placed to receive such a son. In his works Shakespeare broke away from the conventional classical rules that the Renaissance and previous practitioners had made so clear. He stood on their shoulders and further developed writing for the stage by the interweaving of plots, and the use of subplots, by shifting the action of the play from place to place, and by combining elements of comedy and tragedy in the same play. Because of this, and because of the remarkable insight that Shakespeare seemed to have into the human condition, his works have enormous emotional strength and depth. In addition the poetical truths within his work ring true and as loudly today as they ever did. The plays are so brilliantly put together that no amount of reinterpretation, of fiddling, of bastardization, has ever succeeded in lessening their remarkable strength and allure. We return time and time again to his work, knowing that on each new journey we will discover more and more.

In Performance

It is calculated that so popular and revered are the works of Shakespeare that throughout the world one of his plays is always in performance somewhere.

WILLIAM SHAKESPEARE (1564–1616)

William Shakespeare was born in Stratford-upon-Avon, Warwickshire, England on St George's day, 23 April 1564. He was the son of John Shakespeare, a glover, and his wife Mary Arden. We know little about his early life, although we do know he had three brothers who survived to adulthood – Gilbert, Edmund and Richard – and a sister, Joan, and it is thought he attended the local grammar school.

In November 1582, at the age of eighteen, Shakespeare married Anne Hathaway, by whom he had firstly a daughter, Susanna, in 1583, and then twins in 1585, Judith and Hamnet. His son died at the age of eleven, in August 1596.

Shakespeare went to London, and by 1592 was well known as an actor and a writer of poetry and plays. His earliest publications were the poems *Venus and Adonis* (1593) and *Lucrece* (1594), both of which were dedicated to Henry Wriothesley, the Earl of Southampton, who became Shakespeare's main patron and may be the dedicatee of the sonnets.

In the Dark

Among the many unknown facts surrounding Shakespeare are the identities of the dedicatee of the sonnets and its so-called 'dark lady'. The sonnets are written as to 'Mr W. H.', and there are up to six people with those initials who were known to Shakespeare. The 'dark lady', to whom many of the sonnets are addressed, could likewise have been any number of women (and possibly men) – usually cited are Jane Davenant, Mary Fitton, Elizabeth Hatton, Emilia Lanier, Lucy Morgan and Penelope Rich.

Along with the Burbages, Shakespeare was a member of the players known as the Lord Chamberlain's Men. By 1598 he was sufficiently well placed that when the Burbages, in dispute concerning the lease of The Theatre, created a new playhouse called The Globe, he could afford to invest in a 10 per cent share of the venture (*see* page 68). Increasingly wealthy, and considered a gentleman of the period, Shakespeare eventually owned houses in London and Stratford, and became a substantial owner of other property and land in Stratford. Shakespeare performed and wrote mostly for his company at The Theatre, and probably also The Curtain. This was then followed by The Globe, and in 1608 grew to include the Blackfriars theatre, which the company leased at this time for the playing of winter performances.

In 1607 Shakespeare's daughter Susanna married a Dr John Hall, and in 1608 Shakespeare became a grandfather on the birth of their daughter Elizabeth. His other daughter did not marry until after his death. His sonnets were first published in 1609 to great acclaim.

Having made a great success of his career, Shakespeare retired back to Stratford, where he died in 1616, on his fifty-second birthday. Tradition says his death may have been partly brought on by rather too strenuous an evening in the company of his friends, amongst whom was fellow playwright Ben Jonson.

The Works of William Shakespeare

The plays of Shakespeare are known from three main sources. The earliest version of 1603 was unauthorized and appears very inaccurate when compared with the later, authorized versions of 1604 and 1623. Published before he had written all his works, this edition contained the text of only sixteen of the plays. Certainly the authorized versions are at least twice as long as the 1603 version, which appears to have been put together from 'memory' rather than

from a written source. The 1623 version, known as the first folio, has an extra seventy or so lines added, and over 250 fewer than the 1604 version; it does, however, contain all the plays except *Pericles*, which was added in a second impression in 1664. Later versions – at least three more in Shakespeare's lifetime alone – tend to follow the 1604 Quarto.

Editors of the plays thus have certain choices to make when publishing them, as do directors when staging them. A comparison of possibly the most famous speech of all, Hamlet's 'To be or not to be' soliloquy, indicates how much variation there can be (*see* box below). The later version is the one that any director will almost definitely choose to stage, as it

---

Hamlet: From the unauthorized Quarto of 1603
SCENE VII
Claudius and Corambis hide behind the arras.
Enter Hamlet.
HAMLET: To be or not to be, I there's the point,
To die, to sleep, is that all? I all:
No, to sleep, to dream, I marry there it goes.
For in that dream of death, when we awake,
And born before an everlasting Judge,
From whence no passenger ever retur'nd,
The undiscovered country, at whose sight
The happy smile, and the accursed damn'd.
But for this, the joyful hope of this,
Whol'd bear the scorns and flattery of the world,
Scorned by the right rich, the rich cursed of the poor?

In Speaking

The English language of Shakespearean England was enormously varied and diverse – no wonder, then, that some of the greatest poetry and drama hails from this period. The fluidity and depth of expression contained within the works of the bard alone have never been surpassed. The language was less rigid than now, even in the way it was spelt – Shakespeare himself in various documents even spelt his own name differently.

Hamlet: From authorized & longer Quarto of 1623
ACT 3 SC I

Enter Hamlet.
HAMLET: To be, or not to be, that is the question:
Whether 'tis nobler in the mind to suffer
The slings and arrows of outrageous fortune,
Or to take arms against a sea of troubles
And by opposing end them. To die – to sleep,
No more; and by a sleep to say we end
The heart-ache and the thousand natural shocks
That flesh is heir to: 'tis a consummation
Devoutly to be wished. To die, to sleep;
To sleep, perchance to dream – ay, there's the rub:
For in that sleep of death what dreams may come,
When we have shuffled off this mortal coil,
Must give us pause – there's the respect
That makes calamity of so long life.
For who would bear the whips and scorns of time,
The oppressor's wrong, the proud man's contumely,
The pangs of despised love, the law's delay,
The insolence of office, and the spurns
That patient merit of the unworthy takes,
When he himself might his quietus make
With a bare bodkin? Who would fardels bear,
To grunt and sweat under a weary life,
But that the dread of something after death,
The undiscovered country, from whose bourne
No traveller returns, puzzles the will,
And makes us rather bear those ills we have
Than fly to others that we know not of?

certainly reads much more fluently and appears the work of a much more skilled mind. However, the text, as with any play, is not considered sacrosanct, and a director is likely to edit even this speech to 'improve' the play for modern audiences (a probable edit is suggested in italics).

Not only is the text in the 1603 edition notably less refined, but also the character we know as Polonius is here called Corambis. The speech also appears in a different part of the play: in the 1603 text it is set at the beginning of Scene vii out of a scheme of seventeen scenes, with no act divisions.

It is important to remember, however, that the acts and scenes that have become the standard format of the works of Shakespeare are the devices of later editors. Generally they follow the classical scheme of changing scene when location changes, or major characters enter or exit.

PLAYS

William Shakespeare is credited with at least thirty-seven plays. In many ways their range and excellence can be seen as a direct result of the theatre history that has come before them, and of course many think they are the, as yet, unchallenged pinnacle of achievement in this art form.

Shakespeare drew on the works of Seneca and Plautus, on medieval traditions, Italian Commedia,

In Repute

Poet John Davies (c.1565–1618), who became writing master to Henry, Prince of Wales, described Shakespeare as 'the English Terence'.

Shakespeare in contemporary performance: from **A Midsummer Night's Dream.**

historical commentaries and folk traditions. To help get to grips with his works they are traditionally divided into a number of groups, which also fall into a rough chronological order:

EARLY COMEDIES

The Two Gentlemen of Verona	1590–91
The Taming of the Shrew	1593
The Comedy of Errors	1594
Love's Labours Lost	1594–95

In History

The main source of the 'Histories' is thought to have been the 1586/7 edition of the 'Chronicles' of Raphael Holinshed (d.c.1581), originally published in 1577.

HISTORIES

Henry VI Pts I, II & III	1592
Richard III	1592–93
King John	1595
Richard II	1595
Henry IV Pts I & II	1596–97
Henry V	1598

In Jest

Tradition has it that *The Merry Wives of Windsor* was written by order of the Queen, who wished to see the character of Falstaff in love.

LATER COMEDIES

A Midsummer Night's Dream	1595–96
The Merchant of Venice	1596–97
The Merry Wives of Windsor	1597–98
Much Ado about Nothing	1598
As You Like It	1599
Twelfth Night	1601
Troilus and Cressida	1602

Measure for Measure	1603
All's Well That Ends Well	1604–05

TRAGEDIES

Titus Andronicus	1592
Romeo and Juliet	1599
Julius Ceasar	1599
Antony and Cleopatra	1606
Coriolanus	1608
Hamlet	1600–01
Othello	1603–04
Timon of Athens	1605
King Lear	1605–06
Macbeth	1606

In Superstition

It has become a tradition that to mention the play *Macbeth* in a theatre is very bad luck. There are a number of theories as to why this is. Firstly it is thought that Shakespeare may have used some 'real' black magic quotations in the text for the witches. Secondly it became the tradition in later years to play *Macbeth* to get a theatre out of financial trouble, because it was seen as a sure-fire success; thus the mention of the play becoming synonymous with possible financial misfortune.

LATE PLAYS

Pericles	1607
A Winter's Tale	1609
Cymbeline	1610
The Tempest	1611
Henry VIII	1613

Although these categories allow us to assimilate Shakespeare's work in some order, we must not be too tied to them. For example, there is another way of representing them: the diagram (page 82) shows that perhaps only the histories fall into a specific timeframe within Shakespeare's life – and even this does not account for *Henry VIII*.

A further late play, *Two Noble Kinsmen* (1613), although not a great work as such, has also increasingly been credited to the Shakespeare canon –

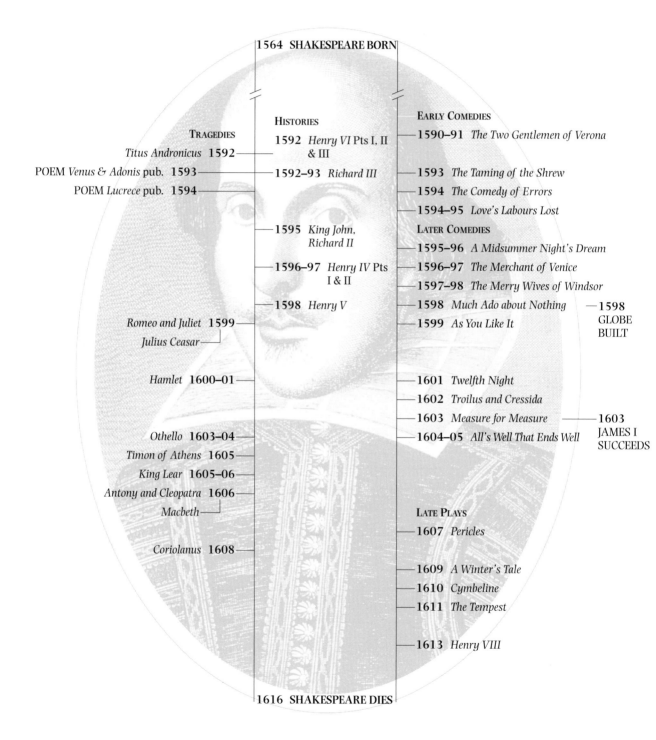

1564 SHAKESPEARE BORN

TRAGEDIES

Titus Andronicus **1592**

POEM *Venus & Adonis* pub. **1593**

POEM *Lucrece* pub. **1594**

Romeo and Juliet **1599**

Julius Ceasar

Hamlet **1600–01**

Othello **1603–04**

Timon of Athens **1605**

King Lear **1605–06**

Antony and Cleopatra **1606**

Macbeth

Coriolanus **1608**

HISTORIES

1592 *Henry VI* Pts I, II & III

1592–93 *Richard III*

— **1595** *King John, Richard II*

— **1596–97** *Henry IV* Pts I & II

— **1598** *Henry V*

EARLY COMEDIES

— **1590–91** *The Two Gentlemen of Verona*

— **1593** *The Taming of the Shrew*

— **1594** *The Comedy of Errors*

— **1594–95** *Love's Labours Lost*

LATER COMEDIES

— **1595–96** *A Midsummer Night's Dream*

— **1596–97** *The Merchant of Venice*

— **1597–98** *The Merry Wives of Windsor*

— **1598** *Much Ado about Nothing*

— **1599** *As You Like It*

—**1598** GLOBE BUILT

— **1601** *Twelfth Night*

— **1602** *Troilus and Cressida*

— **1603** *Measure for Measure*

— **1604–05** *All's Well That Ends Well*

—**1603** JAMES I SUCCEEDS

LATE PLAYS

— **1607** *Pericles*

— **1609** *A Winter's Tale*

— **1610** *Cymbeline*

— **1611** *The Tempest*

— **1613** *Henry VIII*

1616 SHAKESPEARE DIES

In Film

Over 1,300 films derive from the plays of Shakespeare. These include Kirosawa's *Ran*, and *Throne of Blood* based on *King Lear* and *Macbeth*; the musical *West Side Story* based on *Romeo and Juliet*; and more recent Hollywood ventures such as *O* based on *Othello*, and *Ten Things I Hate About You* based on *The Taming of the Shrew*.

although if so, it seems likely here that Fletcher may have shared authorship (*see* page 94).

On Shakespeare's death, greedy publishers ascribed many other works to him, but few of these are now given credence. It is thought, however, that Shakespeare may well have contributed to *Edward III* (*c.*1596), and may also have written an act of *Sir Thomas More* (the latter being the acknowledged work of six playwrights).

Extracts from Shakespeare's Works

No single extract can possibly reveal the scope of Shakespeare's work, so instead here is a collection of quotes to display some of the many aspects of his work: the poetry, the wit, the use of language, the range of ideas and themes. They are loosely based around the theme of 'night'.

O! She doth teach the torches to burn bright. It seems she hangs upon the cheek of night like a rich jewel in an Ethiop's ear. *Romeo and Juliet* Act 1 Sc v

Come, civil night, Thou sober-suited matron, all in black. Ibid, Act 3 Sc ii

In Language

There are over 21,000 different words used in the works of Shakespeare, and over 2,000 of them originate – that is, they were first found – in these plays.

... all the world be in love with night, and pay no worship to the garish sun. Ibid, Act 3 Sc ii

I must become a borrower of the night. *Macbeth* Act 3 Sc i

The shard-borne bettle with his drowsy hums hath rung night's yawning peal. Ibid, Act 3 Sc ii

Come, seeling night, scarf up the tender eye of pitiful day. Ibid, Act 3 Sc ii

Light thickens; and the crow makes wing to the rooky wood; Good things of day begin to droop and drowse, while night's black agents to their preys do rouse. Ibid, Act 3 Sc ii

The black bat night has flown. *Macbeth*

In the dead and vast and middle of the night. *Hamlet* Act 1 Sc ii

What may this mean, that thou, dead corse, again in complete steel, revisit'st thus the glimpses of the moon, making night hideous? Ibid, Act 1 Sc iv

'Tis now the very witching time of night, when churchyards yawn and hell itself breathes out contagion to this world. Ibid, Act 3 Sc ii

This will last out a night in Russia, when nights are longest there. *Measure for Measure* Act 2 Sc i

O polished pertubation! Golden care! That keep'st the ports of slumber open wide to many a watchful night! *Henry IV, Pt II* Act 3 Sc v

Now entertain conjecture of a time when creeping murmur and the poring dark fills the wide vessel of the universe. From camp to camp, through the foul womb of night, the hum of either army stilly sounds. *Henry V* Act 4 Chorus

This is the night that either makes me or fordoes me quite. *Othello* Act 5, Sc i

Let's have one other gaudy night.
Antony and Cleopatra Act 3 Sc xi

LORENZO: In such a night Troilus me-thinks mounted the Troyan walls, and sighed his soul toward the Grecian tents where Cressid lay that night.
JESSICA: In such a night did Thisbe fearfully o'ertrip the dew, and saw the lion's shadow ere himself, and ran dismay away.
LORENZO: In such a night stood Dido with a willow in her hand upon the wild sea-banks, and waft her love to come to Carthage.
JESSICA: In such a night Medea gathered the enchanted herbs that did renew old Aeson.
The Merchant of Venice Act 5 Sc i

O, I have passed a miserable night, so full of ugly sights, of ghastly dreams, that, as I am a Christian faithful man, I would not spend another such a night, Though 'twere to buy a world of happy days, so full of dismal terror was the time!
Richard III Act 1 Sc iv

Fortune, good night, smile once more, turn thy wheel! *King Lear* Act 2 Sc i

'Tis a naughty night to swim in. Ibid, Act 3 Sc ii

How sweet the moonlight sleeps upon this bank! Here we sit, and let the sounds of music creep in our ears: soft stillness and the night become the touches of sweet harmony. *The Merry Wives of Windsor* Act 5 Sc i

The man that hath no music in himself, nor is moved with concord of sweet sounds, is fit for treasons, stratagems, and spoils; The motions of his spirits are dull as night, and his affections dark as Erebus: Let no such man be trusted. Ibid, Act 5 Sc i

THE JACOBEAN PERIOD

King James I was as passionate a lover of theatre as Elizabeth I, and therefore little changed in theatrical life on his succession to the throne in 1603. James was certainly as happy to give his name to the art form as his predecessor. Shakespeare's company was itself privileged to receive a royal patent in that year, changing the company name from the Chamberlain's Men to the King's Men.

The period leading up to the succession (1600–02) also saw the so-called **War of Theatres** between rival companies, where Ben Jonson and one set of playwrights wrote critical satires attacking another set, who themselves fought back in similar style. This latter group included Marston, Dekker, and others (see individual entries below).

Many of Shakespeare's great works were written in the Jacobean period (*see* chart on page 82) – but he was not alone, and many other great playwrights were working alongside him, or were soon to follow.

Ben Jonson (1572–1637)

Benjamin Jonson was a close contemporary of William Shakespeare, and many of his plays were written, like Shakespeare's, for the King's Men. In fact Shakespeare is listed as having acted in the first performances of two of Jonson's plays, *Everyman in his Humour* and *Sejanus*.

Jonson led a very colourful life. Although well educated at Westminster School, he was briefly apprenticed to his stepfather as a bricklayer; he then undertook military service abroad, was several times imprisoned, and is known to have killed the actor Gabriel Spencer in a duel in 1598. He converted to Roman Catholicism whilst awaiting trial for this act, and was eventually acquitted; however, after a period of twelve or so years, he abandoned this calling. He was also questioned concerning the Gunpowder Plot, but was not implicated. Jonson was an actor for a short period, although not a very good one by all accounts: historian John Aubrey said of him, 'Ben Jonson was never a good Actor, but an excellent instructor.'[ii]

Jonson wrote in many idioms – poetry, epigram, epistle, satire, and literary theory. In his day Jonson was seen as much more a man of letters than Shakespeare, and in 1616 he was granted a royal pension, making him the Poet Laureate of his time. He was also honoured with honorary degrees from both Oxford and Cambridge. Jonson's collected 'workes' were published in folio in 1616, and uniquely included his plays. It is thought that without this example we may well not have had the Shakespeare folio of 1623.

Ben Jonson.

It is as a playwright that Jonson is chiefly remembered. He wrote initially as a journeyman for the theatre manager Philip Henslowe, but many of these works have not survived (*see* the early plays below). It is thought that he may have added substantially to the text of Kyd's play *The Spanish Tragedy* of 1589. However, Jonson can only really be said to have come into his style with *Everyman in his Humour* in 1598. He wrote many comedies and satires, and was greatly influenced by the works of Aristophanes (*see* page 22), and a good number of tragedies.

Jonson also wrote thirty-three court masques for King James I, most of them in collaboration with the great architect and stage designer Inigo Jones (*see* page 87). His first was *The Masque of*

Blackness in 1605, and others included *Masque of Queens* (1609), *Love Restored* (1612) and *Oberon, the Fairy Prince* in which the young Prince Henry, elder son of King James, appeared, shortly before his death in 1611.

Jonson was the leading figure in the 'War of Theatres'. His play *Poetaster* was written for the child players of Blackfriars known as 'The Chapel Children', and satirized adult actors and playwrights, John Marston and Thomas Dekker in particular. There is even a reference to the rivalry between the boys' and men's companies in Shakespeare's *Hamlet*: in Act II, Scene ii, Hamlet is in conversation with Rosencrantz, and the latter states:

> there is, sir, as aery of children, little eyases,
> that cry out on the top of question,
> and are most tyrannically clapped for't:
> these are now in fashion,
> and so berattle the common stages
> – so they call them –
> that many a wearying rapiers
> are afraid of goose quills and dare come thither.

Jonson suffered ill fortune in later life. He was not popular with King Charles I, who had succeeded to the throne in 1625 and replaced Jonson as writer of royal masques in 1630 after Jonson had fallen out with Inigo Jones over the masque *Chloridia*. Jonson's library burned down, and he ended his life with severe paralysis, unable to find a publisher for a second volume of his 'workes'. He died on 6 August 1637.

PLAYS
Hot Anger Soon Cold
A lesser work, written whilst in the pay of Henslowe.

Richard Crookback
Another lesser work, also written whilst in the pay of Henslowe.

The Isle of Dogs (1596)
This notorious co-written piece (with Nashe – *see* page 75) was considered seditious, and its performance at The Swan led to many of those involved being imprisoned – Jonson among them.

Everyman in his Humour (1598)
Shakespeare played the character 'Kno'well' on its first performance.

Everyman out of his Humour (1599)

The Case is Altered (1599)

Cynthia's Revels (1600)

The Poetaster (1601)
A satire in which Jonson attacks fellow playwrights, including Marston and Dekker. A 'poetaster' is a would-be poet. This play leads to the so-called 'War of Theatres' – *see* page 84.

Sejanus, his fall (1603)
A well-crafted classical history, not popular in its day, but a piece that also led to Jonson being imprisoned.

Eastward Ho! (1605)
Written with Marston and Chapman, a passage defaming the Scots was thought sufficiently inflammatory to have them all imprisoned, but friends interceded and they were released without charge.

Volpone; or, the fox (1606)
Written for the King's Men, this comic play has much in common with morality plays, both in its moralizing intent, and because its characters are metaphors,

taking, as they do, their names and characteristics from the humanly perceived characteristics of animals. 'Volpone' is Italian for 'fox', and other characters include Mosca the flea, Corvino the raven, Corbaccio the crow, and the lawyer Voltore, the vulture. The play is considered one of Jonson's greatest pieces.

Epicaena; or, the Silent Woman (1609)
Written for the King's Men, and influenced by Aretino's play *Il Marescalco* – *see* page 48.

The Alchemist (1610)
Written for the King's Men – a tragedy.

Catiline, his conspiracy (1611)
Another attempt to curry favour with a well-crafted classical history, but again, one not popular in its day.

Bartholomew Fair (1614)
A great rumbustious episodic comedy of life in contemporary London. Almost as successful an historic document as a great entertainment.

The Devil is an Ass (1616)
Considered a typical 'city comedy' of the period.

Staple of News (1625)
Jonson's last great play.

The following is an extract from *Volpone*, in which Volpone is about to entertain a number of his sycophantic followers from his feigned sickbed; first amongst them is Voltore, the advocate. He addresses his servant, Mosca:

The Fox

The printed text of *Volpone* begins with the following 'Argument':

V olpone, childless, rich feigns sick, despairs,
O ffers his state to hopes of several heirs,
L ies languishing; his Parasite receives
P resents of all, assures, deludes; the weaves
O ther cross-plots, which ope themselves, are told.
N ew tricks for safety are sought; they thrive; when, bold,
E ach tempts th' other again, and all are sold.

VOLPONE:
Fetch me my gown,
My furs, and night-caps; say my couch is changing,
And let him entertain himself a while
Without i' th' gallery [*Exit Mosca*]
Now, now, my clients
Begin their visitation! Vulture, kite,
Raven, and gorcrow, all my birds of prey,
That think me turning carcass, now they come.
I am not for 'em yet.
[*Enter Mosca with the gown, furs, etc.*]
How now? The news?

MOSCA:
A piece of plate, sir.

VOLPONE:
Of what bigness?

MOSCA:
Huge, massy, and antique, with your name
    inscribed,
And arms engraven.

VOLPONE:
Good! And not a fox
Stretched on the earth, with fine delusive sleights
Mocking a gaping Crow – ha, Mosca?

MOSCA:
Sharp, sir.

VOLPONE:
Give me my furs. Why dost thou laugh so, man?

MOSCA:
I cannot choose, sir, when I apprehend
What thoughts he has, without, now, as he walks:
That this might be the last gift he should give;
That this would fetch you; if you died today,
And gave him all, that he should be tomorrow;
What a large return would come of all his ventures;
How he should worshipped be, and reverenced;
Ride with his furs, and foot-cloths; waited on
By herds of fools and clients; have a clear way
Made for his moyle, as lettered as himself;
Be called the great and learnèd advocate:
And then concludes, there's nought impossible.

VOLPONE:
Yes, to be learnèd, Mosca.

MOSCA:
O, no; rich implies it. Hood an ass with reverend purple,
So you can hide his two ambitious ears,
And he shall pass for a cathedral doctor.

VOLPONE:
My caps, my caps, good Mosca. Fetch him in.

MOSCA:
Stay sir; your ointment for your eyes.

VOLPONE:
That's true; dispatch, dispatch. I long to have posses-
sion
Of my new present.

MOSCA:
That, and thousands more,
I hope to see you lord of.

VOLPONE:
Thanks, kind Mosca.

MOSCA:
And that, when I am lost in blended dust,
And hundreds such as I am, in succession -

VOLPONE:
Nay, that were too much, Mosca.

MOSCA:
You shall live still to delude these harpies.

VOLPONE:
Loving, Mosca!
'Tis well. My pillow now, and let them enter.
[*Exit Mosca*]
Now, my feigned cough, my phthisic, and my gout,
My apoplexy, palsy, and catarrhs,
Help, with your forcèd functions, this my posture,
Wherein, this three year, I have milked their hopes.
He come, I hear him – uh! uh! uh! uh! O!
[*Volpone gets into bed*] [*Enter Mosca with Voltore*]

Inigo Jones (1573–1652)

Jones was born in London, and became one of the most influential architects of all time. He learned his skills in Italy where he much admired the Palladian style, and he first designed in Denmark for the Danish king, Frederick IV, who then sent him well recommended to the court of his brother-in-law, James I of England.

Jones initially made his mark in England working on the court masques with Ben Jonson and he later introduced to the English stage the proscenium arch

The proscenium stage of Inigo Jones.

as a means to 'frame' the stage (*see* diagram). At Christ Church, Oxford, on the occasion of a visit to the university by the king, Jones used the device of revolving screens or 'periactoids' to change scenery, another Italian idea of classical origin. Jones is also credited with bringing other innovations to England: the use of perspectivized scenery, backcloths, painted flats, and even the very notion of scene changes themselves!

Jones later became famous as an architect. In 1610 he became surveyor of works to Prince Henry, returning to study in Italy on the latter's death. In 1615 he became surveyor general of the royal buildings, designing the queen's house at Greenwich, the Banqueting House, Whitehall, the Queen's Chapel at St James's Palace, St Paul's Church, the piazza at Covent Garden, Lincoln's Inn Fields and many country houses. His influence on British architecture remains quite considerable.

John Marston (*c.*1575–1634)

Marston was born in Coventry, and initially followed a career as a lawyer. His first works were satirical and highly sexually charged poetry: *The Metamorphosis of Pygmalion's Image* and *The Scourge of Villainy* in 1598. His first plays were for the Admiral's Men, and then after for the Children

of Paul's Company, also known as the 'Paul's Boys'.

Marston took part in the so-called 'War of Theatres' (*see* page 84), attacking Jonson in *Jack Drum's Entertainment*, which has not survived, and *What you Will*. He is also known to have collaborated with Dekker in his play *Satiromastix* (1601), which also sought to vilify Jonson. In Jonson's replying play *Poetaster*, Marston is seen as the character Crispinus, ridiculed for both his writing and his looks – he is described as having red hair and puny legs! Scholars have also found evidence that suggests that Marston assisted Shakespeare in the co-writing of *Troilus and Cressida* in 1602.

From 1604 onwards Marston was manager of the 'Children of the Revels', for whom he wrote all his remaining plays. The rivalry with Jonson was also ended, as by 1605 they were both in trouble for their collaboration in the play *Eastward Ho!* (*see* page 86) – although unlike his colleagues, Jonson and Chapman, Marston was not imprisoned. However, he was incarcerated in 1608 when he offended James I with a play now lost. At this point he stopped writing plays, leaving an unfinished work – *The Insatiate Countess*. Marston lived until 1634, ending his life as an ordained priest.

PLAYS
The History of Antonio and Mellida (1599)
A tragedy written for the Children of Paul's company.

Antonio's Revenge (1599)
A sequel to the former play and also written for the Children of Paul's.

Jack Drum's Entertainment (*c.*1601)
No longer in existence, as no copy has survived.

What you Will (1601)
A comedy.

The Malcontent (1603/4)
A comedy, thought to have included some passages contributed by John Webster (*see* page 92).

The Dutch Courtesan (1604/5)
A typical 'city comedy' of the period (*see* page 92).

Eastward Ho! (1605)
Written in collaboration with Jonson and Chapman (*see* notes on page 86).

The Parasitaster (1606)
A comedy.

Sophonisba (1606)
A comedy.

The Insatiate Countess (1613)
A tragedy, his last work, and left unfinished.

Thomas Dekker (*c*.1572–1632)

Dekker was born in London, and little is known of his early life. He wrote over forty plays, some in collaboration, from 1598 to 1602, for the Admiral's or the Worcester's Men, of which only six are extant. Dekker seems to have written many of his works in collaboration, and in later life he also took to the writing of pamphlets.

Dekker's play *Satiromastix* (1601) was written in collaboration with John Marston (*see* page 88). It is a satire on the world of Ben Jonson and a reply to Jonson's attacks in his play *Poetaster*. Dekker was thus a feature player in the so-called 'War of Theatres' (*see* page 84), and this resulted in Jonson describing Dekker as 'a rogue' – although the two men later collaborated together on Court entertainments, so the quarrel must have been patched up.

In later years Dekker produced the Lord Mayor of London's pageant on a number of occasions.

Warburton's Cook

The loss of the only existing copy of many of Dekker's plays is one of the major 'crimes' attributed to Warburton's cook! Antiquarian John Warburton (1682–1759) had in his care over sixty manuscripts of plays from this period. Through a complete lack of understanding and care, his cook, Betsy Baker, used them to line pie dishes and the like. Other losses to the culinary arts include works by Ford and Massinger.

Despite his success, throughout his life Dekker had trouble with money, and it is thought he ended his days in debt.

PLAYS
Old Fortunatus (*c*.1600)
A comedy.

Shoemaker's Holiday (*c*.1600)
An ebullient comedy, based on a story by the contemporary author Thomas Deloney, and Dekker's most famous work. It concerns the rise to fame of shoemaker Simon Eyre, who becomes Lord Mayor of London.

Satiromastix (1601)
A satire written in collaboration with John Marston (*see* page 88).

Patient Grissil (1603)
Written in collaboration with Chettle and Haughton. Hardly any work survives of the plays of Henry Chettle (*c*.1560–*c*.1607) and John Haughton (*c*.1575–1605). Chettle's only extant work is *The Tragedy of Hoffman* (1602), and Haughton's the comedy *Englishmen For My Money* (1598).

The Honest Whore (1604)
Written in two parts, with the second part not appearing until 1630. It is thought that Middleton may have had a hand in writing the first part.

The Roaring Girl (*c*.1610)
A comedy, written with Thomas Middleton. Dekker and Middleton took as their model for *The Roaring Girl* a notorious thief of the period: Mary Frith, known as 'Cutpurse Moll'. She may have been an actor – unusual in this period for a woman – but 'Moll' always wore men's clothing and smoked a pipe! Professionally she was also a bawd, a fence, a prostitute, and ran a school for thieves in Aldersgate Street, London. She also robbed the parliamentary commander, Colonel Fairfax, during the Civil War. She died of dropsy in 1650.

The Virgin Martyr (*c*.1610)
A tragedy, written in collaboration with Massinger.

The Witch of Edmonton (c.1621)
A tragi-comedy written in collaboration with Ford and Rowley and probably others – its title page reads 'by Dekker, J. Ford, W. Rowley, etc.'.

Match Me in London (pub. 1631)
His last solo work.

Thomas Heywood (*c*.1575–1641)

Heywood was an actor and a playwright. He appeared with the Admiral's and Worcester's Men, working, like Jonson, for the theatre manager Philip Henslowe. He wrote many more plays than have survived, claiming to have had 'an entire hand, or at least a main finger' in 220 plays. He also wrote prose works, among them *Apology for Actors* of 1612.

Heywood gave up acting and writing plays in 1619 on the death of Queen Anne, though he took up being a playwright again in 1630. He also wrote a prologue to Marlowe's *The Jew of Malta* and a number of Lord Mayor's pageants.

PLAYS
Edward IV (1599)
A history written in two parts and in collaboration with Chettle (*see* page 89) and others.

Four Prentices of London (1600)
A romantic comedy, later satirized by Francis Beaumont in his play *Knight of the Burning Pestle* of 1607 (*see* page 94).

A Woman Killed with Kindness (1603)
Heywood's masterpiece, a play that still stands the test of time, dealing as it does with a women's infidelity and her husband's attitude to it.

If You Know Not Me, You Know Nobody (1604/5)
A two-part chronicle of the early years of Queen Elizabeth I.

The Wise Woman of Hogson (1604)

The Rape of Lucrece (c.1608)

Golden Age, Silver Age, Brazen Age, Iron Age (1611–13)
A cycle of plays depicting the lives of the Gods during the Trojan War.

The Fair Maid of the West (c.1630)
A romantic melodrama.

The English Traveller (c.1633)
A tragedy with a comic sub-plot.

William Rowley (*c*.1585–*c*.1640)

Rowley was a comic actor, known for his portrayal of fat men, and a performer in the companies of Prince Charles's Men and the King's Company. As a writer of plays Rowley is known for his collaboration with Thomas Middleton, with whom he wrote his best work. He also wrote pieces alongside Heywood, Webster, Ford, Massinger and Ford. He also wrote poetry.

Samuel Rowley

William Rowley, should not be confused with Samuel Rowley of very similar dates (*c*.1575–1624). Samuel Rowley was also a playwright, but his only surviving play is *When You See Me, You Know Me* (1603), a life and times of King Henry VIII. He was however said to have had a hand in the writing of *The Taming of the Shrew c.*1589.

PLAYS
A Fair Quarrel (1617)
Written with Middleton (*see* page 91).

The Spanish Gypsy
Written with Middleton.

The Changeling (1622)
Written with Middleton.

All's Lost by Lust (1622)
A play in which Rowley himself played the role of clown.

A New Wonder (1632)

A Match at Midnight (1633)

A Shoomaker a Gentleman (1638)

Fortune by Land and Sea
Written in collaboration with Thomas Heywood.

The Thracian Wonder (pub. 1661)
Written in collaboration with John Webster.

Thomas Middleton (*c.*1570–1627)

Middleton was born in London, and wrote prose and poetry before he turned to drama. His first plays were for the Admiral's Men and later for the Paul's Boys. His early works, often in collaboration with Dekker, Drayton, Munday and Webster, are mostly lost, although he is thought to have played a part in the writing of Dekker's plays *The Honest Whore* and *The Roaring Girl* (*c.*1610).

Middleton's later work, much in association with William Rowley, is remarkable for its intense realism, certainly when compared with that of his contemporaries. Middleton also wrote pageants for the city companies in London, and in 1620 was appointed chronologer to the City.

PLAYS
A Trick to Catch the Old One (1604/5)

Michaelmas Terme (1607)

The Familie of Love (1608)

A Mad World, my Masters (1608)
A typical 'city comedy' of the period (*see* page 92).

A Chaste Maid in Cheapside (1611)
Considered perhaps his greatest work.

A Fair Quarrel (1617), with Rowley.

Women Beware Women (1621)
Another great work of the period.

The Changeling, a tragedy (1622) with Rowley.
A play of great worth and often still performed.

The Spanish Gypsy (1623), with Rowley.

More Dissemblers besides Women (pub. 1657)

No Wit, no Help like a Woman's (pub. 1657)

A Game of Chess (1624)
A satire aimed at the public dislike for a Spanish marriage for Prince Charles, and a play in which William Rowley created the role of the fat bishop. The politics of this piece caused it to be eventually banned.

The Witch (*c.*1627)
A tragedy that bears interesting comparison with Shakespeare's *Macbeth*. (The 'Hecate' scenes in *Macbeth* are generally thought to be interpolations authored by Thomas Middleton.)

Anything for a Quiet Life (pub. 1662)

The Widdow (pub. 1652)
A collaboration with Ben Jonson and John Fletcher.

Detail from **The Witch** *– a modern staging, directed by Robin Midgley.*

JACOBEAN TRAGEDY

As time passed, and tastes inevitably changed, the variety of work of the Elizabethan era became somewhat eclipsed by a newly emerging genre that to some extent sang on fewer notes. Also known as 'revenge tragedy', this drama of reprisal and retribution was in style and content often bloody, and even tortuously violent. It spoke of enraged passion, twisted and elaborate plots, and dark machinations. The fashion for this kind of drama may be said to start with Kyd's *Spanish Tragedy*, and is typified by the two great works of Webster. Earlier pieces, such as Marlowe's *Edward II*, and even Shakespeare's *Hamlet*, also fit the definition of revenge tragedy. It can therefore be described as high drama, of plot and counterplot, where revenge is 'a dish best served cold'. *Hamlet* is probably the best known example, although not by any means the darkest – indeed, *Titus Andronicus*, Shakespeare's other entry into this genre, is much bleaker.

Revenge tragedies contain, as their name suggests, a hero or heroine who grapples with conscience or custom before deciding to enact revenge for a dastardly deed done either to them, or to a near relative. In *Hamlet*, of course, the eponymous hero spends a large part of the play being indecisive about whether he should revenge the assassination of his father by his uncle. In other works this process is a lot quicker, leaving room for counter revenge and counter-counter revenge! The Jacobean period seems also to have been one where fascination with bodily functions leads in these plays to a keen interest in, and different and even strange, punishments or tortures. Archetypal examples of this genre are Kyd's *Spanish Tragedy* and Tourneur's *Revenger's Tragedy* of 1607.

On a lighter note, the comedies of the period are often classified as 'city' or 'country' comedies, because they take the form of knowing city pieces or country bumpkin farces. Examples of these comedies are Marston's *The Dutch Courtesan* and Middleton's *A Mad World, my Masters*. As a general note, however, it is the tragedies from this period that have stayed in the imagination and on our stages.

John Webster (*c.*1580–*c.*1630)

Webster was a declaimed Londoner, and little else is known of his life, although it is possible he was also an actor. Of his plays, two have seriously stood the test of time: *The White Devil* and *The Duchess of Malfi* remain stalwarts of the classical repertoire and are often revived. They are plays of great passion, both romantic and political. Perhaps more than anything their sense of horror mixed with poetry defines the term 'Jacobean Tragedy'. Amongst his contemporaries, Webster can perhaps be said to stand closest to Shakespeare in the power of his work.

PLAYS
Appius and Virginia (*c.*1608)

The White Devil (1612)

The Duchess of Malfi (1614), *see* extract below.

The Devil's Law Case (1623)

The following extract is from *The Duchess of Malfi*. To set the scene: for political reasons the Duchess of Malfi is forbidden to marry by her brothers, who hold high office. But the Duchess falls in love with her steward Antonio and secretly marries him, later also conceiving a child by him. Her suspicious brothers place in her household a spy – Bosola. The Duchess and Antonio flee to avoid confrontation, but the Duchess is captured and murdered by Bosola. Struck by his victim's courage in death, and aware that they now desire his removal, Bosola seeks to revenge the Duchess's death on her brothers – only to kill Antonio in mistake for one of them. Further revenge and counter revenge ensue before the play comes to its dark conclusion. The following extract comes from the Duchess's last moments:

Act Four, Scene ii.
[*Enter Executioner with a coffin, cords, and a bell*]
BOSOLA:
Here is a present from your princely brothers,
And may it arrive welcome, for it brings
Last benefit, last sorrow.

DUCHESS:
Let me see it.
I have much obedience, in my blood,
I wish it in their veins, to do them good.

BOSOLA:
This is your last presence chamber.

CARIOLA:
O my sweet lady!

DUCHESS:
Peace; it affrights not me.

BOSOLA:
I am the common bellman,
That usually is sent to condemn'd persons,
The night before they suffer.

DUCHESS:
Even now thou said'st thou wast a tomb maker?

BOSOLA:
Twas to bring you
By degrees to mortification. Listen: [*He rings the bell.*]
Hark, now every thing is still,
The screech-owl and the whistler shrill
Call upon our Dame, aloud,
And bid her quickly don her shroud.
Much you had of land and rent,
Your length in clay's now competent.
A long war disturb'd your mind,
Here you perfect peace is sign'd.
Of what is't fools make such vain keeping?
Sin their conception, their birth, weeping:
Their life, a general mist of error,
Their death, a hideous storm of terror.
Strew your hair with powders sweet:
Don clean linen, bathe your feet,
And, the foul fiend more to check,
A crucifix let bless your neck.
'Tis now full tide 'tween night and day,
End your groan, and come away.
[*Executioners approach*]

George Chapman (*c.*1559–1634)

Chapman was born in Hitchen, Hertfordshire, a poet and dramatist who wrote for the Admiral's Men and later completed the last, unfinished work of Marlowe, *Hero and Leander.* Much of his work seemed to excite censure and controversy (*see*

below). Possibly because of this, he concentrated most of his literary efforts on poetry, and in the period these works were thought to have rivalled the poetical outpourings of Shakespeare.

PLAYS
Bussy d'Amboise (1604)

Eastward Ho! (1605)
A controversial play written with Jonson and Marston (*see* notes on page 86).

Charles, Duke of Biron (1608)
Chapman was again in trouble with this play, which offended the French Ambassador.

John Ford (1588–1639)

John Ford was born in Devon and is one of the unfortunate playwrights to have suffered at the hands of Warburton's cook (*see* page 89); as such he is only really known for three surviving plays; however, they are works of note.

PLAYS
'Tis pity she's a Whore (*c.*1628)
Ford's masterpiece and a great play of the period. Dealing with the intense subject of incest, this piece has remained fresh and relevant long after many of its fellows have faded into obscurity. Ford's portrayal of siblings in love still arouses emotions and reactions in us at the deepest level.

The Broken Heart

Love's Sacrifice (*c.*1632)

Cyril Tourneur (*c.*1575–1626)

Tourneur served his country in military and diplomatic fashion, as well as being a poet and a dramatist. He was at one time a diplomatic courier before later becoming secretary to Sir Edward Cecil. In this service he was part of an unsuccessful raid on Cadiz in 1625, and it may well have been that he died from his wounds received on this occasion. As a dramatist Tourneur collaborated with others, notably Fletcher.

PLAYS
Revenger's Tragedy (1607)
Of disputed authorship, but now generally thought to be Tourneur's work.

The Atheist's Tragedy (c.1608)
An inferior work that led to the dispute concerning the vastly superior earlier work.

The Nobleman (c.1612)
Listed as a tragi-comedy, but now lost.

Beaumont & Fletcher
At one time over fifty plays were ascribed to this partnership, and even today they are mostly known for their joint work.

John Fletcher (1579–1625)
Fletcher was a professional author; his earliest known work appears as a solo piece, but thereafter he is known to have worked often with others, notably Massinger (*see* page 95), Rowley, Jonson, Middleton, and possibly Shakespeare. But the majority of his collaborations seem to have been with Beaumont. Fletcher died of the plague in 1625.

Contemporary records suggest that Fletcher co-wrote a play, now lost, called *The History of Cardenio,* with Shakespeare. It is also thought that he may have had a hand in Shakespeare's *Henry VIII* and *Two Noble Kinsmen.*

Fletcher's solo efforts date from 1608–20, and are mostly comedies and romances:

PLAYS
The Faithful Shepherdess
A light, pastoral piece.

Wit without Money

Valentinian

The Loyal Subject

The Mad Lover

The Humorous Lieutenant

Women Pleased

The Wild Goose Chase
Adapted by George Farquhar as *The Inconstant* in 1702 (*see* page 113).

The Pilgrim
Later used by John Vanbrugh as the basis for his own play of the same name, written in 1700 (*see* page 112).

The Island Princess

Monsieur Thomas

The Woman's Prize; or, The Tamer Tamed
A sequel to *The Taming of the Shrew.*

A Wife for a Month

Rule a Wife and have a Wife

The Chances (1623)

Sir Francis Beaumont (1584–1616)
Although he trained as a lawyer, it seems he never practised. Nearly all of his plays were co-written with John Fletcher, though two pieces are credited to him alone: *Knight of the Burning Pestle* (1607), which in imitation of Jonson seeks to satirize Heywood's *Four Prentices of London* of 1600; and *The Women Hater* (1607), a comedy.

As a pair, Beaumont and Fletcher are said to have taken over the main writing role for the King's Men from William Shakespeare in around 1609. Below are listed their joint plays:

PLAYS
Four Plays in One (c.1608)
Four short plays.

Philaster (1610)

The Maid's Tragedy (1611)

A King and No King (1611)

The Scornful Lady (1613)

The Coxcomb (1612)

Cupid's Revenge (c.1612)
A tragedy.

The Captain (c.1612)
A comedy.

The Honest Man's Fortune (c.1613)

Bonduca (c.1613)

The Knight of Malta (1619)
A tragi-comedy.

Thierry and Theodoret (c.1620)

Love's Cure (c.1620)

Philip Massinger (1584–1640)

Massinger was born in Salisbury and spent most of his writing career working exclusively for the King's Men. He wrote often in collaboration, and much of his work, some twenty or so plays, is now lost, another victim of Warburton's cook (*see* page 89). His most notable pieces are *A New Way to Pay Old Debts* and *The City Madam*.

His works written in collaboration with Fletcher include *Sir John van Olden Barnavelt* (1619), *The Beggar's Bush* (1622), *The False One*, *The Elder Brother*, and *The Spanish Curate* (c.1622). With Dekker he wrote *The Virgin Martyr* (c.1610).

Massinger is also often cited as another possible collaborator with Shakespeare on the plays *Two Noble Kinsmen* and *Henry VIII*.

PLAYS
The Fatal Dowry (1619)
A tragi-comedy that may have been written in collaboration with Nathan Field (*see* page 90).

The Virgin Martyr (1620)
Another possibly collaborative work, this time with Dekker (*see* page 89).

The Duke of Milan (1620)
A romantic comedy.

A New Way to Pay Old Debts (c.1623)
A satirical work thought to owe its concept to Middleton's *A Trick to Catch the Old One* of 1604/5. Much revived, the central role of Sir Giles Overreach remains a performer's delight.

The Bondman (1623)
A tragi-comedy.

The Parliament of Love (1624)

The Roman Actor (1626)

The Great Duke of Florence (1627)
A romantic comedy.

The Renegado (1630)

The Picture (1630)

The City Madam (c.1632)
A comedy written in collaboration with Field.

The Maid of Honour (1632)

The Emperor of the East (1632)

The Guardian (1633)
A comedy written in collaboration with Dekker.

The Bashful Lover (c.1639)

The Unnatural Combat (1639)

Richard Brome (c.1590–1652)

Little is known of Brome's life, but it is thought he may have been a secretary or close companion to Ben Jonson, whose influence (if not collaboration) shows in his surviving work. A lost comedy called *A Fault in Friendship* (1623) was said to have been written in conjunction with Jonson's son. Of his surviving plays, some fifteen, the best pieces are *The City Wit* and *The Joviall Crew*. Brome seems to have continued writing right up to the closing of the theatres in 1642.

Lesser Playwrights of the Period

PLAYWRIGHT	NOTES	WORKS
Elizabeth Cary (1586–1629)	Daughter of Lord Tanfield.	*Miriam the Fair, Queen of Jewry*
John Day (1574–1640)	Mostly wrote for children's companies. Last play listed here was written for Will Kempe with Rowley and Wilkins.	*The Blind Beggar of Bethnal Green, Law Tricks, The Isle of Gulls, Humour out of Breath, The Travels of Three English Brothers*
Michael Drayton (1563–1631)	A friend of Shakespeare,with Hathway, Munday & Wilson and mostly a poet, this one piece is a defence of the Falstaff of *Henry IV*.	*Sir John Oldcastle*
Stephen Gosson (1554–1624)	A puritan convert who came to attack the theatre.	*Catiline's Conspiracy, Captain Mario, Praise at Parting*
Richard Hathway (1586–?)	Part author of many plays.	*See* Drayton, above
Thomas Hughes (*c.*1557–*c.*1623)	Performed at court and part written by William Fulbecke, with dumb shows by Francis Bacon.	*The Misfortunes of Arthur*
Thomas Legge (1535–1607)	Written in Latin but said to have influenced Greene, Marlowe and Shakespeare.	*Richardus Tertius, The Destruction of Jerusalem*
Anthony Munday (1560–1633)	Actor and dramatist (*see* Middleton, page 91, and Drayton above.)	*John a Kent and John a Cumber, The Life and Death of Robin Hood*
Henry Porter (unknown)	Co-wrote also with Chettle and Jonson.	*The Two Angry Women of Abingdon*
George Ruggle (1575–1622)	A scholar and satirist.	*Club Law, Ignoramus*
Thomas Tomkis (*c.*1580–1634)	First public appearance of Oliver Cromwell as an actor of four years old.	*Lingua, Albumazar*
Arthur Wilson (1595–1652)	Historian and dramatist.	*The Inconstant Lady*
Robert Wilson (d.1600)	Actor and dramatist.	*Three Ladies of London, Three Lords & Three Ladies of London, Cobbler's Prophecy*

Brome is the earliest playwright for which a contract of employment has been discovered; it was drawn up in his name on 20 July 1635.

PLAYS

The Northern Lass (1632)
Brome's earliest surviving play.

The City Wit (c.1632)

The Sparagus Garden (c.1635)
A robust satire or comedy of manners.

The Antipodes (1638)

The Queen's Exchange
A romantic comedy.

The Queen and the Concubine
A romantic comedy.

The Joviall Crew (1641)

James Shirley (1596–1666)

Shirley was born in London. Initially he was a teacher by profession, becoming headmaster of a grammar school in St Albans in 1623. On losing this job in 1625, on his conversion to Roman Catholicism, he became a schoolmaster and a dramatist. He took part in the civil war under the leadership of the Earl of Newcastle. He wrote some thirty-six plays, and was considered one of the leading playwrights of his time. Shirley was particularly known for his comedies, which played again with great popularity during the early years of the Restoration. He died in 1666 of ill health as a consequence of the Great Fire of London.

PLAYS

The Maid's Revenge (1626)
A tragedy.

The Witty Fair One (1628)
A comedy.

The Traitor (1631)
A tragedy.

Love's Cruelty (1631)
A tragedy.

Changes, or Love in a Maze (1632)
Being a series of dialogues or interchanges of affection between three pairs of lovers.

Hyde Park (1632)
A comedy.

The Gamester (1633)
A comedy.

The Coronation (1635)

The Lady of Pleasure (1635)
A comedy.

The Imposture (1640)

The Cardinall (1641)
A tragedy. Samuel Pepys reported seeing it in 1667.

The Sisters (1642)
A comedy.

The playwrights listed above are the most notable of the period. Others, of interest to scholars of the period, but whose work is either considered less able, or has simply not survived, are listed in the box (*left*). Also notable in this period is Sir Francis Bacon, who for a time was thought a creditable author of the works of Shakespeare. This misplaced notoriety rather overlooks the important contribution Bacon made to the fields of statesmanship, history and science. Bacon died of pneumonia after an experiment to preserve a fowl by stuffing it with snow!

CONCLUSION

The period around the life of William Shakespeare was enormously productive theatrically, and possibly the most diverse of any time. Even the expansiveness of the twentieth century pales when one considers the relative population sizes. But this fecund time comes to an abrupt end with the rise of the puritans, and the closure of all theatres in England in 1642.

6 THEATRE OF THE ENGLISH RESTORATION

We saw a new play acted yesterday ... it is the most entire piece of mirth,
a complete farce from one end to the other, that certainly was ever write.
I never laughed so in all my life; I laughed till my head [ached] all evening
and night with my laughing, and at the very good wit therein.
SAMUEL PEPYS [i]

You are walking down Portugal Street towards the newly opened theatre at Lincoln's Inn Fields, your heart in your mouth. You know that the theatre is different in shape and size from The Swan, which had been your favourite place in which to enjoy the raucous entertainment of the good old days before the last king got the chop. However, you have every hope that the performances within its intimate tennis-court-shaped walls will be just as enjoyable. You have been forced to wait several long frustrating puritanical years for the chance to once again witness the flamboyant performers parade before you in their ingeniously plotted stories. Finally, in the oppressive heat of a June fading fast into August, they are back. You are glad that although the theatre here is changed in shape somewhat the fare seems very familiar. The first plays announced for this new Carolean era are two old favourites: The Siege of Rhodes *and* Hamlet, *and you hear that for the latter it is intended to give the audience paintings, or some such, on stage to show where any scene is taking place. Even better, your favourite tragedian Thomas Betterton is to play the title character. You quicken your pace, tears welling up, as your sense of expectation nearly overwhelms you.*

OPPOSITE PAGE AND RIGHT:
Restoration drama. Modern
productions in period costume.

INTRODUCTION

The puritan ethic, starting under Cromwell's leadership, meant that from 1642 until 1660, theatre was outlawed as a licentious and irreverent pastime. This eighteen-year period of darkness on the English stage during the interregnum was in fact a relatively short period and, on the restoration of the monarch, theatres quickly reopened. Yet despite what in historical terms might seem a short gap, the flourish of renewed theatrical activity on the restoration of

Charles II in 1660 was distinctly different from the theatre that had preceded it, and had been so abruptly curtailed.

Many of the practices of the earlier period could not be continued; the links with popular tradition were broken, and much of the knowledge and many of the methods of the period which had been passed down for many years were lost. As part of this, a whole generation of performers had been lost. There were, for example, no new boy actors trained to take on the young female roles, and no juveniles waiting to take on the older roles. In addition, the theatre buildings themselves were gone or in terrible repair. While new buildings were being built, theatrical events took place in any available large space: inn courts, private halls and even tennis courts were used, and the rectangular nature of these spaces can be seen to have influenced the theatres that were to follow.

Alongside the loss of English traditions, many French conventions returned to England with the English court, not the least of which involved the staging of drama. Theatres became more like the

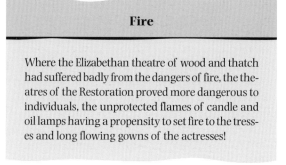

Fire

Where the Elizabethan theatre of wood and thatch had suffered badly from the dangers of fire, the theatres of the Restoration proved more dangerous to individuals, the unprotected flames of candle and oil lamps having a propensity to set fire to the tresses and long flowing gowns of the actresses!

ones designed by Inigo Jones for short-lived entertainments and royal spectacles – his ideas had, after all, been born on the continent (*see* page 87). As a consequence of this, theatre now moved permanently indoors, and remained there. This change of performance space was further reinforced when the London theatres had to close in 1665 because of the plague, and the court moved to Oxford (*see* Dryden, page 107).

In the new theatres, candles and, later, oil lamps were used for illumination, even though windows

The Restoration stage.

were often built above the stage and audience; candelabra were hung or supported above, at the side, and within the scenery. The footlight became a prominent source of available light, coming, as it did, from so close to the performers. The stage area was now backed and framed with scenery and structure, the acting area itself thrusting forward to the audience from within this frame (*see* diagram).

THE FIRST PRACTITIONERS OF THE RESTORATION STAGE

Immediately following the king's restoration, two characters who had been heavily involved with the theatre before the civil war were allowed to hold sway over the re-establishment of the theatre business in England. With warrants from the newly throned king, William Davenant and Thomas Killigrew, both theatre managers and writers of plays, had an almost complete monopoly on the hiring and firing of performers. Before the interregnum Davenant and Killigrew had written plays and masques for the court. They now both worked hard to re-establish theatrical life in England, and subsequently both opened playhouses and established theatre companies.

Shakespeare's Heir

Davenant was reputed to be the illegitimate son of William Shakespeare, by the hostess of a famous hostlery. There seems little doubt that there may have been some connection here, but it is more likely that he was in fact only the boy's godfather.

William Davenant (1606–68)

Prior to the break in royal rule, Davenant produced plays and masques in a Jonsonian manner, becoming Poet Laureate in 1638. During the civil war he fought on the Royalist side, and was knighted in 1643. During the Commonwealth he managed to get permission to stage a few events under the auspices of music and education (*see* below). On the return of the king he obtained a patent and opened the Lincoln's Inn

Lincoln's Inn Fields

The Lincoln's Inn Fields Theatre, which opened in 1661, was also known as the Duke's House. Originally a traditional indoor tennis court, it can claim to be the first English theatre to have had a proscenium arch and to have used movable scenery. Used as a theatre until *c*.1733, the building lasted until 1848.

Fields Theatre, where the company leading actor was Thomas Betterton (*see* page 102).

Davenant was also responsible for several adaptations of the works of Shakespeare, and encouraged innovations in the use of stage machinery and extravagant scenic elements.

PLAYS
The Siege of Rhodes (1656)
This piece, written in two parts, uses a lot of music to accompany the action, and can therefore be identified as more of a masque than a play; it is also sometimes claimed as the first English opera. It was the first play to be performed, as a revival, in the Lincoln's Inn Fields Theatre on its opening in June 1661.

The Spaniards in Peru (1658)
Written to inform the masses of the doings of the Conquistadors.

Sir Francis Drake (1659)
In common with its predecessor, this was written at the end of the Commonwealth and as a piece decidedly to educate rather than entertain!

Thomas Killigrew (1612–83)

Killigrew practised as a playwright before the execution of Charles I, and then after the Restoration founded Drury Lane Theatre in 1662; he also became Master of the King's Revel in 1673. His only known play is *The Parson's Wedding* (1640), an early success based on a play by Calderón (*see* page 63). The piece was of a rather risqué nature, and on revival in 1664 was said to have made 'even Mr Pepys blush'!

101

The New Style of Theatre and its Performers

The Restoration period also differed markedly in tone from the pre-civil war era. Although the monarchy had been restored, the mood of the populace was much altered by the events leading to, and playing a part in, the interregnum. The certainties that had suffused the work of Shakespeare, certainties concerning queen and country, and religious faith, were no longer so secure. The excesses of war and the puritan ethics had had much the same effect as would the two world wars of a much later century: the very foundations of belief had been rocked, and thus the dramatic art that accompanied this feeling was one of criticism, and overt – and seemingly often obscene – abandonment and exuberance. Sentimentality and outrageousness walked hand in hand alongside cynicism and a keen sense of commerce; all this in differing measures of course, depending on who was writing. Although the period started with revivals of the works of Jonson, and of Beaumont and Fletcher, soon new work from new writers joined the fray, and as one would imagine, the comedies of this period were particularly notable.

Of the male performers of this period there is perhaps no better example than that of **Thomas Betterton** (c.1635–1710), whose name pops up time and again in what follows. Betterton was the leading man of his day, and an actor/manager. The son of a cook to Charles I, Betterton acted at Lincoln's Inn Fields and other theatres, before undertaking a number of Shakespearean leads at the theatre in Drury Lane, thus making his name. He later performed back at Lincoln's Inn and also at the Haymarket. At the latter he appeared in the first performance of Congreve's *Love for Love*. He made his final appearance in 1710, and was buried in Westminster Abbey.

For the first time in England, women began to take their rightful place on stage among the men. First among them were renowned performers such as Mrs Barry, Mrs Colman, Mrs Mountfort and, most infamous of all, Nell Gwyn. As the ladies took their place, so eventually did the writing for them grow and develop, and quickly they, too, became as associated with roles and writers as the men. For example, a great public favourite of the time, Mrs Bracegirdle, became intrinsically linked with the heroines of Congreve's comedies. It is also from this period that the first real professional female writer (in any medium) can be dated: her name was Aphra Behn (*see* page 110).

The Playwrights of the Restoration

GEORGE ETHEREGE (1634–91)

Etherege was the first great writer of the Restoration period, and notable for his social comedy of manners: the best example of this was his most popular piece *The Man of Mode* of 1676, which clearly shows the influence of the work of Molière. It is therefore Etherege who can be said to set the tone for the greater comedies that were to follow.

Etherege was also considered quite a rake about town, fathering a daughter by actress Mrs Barry, and numbering amongst his friends the notorious Earl of Rochester. However, he was also appointed ambassador to Constantinople (1668–71) and later to the imperial court at Ratisborn, after which he was knighted.

PLAYS

The Comical Revenge; or, Love in a Tub (1664)
A very successful debut play; although not really an archetypal Restoration comedy, it nevertheless earned Etherege a strong reputation.

She Would if she Could (1668)
Perhaps a more characteristic comedy of the period.

Rochester

The rather debauched 2nd Earl of Rochester, as well as being friend to many playwrights, was also used as a model by them for a number of characters in their plays. The part of Dorimant in *The Man of Mode* being one of them.

The Man of Mode (1676)

A full-blown Restoration comedy, and one that set the seal on Etherege's reputation. This play is particularly notable for its foppish characters, including the wonderful Sir Fopling Flutter.

The following is an extract from *The Man of Mode* by George Etherege. Despite being the character that everyone associates with this play, Sir Fopling Flutter does not, in fact, make his first entrance until Act III. Nevertheless, the immediacy with which he comes to us works even when the play is read.

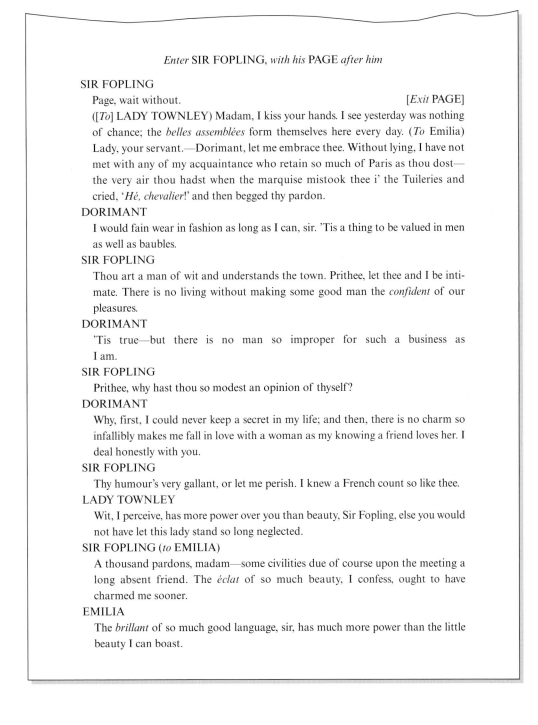

Enter SIR FOPLING, *with his* PAGE *after him*

SIR FOPLING

Page, wait without.   [*Exit* PAGE]

([*To*] LADY TOWNLEY) Madam, I kiss your hands. I see yesterday was nothing of chance; the *belles assemblées* form themselves here every day. (*To* Emilia) Lady, your servant.—Dorimant, let me embrace thee. Without lying, I have not met with any of my acquaintance who retain so much of Paris as thou dost—the very air thou hadst when the marquise mistook thee i' the Tuileries and cried, '*Hé, chevalier!*' and then begged thy pardon.

DORIMANT

I would fain wear in fashion as long as I can, sir. 'Tis a thing to be valued in men as well as baubles.

SIR FOPLING

Thou art a man of wit and understands the town. Prithee, let thee and I be intimate. There is no living without making some good man the *confident* of our pleasures.

DORIMANT

'Tis true—but there is no man so improper for such a business as I am.

SIR FOPLING

Prithee, why hast thou so modest an opinion of thyself?

DORIMANT

Why, first, I could never keep a secret in my life; and then, there is no charm so infallibly makes me fall in love with a woman as my knowing a friend loves her. I deal honestly with you.

SIR FOPLING

Thy humour's very gallant, or let me perish. I knew a French count so like thee.

LADY TOWNLEY

Wit, I perceive, has more power over you than beauty, Sir Fopling, else you would not have let this lady stand so long neglected.

SIR FOPLING (*to* EMILIA)

A thousand pardons, madam—some civilities due of course upon the meeting a long absent friend. The *éclat* of so much beauty, I confess, ought to have charmed me sooner.

EMILIA

The *brillant* of so much good language, sir, has much more power than the little beauty I can boast.

SIR FOPLING

I never saw anything prettier than this high work of your *point d'Espagne*.

EMILIA

'Tis not so rich as *point de Venise*.

SIR FOPLING

Not altogether, but looks cooler, and is more proper for the season. —Dorimant, is not that Medley?

DORIMANT

The same, sir.

SIR FOPLING [*to* MEDLEY]

Forgive me, sir; in this *embarras* of civilities I could not come to have you in my arms sooner. You understand an equipage the best of any man in town, I hear.

MEDLEY

By my own you would not guess it.

SIR FOPLING

There are critics who do not write, sir.

MEDLEY

Our peevish poets will scarce allow it.

SIR FOPLING

Damn 'em, they'll allow no man wit who does not play the fool like themselves and show it! Have you taken notice of the gallesh I brought over?

MEDLEY

Oh, yes! 'T has quite another air than the English makes.

SIR FOPLING

'Tis as easily known from an English tumbril as an Inns of Court man is from one of us.

DORIMANT

Truly there is a *bel air* in galleshes as well as men.

MEDLEY

But there are few so delicate to observe it.

SIR FOPLING

The world is generally very *grossier* here, indeed.

LADY TOWNLEY [*to* EMILIA]

He's very fine.

EMILIA

Extreme proper!

SIR FOPLING

A slight suit I made to appear in at my first arrival—not worthy your consideration, ladies.

DORIMANT

The pantaloon is very well mounted.

SIR FOPLING

The tassels are new and pretty.

MEDLEY

I never saw a coat better cut.

SIR FOPLING

It makes me show long-waisted, and, I think, slender.

DORIMANT

That's the shape our ladies dote on.

MEDLEY

Your breech, though, is a handful too high, in my eye, Sir Fopling.

SIR FOPLING

Peace, Medley, I have wished it lower a thousand times, but a pox on 't, 'twill not be!

LADY TOWNLEY

His gloves are well fringed, large, and graceful.

SIR FOPLING

I was always eminent for being *bien ganté*.

EMILIA

He wears nothing but what are originals of the most famous hands in Paris.

SIR FOPLING

You are in the right, madam.

LADY TOWNLEY

The suit?

SIR FOPLING

Barroy.

EMILIA

The garniture?

SIR FOPLING

Le Gras.

MEDLEY

The shoes?

SIR FOPLING

Piccar.

DORIMANT

The periwig?

SIR FOPLING

Chedreux.

LADY TOWNLEY, EMILIA

The gloves?

SIR FOPLING

Orangerie—you know the smell, ladies. —Dorimant, I could find in my heart for an amusement to have a gallantry with some of our English ladies.

DORIMANT

'Tis a thing no less necessary to confirm the reputation of your wit than an duel will be to satisfy the town of your courage.

SIR FOPLING

Here was a woman yesterday—

DORIMANT

Mrs Loveit.

SIR FOPLING

You have named her!

DORIMANT

You cannot pitch on a better for your purpose.

SIR FOPLING

Prithee, what is she?

DORIMANT

A person of quality, and one who has a rest of reputation enough to make the conquest considerable. Besides I hear she likes you too.

SIR FOPLING

Methoughts she seemed, though, very reserved and uneasy all the time I entertained her.

DORIMANT

Grimace and affectation! You will see her i' the Mall tonight.

SIR FOPLING

Prithee, let thee and I take the air together.

DORIMANT

I am engaged to Medley, but I'll see you at St James's and give you some information upon the which you may regulate your proceedings.

SIR FOPLING

All the world will be in the Park tonight.— Ladies, 'twere pity to keep so much beauty longer within doors and rob the Ring of all those charms that should adorn it. — Hey, page!

Enter PAGE

See that all my people be ready.   [PAGE] *goes out again*
Dorimant, *à revoir*.   [*Exit* SIR FOPLING]

William Wycherley (1640–1716)

Wycherley was born near Shrewsbury and trained as a lawyer; however, after associating with Etherege, the Earl of Rochester and the like, he decided he preferred acting, theatrical management and writing. In content his work was often intensely crude, if not obscene, but it was also savage in its intent to reveal the hypocrisy of the age. Wycherley's portrayal of all the vices of the period is thus both excellent theatre and most pointed social comment. Like others at this time, his work clearly displays the influence of Molière.

After his last piece in 1676, Wycherley seemed to tire of writing, and simply lived the sort of life he had so keenly and critically described in his work. In 1679 he lost the patronage of Charles II by marrying the Countess of Drogheda. On her death in 1681 he was imprisoned for the debt of her estate; however, James II had him released and awarded him a pension. He then lived a rather reclusive life, married again, wrote poetry, and formed a literary friendship with the young Alexander Pope. He died in 1716.

PLAYS

Love in the Wood; or, St. James's Park (1671)
His first play is a dark satire on society's sexual and financial greediness. Within it are all the themes that are to be better used in his subsequent efforts.

The Gentle Dancing Master (1672)
This play is based on Calderón's play *'El Maestro de Danzar'* (*see* page 63), and is therefore not a very typical piece in that it plays more gently than his other work.

The Country Wife (1675)
Wycherley's most famous work, and one that portrays the social ills and dealings of the period that he seemed to know, and sum up, so well.

The Plain Dealer (1676)
His last, and possibly his best piece.

Charles Sedley (*c.*1639–1701)

A younger son of a baronet; Charles inherited the title on his brother's death. He was a comrade of Rochester and his cronies; however, later he became an MP for Romney. He was only a minor figure as a dramatist, although he was well known in his time for his wit and extravagance. He was influenced by Molière and Etherege, and wrote two tragedies (now lost), and two comedies, for which he is better known.

PLAYS

The Mulberry Garden (1668)
Said to be partly derived from Molière's *L'École des Maris* (*see* page 60), and Etherege's *The Comical Revenge*.

Bellamira; or, The Mistress (1687)
A comedy based on *Eunuchus* by Terence (*see* page 28).

John Dryden (1631 – 1700)

A prolific writer, poet, satirist and playwright. He was born in Northamptonshire, and was famous for his 'heroic tragedies', which put him somewhat out on a limb compared to the other Restoration dramatists. Never an extremist, he was much satirized – notably in the play *The Rehearsal* (1671) by Buckingham (qv), and on other occasions by such as the notorious Earl of Rochester.

On the death of Sir William D'Avenant in 1668, Dryden was made Poet Laureate, only the second person to officially hold the title. In addition he was appointed Historiographer Royal in 1670.

After the success of *All for Love* in 1678, Dryden paused in his work as a dramatist, although he did co-author two plays with Nathaniel Lee (*see* page 109). He did, however, continue to write poetry, articles and satires, the last of these displaying his growing interest in the politics of the day. His poems became a means by which he made strong political points, and for a time a so-called 'paper war' raged, in which Thomas Shadwell, amongst others, wrote rebuffs and counter-rebuffs, some of which naturally opposed Dryden's own written beliefs.

With the Protestant revolution of 1688 Dryden lost the laureateship to Shadwell, and returned his attention to the theatre. He contributed to the libretto of Purcell's opera *King Arthur* (1691), and wrote translations of the classics, including Virgil, Persius and Juvenal. His last work were adaptations of the work of Ovid, Boccaccio and Chaucer. He died at the end of the century, having enjoyed great success, and was buried in Westminster Abbey.

Apart from his tragedies, Dryden is also known for his tragi-comedies, of which the best known are *All for Love* and *Marriage à-la-Mode*. He also wrote, less successfully, new versions of Shakespeare's *Troilus and Cressida* and *The Tempest*, as well as *Amphitryon* by Plautus.

PLAYS

The Wild Gallant (1663)
His first play, but of little note otherwise.

The Rival Ladies (1664)
A more popular piece, written in rhyming couplets, and little revived nowadays.

The Indian Queen (1664)
Co-written with Sir Robert Howard.

The Indian Emperor (1665)
This was the work that helped make Dryden's reputation as a dramatist. It was first played at Oxford, where the court had moved after the plague had shut the London theatres, and saw the heroic style well established.

Secret Love; or, The Maiden Queen (1667/8)
A popular piece in the newly re-opened theatres, that featured Nell Gwyn as Florimell, a mad woman who has to take on manly guise to succeed in her aims.[ii] Samuel Pepys said of *The Maiden Queen* 'A new play of Dryden's, mightily commended for the regularity of it and the strain and wit; and the truth is, there is a comical part done by Nell ... that I never can hope ever to see the like done again by man or woman.'

Sir Martin Mar-All; or, The Feign'd Innocence (1667)

An Evening's Love; or, The Mock Astrologer (1668)

Tyrannic Love; or, The Royal Martyr (1669)
A play that deals with the lust of Emperor Maximin for the martyr St Catherine.

The Tempest (1670)
An adaptation of Shakespeare's play, co-authored with Sir William D'Avenant (qv).

Almanzor and Almahide; or, The Conquest of Granada (1670/1)
A historical play concerned with religious and social controversy.

Marriage à-la-Mode (1671)
Dryden's great comic masterpiece, quite classical in style and with two distinct plots, one heroic and the other mannered.

The Assignation; or, Love in a Nunnery (1672)

Amboyna; or, the Cruelties of the Dutch to the English Merchants (1673)
A piece written as anti-Dutch propaganda and of little interest today.

The State of Innocence (1674)
An ill-advised musical adaptation of Milton's epic poem *Paradise Lost*. Written for the newly opened Theatre Royal, but never performed.

Aureng-Zebe (1675)
A heroic tragedy, and his last written in rhyming couplets, it tells a love story set in the India of the Mogul dynasties.

All for Love (1678)
Subtitled *The World well Lost*, and his first written in blank verse, this play very successfully takes as its source Shakespeare's *Antony and Cleopatra*, and uses it to very different ends. This play deals with the last two hours of the main protagonists' lives, and displays a sensitive and moving vision of the conflict between love, honour and duty. As such it is considered one of the great masterpieces of the period.

Oedipus (1679)
The classical story co-written with Nathaniel Lee (qv).

Troilus and Cressida (1679)
New version of Shakespeare's play of the same name.

The Kind Keeper; or, Mr Limberham (1680)

The Duke of Guise (1682)
Co-written with Nathaniel Lee (qv).

Don Sebastian (c.1690)
A comedy, and Dryden's return to drama after a break of twelve years.

Amphitryon (1690)
An adaptation of the play of the same name by Plautus (qv).

Cleomenes: The Spartan Hero (1692)

Love Triumphant (1694)
An unsuccessful work and his last for the stage, as indeed is announced in the prologue.

George Villiers, the 2nd Duke of Buckingham (1628–87)

Villiers was a playwright and politician who is best remembered for his play *The Rehearsal* (1671), which made fun of Dryden and his 'heroic drama'. This play also proved a firm basis for Sheridan's play *The Critic*. Buckingham was himself satirized by Dryden in his political poem *Absalom and Achitophel*, where he appears as the character Zimri. Buckingham also wrote a popular version of Fletcher's play *The Chances* in 1623.

Thomas Shadwell (1642–92)

Shadwell was born in Norfolk and studied law before embarking on a literary career. He became Poet Laureate after Dryden, whom he satirized, especially in his poem *The Medal of John Bayes* (1682). Shadwell was himself targeted by Dryden in his satirical poem *Mac Flecknoe*, subtitled *A Satire on the True-Blue Protestant Poet*, of 1678 (published 1682); in this poem Shadwell is unfavourably compared to Christ, Romulus, Elijah and a piece of faeces! The damage done to Shadwell's reputation by this attack was something from which he never really recovered.

PLAYS
The Sullen Lovers; or, the Impertinents (1668)
Based on Molière's *Les Fâcheux*, and similar to the work of Jonson.

The Humorists (1670)

Epsom Wells (1672)

The Enchanted Isle (1674)
An adaptation of *The Tempest* as an opera, much criticized for allowing the spectacle of its first production to take over the play.

Psyche (1675)
Another of his operatic works.

The Libertine (1675)
A weak example of the kind of heroic drama more typical of Dryden.

The Virtuoso (1676)

Timon of Athens (1678)
Adapted from Shakespeare, and again an attempt at Drydenesque heroic tragedy.

The Squire of Alsatia (1688)

Bury Fair (1689)

Nathaniel Lee (c.1653–92)

An actor and playwright who authored mostly tragedies, based on stories taken from ancient history. He twice collaborated with Dryden (*see* page 107), and by today's standards his plays were rather melodramatic and hysterically overblown. Lee seemed to have been like this in life also, suffering from bouts of mental instability, one of which saw him incarcerated from 1684 to 1689. He died insane in the famous asylum of the period known as Bedlam, in 1692. His plays remained popular for some time after his death.

PLAYS
Nero (1674)

Sophonisba (1675)

Glorian (1676)

The Rival Queens; or, The Death of Alexander (1677)
Betterton took the role of Alexander in the first performance of this play.

Mithridates (1678)

Oedipus (1679)
A collaboration with Dryden.

Thoedosius (1680)

Lucius Junius Brutus (1680/1)

The Princess of Cleve (1681)
A satirical play on the sexual mores of the period, and which includes a brutally accurate portrait of the Earl of Rochester in the character of Nemours.

The Duke of Guise (1682)
Another collaboration with Dryden.

The Massacre of Paris (1690)

Aphra Behn (1640–89)

Brought up in Guiana in the West Indies, Mrs Behn can claim to be the first professional female dramatist. She also wrote poems and novels, two of the latter being dramatized by Thomas Southerne (*see* below). Behn is said to have had an exciting life, with careers as adventurer and spy, and on at least one occasion she was imprisoned for debt. As a dramatist her early work is rather derivative; she is best known for her topical comedies, and for her ability to deal even-handedly with issues concerning both sexes. She is buried in Westminster Abbey.

The great Restoration actor Thomas Betterton appeared in Behn's play *The Forced Marriage*, but more unusually, so did Thomas Otway (qv), the dramatist, whose only stage appearance it appears to have been!

PLAYS
The Forced Marriage; or, The Jealous Bridegroom (1670)
A tragi-comedy featuring Betterton.

The Town Fop (1676)

The Rover; or, The Banished Cavalier (1677)
A comedy of intrigue typical of Behn's most successful work. This play, and its sequel of 1681, concerns the adventures of English cavaliers during the exile of Charles II.

Sir Patient Fancy (1678)

The Feign'd Curtizans; or, A Night's Intrigue (1678)

The Roundheads; or, The Good Old Cause (1681)

The Revenge; or, A Match in Newgate (1680)
Adapted by Aphra Behn from *The Dutch Courtesan* (1604) by John Marston.

The Second Part of the Rover (1681)

The City Heiress; or, Sir Timothy Treat-All (1682)
A successful piece of political intrigue, but one that leans heavily on Middleton's *A Mad World My Masters* (*see* page 91).

Lucky Chance (1686)

The Emperor of the Moon (1687)
Although less popular at the time than Behn's earlier work, this was a comedy, farcical in nature, and based on a Commedia dell'arte scenario popular at the time. As such it can be seen as a possible forerunner of the English pantomime, and did remain in the repertoire for some time.

Thomas Southerne (1660–1746)

Southerne was born in Dublin, but came to London to study law. Whilst a dramatist in his own right, he also wrote prologues and epilogues for a number of the plays of Dryden, and adapted two of the novels of Aphra Behn for the stage. Southerne wrote tragedies in a style said to have influenced the best work of the eighteenth century, a mixture of the sentimental and the heroic. His lighter works are typical 'comedies of manners', but are somewhat overloaded with content and confusing in plot. They do, however, show the beginnings of the more sophisticated style that we shall find in Congreve and Vanbrugh.

PLAYS

The Loyal Brother; or, The Persian Prince (1682)
Southerne's first play, a tragedy, but also a eulogy to the Duke of York.

Sir Anthony Love; or, The Rambling Lady (1690)
A comedy.

The Wives' Excuse; or, Cuckolds Make Themselves (1691)
A comedy.

The Maid's Last Prayer; or, Any, Rather than Fail (1693)
A comedy.

The Fatal Marriage; or, The Innocent Adultery (1694)
A tragedy based on the novel of the same name by Aphra Behn.

Oroonoko (1695)
The second of two plays based on the novels of the same name by Aphra Behn.

Money the Mistress (1726)
Southerne's last piece, a less-than-successful comedy.

Thomas Otway (1652–85)

Otway was born in Milland, a small village in Sussex, and tried his hand at acting before turning to writing. He is known to have performed in *The Forced Marriage* by Aphra Behn. In 1678 he enlisted in the army and served in Holland, receiving a commission; he returned the same year. Alongside his plays, Otway is known to have written poetry, prologues and epilogues. He is also known to have held strong political views, opposing the rise of the Whig party of the time.

Otway's best work displays an unusual sensitivity to character for the period. This, combined with an acute sense of the satiric, means that he is seen as a leader in his field. His best work, *The Orphan* and *Venice Preserv'd*, can be described as among the finest English blank-verse tragedies.[iii] His comedies are not generally held in such high regard – indeed

in his own time Otway failed to attract a sponsor or patron, and he ended his days in poverty, dying at the age of thirty-three.

Unrequited Love

Otway was forlornly and unrequitedly in love with actress Mrs Barry, who starred in his plays *Alcibiades*, *The Orphan* and *Venice Preserv'd*. In the last two of these she starred with fellow actor Thomas Betterton.

PLAYS

Alcibiades (1675)
Otway's first play, a successful tragedy, in the tradition of heavily rhymed verse and great turns of rhetoric.

Don Carlos (1676)
A tragedy, written in rhyming couplets, but containing some quite delicate characterization for the period.

Titus and Bérénice (1676)
Based on *Bérénice* by Racine, whom Otway held in the greatest respect, and by whom he was strongly influenced.

The Cheats of Scapin (1676)
An adaptation of Molière's *Les Fourberies de Scapin*, and originally performed as an after-piece to the previous play, *Titus and Bérénice*, one of Otway's more successful comedies.

Friendship in Fashion (1678)
A comedy.

The Soldier's Fortune (1680)
A comedy.

The Orphan; or, the Unhappy Marriage (1680)
One of Otway's most successful pieces.

The Atheist (1683)
A comedy, and sequel to *The Soldier's Fortune*.

Venice Preserv'd; or, a Plot Discovered (1682)
Another of Otway's better pieces, and one that clearly shows the influence of the work of Racine (*see* page 83).

John Vanbrugh (1664–1726)

Vanbrugh was born in London to a wealthy family whose money came from the sugar trade. Like many of his time, Vanbrugh can be said to have pursued more than one profession. He was commissioned in the Earl of Huntingdon's regiment (the 13th Foot) and imprisoned as a spy by the French, spending some time in the infamous Bastille in Paris (1690–92). After leaving the armed services, Vanbrugh turned to playwriting and then moved on.

Turning next to architecture, Vanbrugh was responsible for many successful buildings, including Castle Howard and Blenheim Palace. His success in this field saw him appointed 'comptroller of the royal works' in 1702, and awarded the heraldic title of Clarenceux King-at-Arms in 1704. In keeping with his theatrical background he designed the Opera House in London's Haymarket in 1705, and the Queen's Theatre in the West End for Betterton's company; subsequently this latter became a home for some of his own plays.

Politically a Whig, Vanbrugh went through a period of bad fortune, losing his title of 'comptroller', only to regain it on the succession to the throne of George I in 1714. He was knighted in 1723, and went on to succeed Sir Christopher Wren as surveyor at Greenwich. His collected works appeared in 1730.

As a playwright, Vanbrugh's best known work is *The Relapse* of 1696. Lacking interest in the nuances and style of the period that was the focus of the work of his contemporary Congreve, Vanbrugh's deals rather in caricature and wit. Many of his lesser works were based on the earlier plays of others, and suffer from being rather garrulous in nature. *The Relapse* and *The Provoked Wife* were both attacked in *A Short View of the Immorality and Profaneness of the English Stage*, a savage attack on the immorality and excesses of Restoration theatre, written by Jeremy

Collier in 1698 (*see* page 114). Vanbrugh replied in *A Short Vindication of The Relapse and The Provok'd Wife from Immorality and Profaneness* in the same year. Congreve (qv) did likewise, *see* page 114.

PLAYS
The Relapse; or, Virtue in Danger (1696)
A sequel to, and parody of *Love's Last Shift* written, earlier in the same year, by Colly Cibber (*see* page 118). The play shows the central character of Loveless, who is left at the end of Cibber's play a reformed man, reverting to perfidious type as his fortunes unfold. *The Relapse* was itself the subject of implied criticism when Richard Brinsley Sheridan (qv) rewrote it for his own audience as *A Trip to Scarborough*, nearly 100 years later, in 1777.

The Provoked Wife (1697)
Another great and typical restoration comedy. Satirized by Colly Cibber in his play *The Provoked Husband* of 1728 (*see* page 119).

Aesop (1697)
Written in two parts and derived from Boursault.

The Country House (1698)
Derived from the works of the minor French playwright Florent Carton Dancourt (1661–1725).

The Pilgrim (1700)
Based on a play by John Fletcher (*see* page 94).

The False Friend (1702)
From the works of Le Sage.

Squire Trelooby (1704)
A less-than-successful play co-written with Congreve (*see* page 114) and the poet William Walsh.

The Confederacy (1705)
One of Vanbrugh's most successful adaptations, a comedy based on *Les Bourgeoises à la mode* of 1692 by Florent Carton Dancourt.

The Mistake (1705)
Taken from a play by Molière (*see* page 60).

The Confederacy, *a modern production in period dress, directed by Peter Fieldson*

The Cuckold in Conceit (1707)
One of Vanbrugh's less successful comedies.

A Journey to London
Vanbrugh's last work, unfinished at his death, but later finished by Colly Cibber as *The Provoked Husband* in 1728.

George Farquhar (1678–1707)

Farquhar was born in Derry in Ireland, and acted briefly in Dublin; however, from 1697, and like most dramatists of the period in England, he practised his art in London. Like Vanbrugh and many others in this period, he served in the army in Holland, and in his case reached the rank of lieutenant. He is said to have given up acting as a result of accidentally injuring a fellow actor on stage.

Farquhar's plays are notable for their sensitivity to the warmer side of character, although they show a distinct change of mood following Jeremy Collier's famous attack on the morality of the theatre of the period in 1698 (*see* page 114). Thereafter the work suffers from over-sentimentality, and the delicate balance between the satire of the pervading Restoration style and Farquhar's innate charm is thrown into disarray for a number of works.

After a period, however, Farquhar found his voice again, and wrote his most successful works: *The Recruiting Officer* and *The Beaux Stratagem.* Although Farquhar lived just long enough to know of the success of these late pieces, his finances were in tatters, and he died a penniless man in 1707.

PLAYS
Love in a Bottle (1698)
A comedy of conspiracy, written for Farquhar's great friend, actor Robert Wilks, and originally staged at Drury Lane. However, this piece was only a moderate success.

The Constant Couple; or, A Trip to the Jubilee (1699)
Farquhar's first real success, particularly for the character of Sir Harry Wildair, who perfectly expresses the playwright's ability to combine the archness of the period with a more humane face. This role was created for Farquhar's friend Robert Wilks.

Sir Harry Wildair (1701)
A less successful sequel to the earlier play, featuring the same main character.

Breeches

The part of Sir Harry Wildair appears in two of Farquhar's plays, and was created for Robert Wilks; however, it became a very popular role for female actors. Such 'breeches' roles were popular in the eighteenth century, and saw talented actresses such as Margaret 'Peg' Woffington and Dorothy Jordon enjoying great success. These 'straight' drag performances were aimed to convince, rather than to satirize. Another example, also played by Woffington, is the role of Lothario in Nicholas Rowe's comedy *The Fair Penitent* (*see* page 123).

The Inconstant (1702)

The first of Farquhar's plays to show the influence of the publication of Collier's critical essay on the drama of the period four years earlier. This piece suffered from a lack of confidence and a sense of identity crisis. It is somewhat apologetic and soft, and finds little with which to replace the barbed wit of the period. Farquhar had turned to others for help here perhaps, as this play is an impoverished adaptation of Fletcher's *The Wild Goose Chase*.

The Twin Rivals (1702)

This piece suffered in much the same way as the other title written by Farquhar in this year.

The Stage Coach (1704)

A slightly richer piece than the two that precede it, and therefore more successful. Possibly written in conjunction with Peter Anthony Motteux (1660–1718), a French writer, editor and translator.

The Recruiting Officer (1706)

This play saw Farquhar back on form, and was clearly written from his own experience: Farquhar, in need of an income, joined the Grenadier Guards in 1703/4, serving as a recruiting officer. The play is most successful for its ideas of grand romantic comedy, rather than for the satire it also attempts. This piece was later used by Bertolt Brecht as the basis for his play *Pauken und Trompetten* (*see* page 180).

The Beaux Stratagem (1707)

Friend and successful actor Robert Wilks gave Farquhar twenty guineas to be able to write this piece. Like the play that precedes it, its strength lies in its romanticism. Also similar to the preceding play, it is set outside fashion-conscious London, and perhaps because of this, contains a welcome breath of vitality. Farquhar died in the year that he wrote it, surviving just long enough to know of its great success.

William Congreve (1670–1729)

Congreve was born in the north of England near Leeds, into a military family, and studied law before turning to the stage. His first work was in prose fiction – the novel *Incognita* of 1692. His first play, *The Old Bachelor*, was written in 1693 with the help of Dryden. From this piece onwards Congreve's reputation as a master of stage comedy was made. Although in total Congreve wrote only a few plays, his brilliant use of the comic idiom is such that the accolade 'the greatest writer of Restoration comedy of manners' is not an overstatement by any means. His work exemplifies the wit and craft of the period.

The criticism contained within Jeremy Collier's *Short View of the Immorality and Profaneness of the English Stage*, written in 1698, was primarily aimed at Congreve and Vanbrugh (*see* page 112), and its harshness led to Congreve abandoning the theatre in pursuit of other interests. Before doing so, however, Congreve answered many of Collier's criticisms in his own piece, *Amendments of Mr Collier's False and Imperfect Citations* (1698), and wrote perhaps his greatest work, *The Way of the World*, in 1700.

One of the themes in Congreve's work was that of marital relationships. Some of his knowledge on this matter could have come from his own relationships, which include the Duchess of Marlborough, who bore him a daughter; and the famous actress of the period, Anne Bracegirdle.

After the turn of the century Congreve, now a wealthy man, reduced his theatrical output, which consisted of: a masque, *The Judgement of Paris* (1701); an opera, *Semele* (1710), used by Handel as the libretto to his own opera of the same name; a prose story, *The Impossible Thing* (1720); and various pieces of editorial work and poetry. In addition he co-wrote a minor stage piece with Vanbrugh. He died in 1729.

PLAYS

The Old Bachelor (1693)

A comedy written with the help of Dryden. Its first performances at Drury Lane included a leading role for Betterton, alongside Congreve's paramour, Mrs Bracegirdle.

The Double Dealer (1693)

Performed by the same Drury Lane company as his preceding work.

Love for Love (1695)

This play opened in the new theatre in Lincoln's Inn Fields under the jurisdiction of Betterton, newly moved from Drury Lane, and including

Anne Bracegirdle in the company playing the role of *Angelica* opposite his *Valentine*.

The Mourning Bride (1697)

Congreve's sole tragedy was not as successful as his comedies, being somewhat over-poetic and introspective. Anne Bracegirdle took on the leading role of Almeria.

The Way of the World (1700)

This piece was not as well received initially as some of his earlier works, but has stood the test of time with the greatest success. Congreve's masterpiece is perhaps the pinnacle of the comedy of manners of this period.

Squire Trelooby (1704)

A less-than-successful play co-written with Vanbrugh (qv) and poet William Walsh.

The following extract is taken from *The Way of the World* by William Congreve. Two of the main characters indulge in the kind of witty repartee that makes this play such a joy to play and to watch:

Enter MRS. MILLAMANT, WITWOUD *and* MINCING

MIRABELL
> Here she comes i'faith full sail, with her fan spread and her streamers out, and a shoal of fools for tenders—ha, no, I cry her mercy.

MRS. FAINALL
> I see but one poor empty sculler, and he tows her woman after him.

MIRABELL
> You seem to be unattended, madam. You used to have the *beau monde* throng after you, and a flock of gay fine perukes hovering round you.

WITWOUD
> Like moths about a candle. I had like to have lost my comparison for want of breath!

MILLAMANT
> Oh I have denied myself airs today. I have walked as fast through the crowd—

WITWOUD
> As a favourite in disgrace; and with as few followers.

MILLAMANT
> Dear Mr. Witwoud, truce with your similitudes; for I am as sick of 'em—

WITWOUD
> As a physician of a good air—I cannot help it madam, though 'tis against myself.

MILLAMANT
> Yet again! Mincing, stand between me and his wit.

WITWOUD
> Do Mrs. Mincing, like a screen before a great fire. I confess I do blaze today, I am too bright.

MRS. FAINALL
> But dear Millamant, why were you so long?

WILLIAM CONGREVE

MILLAMANT
Long! Lord, have I not made violent haste? I have asked every living thing I met for you; I have enquired after you as after a new fashion.

WITWOUD
Madam, truce with your similitudes! No, you met her husband and did not ask him for her.

MIRABELL
By your leave Witwoud, that were like enquiring after an old fashion, to ask a husband for his wife.

WITWOUD
Hum; a hit, a hit, a palpable hit, I confess it.

MRS. FAINALL
You were dressed before I came abroad.

MILLAMANT
Ay, that's true—oh but then I had—Mincing what had I? Why was I so long?

MINCING
Oh mem, your la'ship stayed to peruse a pecquet of letters.

MILLAMANT
Oh ay, letters—I had letters—I am persecuted with letters—I hate letters—nobody knows how to write letters; and yet one has 'em, one does not know why. They serve one to pin up one's hair.

WITWOUD
Is that the way? Pray madam, do you pin up your hair with all your letters? I find I must keep copies.

MILLAMANT
Only with those in verse, Mr. Witwoud, I never pin up my hair with prose. I fancy one's hair would not curl if it were pinned up with prose. I think I tried once Mincing?

MINCING
Oh mem, I shall never forget it.

MILLAMANT
Ay, poor Mincing tift and tift all the morning.

MINCING
Till I had the cremp in my fingers I'll vow mem, and all to no purpose. But when you la'ship pins it up with poetry, it sits so pleasant the next day as anything and is so pure and so crips.

WITWOUD
Indeed, so crips?

MINCING
You're such a critic, Mr. Witwoud

THE WAY OF THE WORLD

MILLAMANT

Mirabell, did not you take exceptions last night? Oh ay, and went away—now I think on't I'm angry—no, now I think on't I'm pleased—for I believe I gave you some pain.

MIRABELL

Does that please you?

MILLAMANT

Infinitely; I love to give pain.

MIRABELL

You would affect a cruelty which is not in your nature; your true vanity is in the power of pleasing.

MILLAMANT

Oh I ask your pardon for that—one's cruelty is one's power, and when one parts with one's cruelty one parts with one's power; and when one has parted with that, I fancy one's old and ugly.

MIRABELL

Ay, ay, suffer your cruelty to ruin the object of your power, to destroy your lover—and then how vain, how lost a thing you'll be! Nay, 'tis true; you are no longer handsome when you've lost your lover. Your beauty dies upon the instant; for beauty is the lover's gift; 'tis he bestows your charms: your glass is all a cheat. The ugly and the old, whom the looking-glass mortifies, yet after commendation can be flattered by it and discover beauties in it; for that reflects our praises rather than your face.

MILLAMANT

Oh the vanity of these men! Fainall, d'ye hear him? If they did not commend use, we were not handsome! Now you must know they could not commend one, if one was not handsome. Beauty the lover's gift! Lord, what is a lover, that it can give? Why, one makes lovers as fast as one pleases, and they love as long as one pleases, and they die as soon as one pleases; and then, if one pleases, one makes more.

WITWOUD

Very pretty. Why, you make no more of making of lovers, madam, than of making so many card-matches.

MILLAMANT

One no more owes one's beauty to a lover, than one's wit to an echo; they can but reflect what we look and say: vain empty things if we are silent or unseen, and want a being.

MIRABELL

Yet to those two vain empty things you owe two of the greatest pleasures of your life.

WILLIAM CONGREVE

MILLAMANT
How so?

MIRABELL
To your lover you owe the pleasure of hearing yourselves praised, and to an echo the pleasure of hearing yourselves talk.

WITWOUD
But I know a lady that loves talking so incessantly she won't give an echo fair play; she has that everlasting rotation of tongue, that an echo must wait till she dies before it can catch her last words.

MILLAMANT
Oh fiction! Fainall, let us leave these men.

MIRABELL (*Aside* to MRS. FAINALL)
Draw off Witwoud.

MRS. FAINALL
Immediately; I have a word or two for Mr. Witwoud.

MIRABELL
I would beg a little private audience too—

Exeunt WITWOUD *and* MRS. FAINALL

Colley Cibber (1671–1757)

Although the son of a famous Danish sculptor (Caius Cibber), Cibber was brought up and educated in England. He started acting in 1690, becoming a mainstay of the Drury Lane Theatre in 1691. Apart from his acting, he is known as a dramatist, a poet and a theatre manager. Also of great note is his descriptive writing on the acting of the period. His part as actor-manager from 1708–32 at Drury Lane foreshadows a trend as yet not fully realized at this time (*see* page 125).

One of Cibber's greatest acting roles was that of Lord Foppington in Vanbugh's play *The Relapse*. This is deeply ironic, as this play was a parody of Cibber's first play *Love's Last Shift*. He also acted successfully in his own plays.

Cibber's plays are possibly not of the first ilk, although his comedies where generally acknowledged to be better than his tragedies; however, even of one of the comedies Congreve said 'it has only in it a great many things that were like wit, that in reality were not wit'. Indeed, many of his plays seem to copy, or borrow only too readily, from others of the period. Despite this, and rather surprisingly, Cibber was made Poet Laureate in 1730, and, not so surprisingly, then underwent fervent attack from other writers, amongst them Alexander Pope, Dr Jonson and Henry Fielding – the latter in his novel *Joseph Andrews*.

In 1740 Cibber published his autobiography entitled *Apology for the life of Mr Colly Cibber, Comedian*. It was within this book that Cibber's greatest legacy, namely wonderful descriptions of Restoration actors and acting, are to be found. These colourful anecdotes include many already mentioned in this chapter, such as Thomas and Anne Bracegirdle (qqv).

Cibber was also responsible for an adaptation of Shakespeare's *Richard III* (1700), preferred for its performance over the Bard's for well over a hundred years, and also a well respected version of Molière's *Tartuffe*, entitled *The Non-Juror* (1717).

PLAYS

Love's Last Shift; or, the Fool in Fashion (1696)
A sentimental comedy parodied in *The Relapse; or, Virtue in Danger*, also of 1696, by Sir John Vanbrugh (*see* page 112). The main character within this piece, Sir Novelty Fashion, is used as a model by Vanbrugh for his brilliant Lord Foppington. It was of this play that Congreve spoke, as quoted above.

She Would and She Would Not; or, The Kind Imposter (1702)
A comedy.

The Careless Husband (1704/5)
One of Cibber's more successful pieces.

The Lady's Last Stake (1707)
A poor comedy.

The Non-Juror (1717)
A highly praised version of Molière's play *Tartuffe*.

The Provoked Husband (1728)
A sequel to Vanbrugh's play *The Provoked Wife* and thus a reply to his criticisms; also partly the completion of *A Journey to London*, Vanbrugh's last work, which had been left unfinished at his death.

Restoration drama, a modern production in period dress.

Conclusion

Congreve's play *The Way of the World*, written in 1700, happens to bring the century to a splendid close as one of the most supreme achievements in the art of the comedy of the period. The dramatic work of the English stage, and dramas from elsewhere in Europe, naturally continued to develop seamlessly into the eighteenth century. The robustness of its style and content, however, before 1700, especially in Restoration England, was unique, with a flavour and a feel very much all of its own. For this reason, 'Restoration drama' is still much studied, much loved, and often performed.

7 THEATRE FOR THE MASSES: 1700–1890

The drama's laws, the drama's patrons give,
for we that live to please, must please to live
DR SAMUEL JOHNSON
(from the Prologue at the opening
of the theatre in Drury Lane)

You know you will not have to wait long now as the auditorium illumination is being dowsed in readiness for the start of the play. This innovation of Garrick's is just another thing that you have not quite got used to, and the unfamiliarity of sitting in the near dark to watch the play sends a tingle up your spine. A fairly full house of many thousands now jostles in the gloom, impatient for the velvet curtain to lift.

INTRODUCTION

George I came to the English throne in 1714, and from around this time the theatre of the period began to establish itself as an art form for the masses, to evolve into a popular form not seen since theatre had left the streets of medieval Europe. At the beginning of the Restoration period in 1660 Charles II had granted licences for two companies (*see* page 101); by 1732 five playhouses existed: The Theatre Royal, Drury Lane; Lincoln's Inn Fields; The Queen's Theatre, Haymarket; The Little Haymarket Theatre; and Goodman's Fields. By 1785 two more had been added: Sadler's Wells and The Royalty. Between them they could accommodate a combined audience of many thousands: by 1792 Lincoln's Inn Fields grew to a maximum capacity of 3,000 people, and by 1794 Drury

Lane could accommodate an amazing 3,611 ticket holders!

The need to accommodate a larger and larger audience meant that the Jacobean forestage began to be pushed back behind the proscenium arch. Initially seating and boxes continued to be placed on and alongside the stage, but eventually a much greater separation occurred between stage and audience than had ever been the case before, and this was further advanced by the placing of the orchestra in a front-of-stage pit area.

As this occurred, so scenic painting became a dominant art form, flat painted cloths being the easy way to change locale on such a vast area, and a medium that worked well hung at the rear of a separated stage area. At the start of this period the auditorium was as brightly lit as the stage; by the end, another tool for the separation of audience and players had evolved, the house lights had dimmed, and true stage lighting began to develop.

The size of these buildings affected the staging of the pieces within them, and as a result acting, like the scenery around it, became grander and more mannered. One of the great innovators in the use of scenic elements in this period was actor-manager David Garrick (*see* below).

Acting manuals from this period describe how the technique of acting was perceived at this time. One such by Aaron Hill, entitled *Essay on the Art of Acting*, divides the passions into ten categories, defining each with a look and an action. In his book of 1730, *A General View of the Stage*, popular actor

OPPOSITE PAGE: *The Georgian stage.*

Robert Wilks (1665–1732) also describes the performing of various emotions: to create the effect of 'admiration' he writes:

> Eyes fixed upon the object; the right-hand naturally extends itself with the palm turned outwards; and the left-hand will share in the action, though so as scarcely to be perceived, not venturing far from the body; but when this surprise reaches the superlative degree, which I take to be astonishment, the whole body is actuated: it is thrown back, with one leg set before the other, both hands elevated, the eyes larger than usual, the brows drawn up, and the mouth not quite shut.

This period also saw a continued refinement of ideas following the criticisms in Collier's 'the short view' essay and the theatre world's reaction to it (*see* page 114). As a result there was an increase in harmless, uncontentious, light drama, and sentiment thus became the key to much that was produced. In addition to, and as part of, this diluting of the outrages of previous years, there occurred a diversification of comedy into such forms as farce, pantomime and melodrama. This apparent need for respectability and an adherence to moral values, this growth in the sentimental values, therefore saw a humanization and growth of a popular theatre for the masses. More than anything it was for this reason that many major works from this period are sparkling examples of the art of comedy, notably those by Sheridan and Goldsmith.

Also in this period came the Licensing Act of 1737, in which Queen Anne saw to it that in this measure the previous strictures on censorship were tightened up and adhered to (*see* page 65).

The Georgian actor.

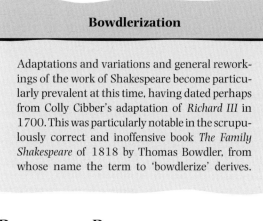

Bowdlerization

Adaptations and variations and general reworkings of the work of Shakespeare become particularly prevalent at this time, having dated perhaps from Colly Cibber's adaptation of *Richard III* in 1700. This was particularly notable in the scrupulously correct and inoffensive book *The Family Shakespeare* of 1818 by Thomas Bowdler, from whose name the term to 'bowdlerize' derives.

PLAYS AND PLAYWRIGHTS

The following are playwrights of the early part of this period – those who shone light on the way ahead.

Richard Steele (1672–1729)

Steele was born in Dublin but educated at Charterhouse, alongside his contemporary, poet Joseph Addison (1672–1719). Steele first came to the public's attention as a poet, although his early stage work – all comedies – clearly displays the move away from the Restoration style. After the lukewarm reception of his early works, Steele turned his attention elsewhere, and from 1706 to 1721 wrote essays and other pieces not for the stage, but took a major role in the politics of the day. On the accession of George I, Steele was appointed supervisor of Drury Lane Theatre (1714–18); he was knighted in 1715.

Richard Steele was also the first person to produce, and subsequently edit, a journal specifically for the theatre – *The Theatre* first appeared in 1719, and was available twice a month. He had previously co-founded *The Tatler* in 1709, and was also associated with other publications that have stood the test of time: namely *The Spectator* from 1711–14, and *The Guardian*.

Steele's final play, *The Conscious Lovers*, shines forth as something much finer than his previous efforts. Steele is thus one of the first playwrights to begin to move away from the main tenets of Restoration drama into something more 'sentimental'.

PLAYS
The Funeral (1701)
Steele's first work for the stage, a comedy that attempted to show the true nature of vice and virtue, rather than the exaggerated version of Restoration comedy.

The Lying Lover (1703)
A comedy.

The Tender Husband (1705)
A comedy.

The Conscious Lovers (1722)
Steele's final work for the stage, an adaptation of *Andria* by Terence (*see* page 28), and a sentimental and moralizing piece. Originally produced by Colley Cibber at Drury Lane.

Nicholas Rowe (1674–1718)
A barrister who turned to poetry and the theatre, Rowe was a friend of poets Alexander Pope (1688–1744) and Joseph Addison (1672–1719). Rowe wrote mostly tragedies, and his plays were, especially for this period, highly charged and dramatically intense. His plays were initially seen at Lincoln's Inn Fields. He became Poet Laureate in 1715, and is buried in Westminster Abbey.

Rowe produced and edited a complete works of Shakespeare in 1709, in which he made the text more intelligible, and for the first time divided the plays into acts and scenes, adding stage directions where he considered they would be useful.

Setting the Scene

Shakespeare's plays in collected form were further divided after Rowe, especially by location. In 1790 Edmund Malone continued this, and was pleased to announce a version with every scene given a formally identified location.

PLAYS
The Ambitious Stepmother (1700)
Rowe's earliest work, and one that established his name as a playwright.

Tamerlane (*c.*1702)
A tragedy, in the central role of which actor Thomas Betterton was highly acclaimed.

The Fair Penitent (1703)
Adapted from Philip Massinger's tragi-comedy, *Fatal Dowry* of 1619, and featuring in its first production, in the role of Calista, an impressive central performance from Mrs Barry. In later productions this role also became a part strongly associated with Sarah Siddons (*see* page 125).

The Biter (1704)
Rowe's only, and unsuccessful, attempt at a comedy.

Ulysses (*c.*1706)
A historical tragedy/romance.

Royal Convert (1707)
With this play he broke from traditionally supplying Lincoln's Inn Fields with his work, as it was first seen at the Haymarket Theatre.

The Tragedy of Jane Shore (1714)
Written for Drury Lane, and supplying another great leading role, initially for actress Anne Oldfield, but later with much acclaim for Mrs Siddons (qv).

The Tragedy of Lady Jane Grey (1715)
A historical tragedy.

John Gay (1685–1732)

Gay was born in Barnstaple, Devon. He was first known as a poet and essayist, and later a playwright. As he made his way in to literary London he befriended many poets and other literary figures, including Alexander Pope and Voltaire. Later, Gay became a member of the Scriblerus Club, which counted among its members fellow poets Pope and John Arbuthnot (the latter was the originator of the archetypal Englishman 'John Bull').

From 1712 Gay was secretary to the Duchess of Monmouth, and then from 1714 also to Lord Clarendon, which kept him financially secure (although he lost most of his later investments in the infamous financial 'South Sea Bubble' fiasco).

As a writer, Gay's first works were less than successful, and his whole career had its up and downs. On the death of Queen Anne in 1714 he once again fell out of favour, as all his political friends went into decline. In 1732 he wrote the libretto for Handel's opera *Alcis and Galatea*. Even after his one truly great success – *The Beggar's Opera* of 1722 – he still managed to reap disapproval with his indulgent lifestyle. Buried in Westminster Abbey, his epitaph reads:

Life is a jest, and all things show it;
I thought so once – and now I know it.

PLAYS
The Mohocks (1712)
A play that Gay himself described as a 'tragi-comical farce', concerning a band of aristocratic brigands. It was Gay's first attempt at writing for the stage, and it was never performed.

The Wife of Bath (1713)
An unsuccessful comedy, of which Jonson simply wrote, 'it received no applause'.

What d'ye Call it (1715)
A burlesque that the audience mistook for a tragedy, and which was therefore also unsuccessful.

Three Hours After Marriage (1717)
A collaboration with Pope and Arbuthnot, which was again not a success. It was Pope's only dramatic excursion. In this case not only did the audience confuse the type of piece that was intended, but so also did the cast! Leading actor Colley Cibber (qv) failed to realize that his part was meant as a parody (of himself, in fact!) and got so angry after the flop of the first night that he and Gay had a fist-fight backstage. Of this piece Samuel Jonson commented that 'it had the fate that such outrages deserve'.

Dione (1719)
A ridiculously improbable pastoral comedy, and another flop.

The Beggar's Opera (1722)
Gay's masterpiece, more a play with songs (some sixty-nine ballads) than an opera. This piece set new records, running for an unprecedented sixty-two nights at the Lincoln's Inn Fields. The play was backed by Gay's patron the Duchess of Queensbury and produced by John Rich, being said to have made 'Gay rich, and Rich gay'.

Jonathan Swift suggested *The Beggars' Opera* to his friend John Gay, and it can probably lay claim to being the most successful play of the eighteenth century. The music was taken from popular airs of the period, selected by Pepusch and set by Linley. For subsequent productions the music has been often rearranged, notably by Frederic Austin in 1920, and Benjamin Britten for Sadler's Wells in 1948.

The play satirizes the taste for Italian opera of the period. It also parodies the upper classes by comparing them with the lowest of classes – the criminal. It later proved of continuing dramatic value when it was adapted by Bertolt Brecht in 1929 as *The Threepenny Opera* (*see* page 180).

Polly (1729)
A sequel to *The Beggar's Opera*, this piece was suppressed by Prime Minister Horace Walpole, who was heartily sick of being lampooned. However, in

published form it still proved very popular. It was finally produced, posthumously, in 1777.

ACTORS AND ACTOR-MANAGERS

This period also saw a continuation in the rising cult of the actor, and the development of the actor-manager as leader of a theatre company. It is to be remembered that although the dual role of manager and lead actor finally faded away, it was to lead to the role of the director – no such beast had as yet been sighted in a theatre. In addition, and starting with Garrick, a new generation of actors came about in this period, and an acting style evolved that could be described as less declamatory and more 'realistic'.

David Garrick (1717–79)

Garrick forged a new 'realism' on stage as an actor and as a manager. His acting in particular was one of great contrast with that of the leading tragedian of his day, James Quin (1693–1766). Against Garrick, Quin's oratorical style soon began to look incredibly old fashioned; his performances – he was a particularly successful Falstaff – were sufficiently histrionic to earn him the sobriquet of 'bellower Quin'.

Garrick made his name initially playing Richard III at Drury Lane in 1742. He then found further success in tragic parts as Hamlet, Lear and Macbeth, and in comedy with Jonson's *The Alchemist*, and with the role of Benedick in *Much Ado About Nothing*.

Garrick also authored or co-authored a number of plays – mostly now long forgotten, and including, as was the tradition then, adaptations of Shakespeare, amongst them *The Taming of the Shrew* (as *Katherine and Petruchio*) and *The Winter's Tale*.

In 1747 Garrick took over the management of Drury Lane, where he was responsible for a number of innovations that showed the way forward to a more modern era. These included appointing the Parisian designer Philip De Loutherbourg (1740–1812), who took the flat surface scenery of the era and used it to create the illusion of the three dimensional. He did this with the use of multi-level scenery and stage lighting designed to fake the appearance of flames, moonlight, and other naturalistic elements. Under Garrick the house lights were dimmed, and the stage became a total painted environment for the actor. Garrick's managership of Drury Lane was only slightly marred by the occurrence of two riots: the first in 1755 was during a performance by French dancers in Noverre's Ballet *The Chinese Festival*, not surprising as England was just about to go to war with France. The second, in 1762, involved an attempt, soon abandoned, to do away with the policy of half price after the third act.

From 1763–65 Garrick toured Europe with his wife, Eva Maria Violetta, a dancer. His farewell appearance was in 1776 when he appeared in *The Wonder, a Woman Keeps a Secret* by Mrs Centlivre. He was buried in Westminster Abbey.

Spranger Barry (1719–77)

Barry was an Irish actor who worked numerous times for, with, and as a rival to, David Garrick. Barry made his name in Dublin, and first appeared at Drury Lane as Othello in 1746. Like Garrick, he was also buried in Westminster Abbey.

John Philip Kemble (1757–1823)

Kemble was part of one of the first theatre dynasties. His father was an actor before him, and J.P. Kemble was brother to Sarah Siddons and Stephen and Charles who also acted, although less successfully. Charles Kemble was then father to Fanny Kemble, who in turn was highly successful.

J.P. Kemble first came to the attention in 1783 as Hamlet, and then continued to be successful in many tragic parts; he did not seem to be overly suited to comedy. His performance style was to build a character slowly to a climax, rarely expressing himself in bouts of extravagant passion or remorse. Considered somewhat stiff by some, his characters were nonetheless thought highly believable for all this.

Kemble also managed theatres, notably Drury Lane and Covent Garden, and introduced the notion of creating costume and scenery specific to a particular performance, rather than taken from stock. Other Shakespeare roles in which he excelled included Julius Caesar, and Coriolanus. It was as the latter that he made his final performance in 1817.

Sarah Siddons (née Kemble) (1755–1831)

Siddons was a renowned tragedian, whose great moment came, after several years of treading the boards, in 1782 when she played in Garrick's production of *Isabella* at Drury Lane. Throughout the rest of her career she was constantly acclaimed as the greatest actress of her generation. Praised for her beauty, gentleness and majesty in many tragic parts (she never played comedy), she was particularly acclaimed as Lady Macbeth, a part she played as her last before retiring in 1812.

Edmund Kean (1787/90–1833)

Perhaps one of the first great popular actors of the period, Kean specialized in evil villains, notably Shylock, Macbeth, Iago, Richard III, Massinger's Sir Giles Overreach, and Marlowe's Barabas from *The Jew of Malta*.

Kean was a foundling, and acted on stage firstly as a boy. His 'realistic' performance of Shylock in 1814 gained him his first real praise, as his later notorious and scandalous behaviour saw him lose favour. He was father to another great actor, Charles Kean (1811–68); his last appearance was as Iago to Charles' Othello, when he collapsed on stage. He died shortly afterwards.

William Charles Macready (1739–1873)

Macready was a rival to Kean. He appeared first in 1810, and had risen to stardom by 1819 playing classic parts such as King Lear, Hamlet and Macbeth. He led his own company as actor-manager on a number of occasions, and his innovations included full rehearsals – and this in a period when it was typical for only the major role holders to walk through their parts in rehearsal, and certainly not the full cast! In

The Astor Place Riot

The Astor Place Riot of 1849 was the final act in a bitter professional rivalry between Macready and American tragedian Edwin Forrest (1806–72). Forrest blamed Macready, of whom he was bitterly jealous, for the failure of his London visit of 1845. When Macready appeared on the New York stage, such was the strength of feeling amongst the crowd over this rivalry that a riot ensued in the theatre and twenty-two people were killed!

performing Shakespeare he also restored the proper text to many of Shakespeare's works, saving them from the hands of so-called 'improvers'.

From 1826 until 1849 Macready appeared often in New York – though after the infamous Astor Place Riot of 1849, he never did again. He retired in 1851 after a final run of performances in perhaps his favourite role: Macbeth.

Fanny Kemble (1809–1893)

Fanny was the daughter of Charles Kemble, and from the very outset seems to have been a great success – although there was perhaps some inevitability to this, as she had the support and full encouraging weight of her father's reputation behind her. Indeed, her first role of Juliet is said to have saved the financial ruin of her father as he floundered in the running of Covent Garden. Other notable roles in an illustrious career include Portia, Beatrice, Lady Teazle, and many parts previously associated with her aunt Sarah Siddons, although unlike her and others in the period, she seems to have been just as strong in comedy as in tragedy.

PLAYWRIGHTS OF THE LATE GEORGIAN ERA

George Colman the Elder (1732–94)

Colman trained as a lawyer, and was to some degree enticed into the theatre by his strong friendship with David Garrick, for whom he wrote his first play, *Polly Honeycombe*. His middle-period works were more successful, however, and are more often revived. Colman also published a successful translation of Terence's comedies in 1765.

Colman risked his friendship with Garrick by taking over as manager of the rival Covent Garden Theatre, in which he promoted the work of Oliver Goldsmith, among others. His tenure of Covent Garden lasted from 1767–74. Later, in 1776, he took over running The Little Theatre in the Haymarket, where he produced many successful plays, among them some by his son, George Colman the younger.

Towards the end of his life Colman suffered increasing bouts of madness. Eventually he retired, handing over the running of the Haymarket to his son in 1790. He died four years later.

George Colman the Younger

George Colman the younger (1762–1836) was, like his father, both playwright and manager. As a writer his work has not survived as well as that of his father, his most notable success being *Inkle and Yarico*, a comedy with songs from 1787. His other plays, all stereotypical five-act comedies, include *The Heir at Law* (1797), *The Poor Gentlemen* (1801) and *John Bull* (1803).

PLAYS

Polly Honeycombe (1760)
Colman's first play, a one-act farce that he was only really happy to acknowledge once he had found fame with his later works.

The Jealous Wife (1761)
With the play below, Colman's most popular and surviving work, inspired by Henry Fielding's novel *Tom Jones*.

The Clandestine Marriage (1766)
The play for which Colman is best known, and the most revived. It, too, was written for David Garrick's company. It was an instant success.

The Man of Business (1774)
Written for Covent Garden, and one of the few successful plays that Colman wrote at this time.

The Suicide (1778)
Another rare success of his late period and written for The Haymarket Theatre.

The Separate Maintenance (1779)
Perhaps the only other success of Colman's late period, and written for The Haymarket Theatre.

Oliver Goldsmith (1730–74)

Playwright, novelist, poet and essayist, Goldsmith was born in Ireland. He studied at Trinity College, Dublin, and then made his way via Scotland, France and Italy to England, arriving in 1756. His first work was as a journalist and essay writer. He became a friend of Dr Jonson, and wrote his famous novel, *The Vicar of Wakefield*, in 1766.

After writing the libretto to *The Captivity* in 1764, Goldsmith turned his skills, rather late in his life, to the writing of plays. He wrote two pieces, his most famous work, *She Stoops to Conquer*, in 1773, the year before he died. Although author of only two pieces for the stage, nevertheless Goldsmith's comedies both stand up well against the brightest of his generation, including those of Sheridan. Much that he wrote was second class, but he left this famous and still produced comedy, one very readable novel and some notable poetry.

Goldsmith's Epitaph

On his death Jonson wrote of Goldsmith: 'No man was more foolish when he had not a pen in his hand, or more wise when he had.' Garrick wrote:

Here lies Nolly Goldsmith, for shortness called Noll,
Who wrote like an angel, but talked like poor Poll.

PLAYS

The Good Natured Man (1768)
A comedy produced at Covent Garden by George Colman (qv) after being turned down by David Garrick for Drury Lane. Not a great success at the time.

She Stoops to Conquer (1773)
Goldsmith's comic masterpiece, also produced by Colman for Covent Garden, and an instant hit. Although of the period, this sparkling work has proved more timeless than many, and is still often seen.

Richard Brinsley Sheridan (1751–1816)

Sheridan was born in Dublin where his father managed The Alley Theatre. Sheridan was sent to school in England at Harrow to study law, but this choice of career was over before it had even begun when Sheridan became involved with a singer, Elizabeth Ann Linley, and fought two duels on her account. After marrying, the couple settled in London. They had met in the fashionable spa town of Bath, and this is the setting for Sheridan's first great work, *The Rivals*.

Although his first work was written for Covent Garden, the majority of Sheridan's works, most of which were penned between 1776 and 1779, were written for Drury Lane, in which he became a major shareholder after buying holdings once owned by David Garrick, who had died in 1779. His managership of Drury Lane saw many ups and downs, and Sheridan is said never really to have recovered from its destruction by fire in 1809.

As a manager of Drury Lane, Sheridan is said to have further encouraged the work of designer Philip De Loutherbourg, whom Garrick had previously championed. Sheridan was responsible, along with his comedies, for the writing of various pantomimes and entertainments that certainly exercised the abilities of De Loutherboug, amongst others, in the creation of spectacle. In this vein Sheridan's pantomimes included a notable *Robinson Crusoe* in 1781, written as an after-piece for Shakespeare's *The Winter's Tale*. He also wrote a number of scenes for various harlequinades, and a comic opera, *The Duenna*, in 1775.

All of Sheridan's plays are comedies of the highest quality, and certainly more than one of them can be seen as a pinnacle of the English comedy of manners. They are vehicles for comic performance that speeds along with a sense of wit and verve uncontested by their rivals. The comic writing has all the ingenuity of previous comedies, but with none of the rudery or crudeness of Restoration works. These sparklingly brilliant pieces are often revived.

After 1779 Sheridan gave up play-writing and turned his attention to politics. He was an MP from 1780 to 1812, and his public speaking was said to rival that of the great Edmund Burke.

PLAYS
The Rivals (1775)
Originally produced for Covent Garden, this play opened to a lukewarm reception. Sheridan therefore rewrote many scenes, and it became a firm favourite from that day to this, second only to *The School for Scandal* as the unrivalled comic masterpiece of its period. This piece contains, amongst

many unforgettable characters, the redoubtable Mrs Malaprop, who gave her name to the word 'malapropism', which describes the hilarity arising from the confusing of one word with another; this is illustrated in the following quotes from the play: 'He's the very pineapple of politeness!'; and 'She's as headstrong as an allegory on the banks of the Nile.'

St. Patrick's Day; or, the Scheming Lieutentant (1775)
A farce.

A Trip to Scarborough (1777)
A reworking for a more prudish audience of John Vanbrugh's play of nearly one hundred years earlier *The Relapse; or, Virtue in Danger* of 1696 (*see* page 112).

The School for Scandal (1777)
Sheridan's masterpiece, possibly the best comedy of the eighteenth century! A brilliantly executed and labyrinthine plot, populated with finely drawn comic characters such as Lady Sneerwell and Sir Benjamin Backbite, and the comic hero Sir Peter Teazle.

The Critic; or, A Tragedy Rehearsed (1779)
Based on Buckingham's *The Rehearsal*.

Pizarro (1779)
Sheridan's last work, an adaptation of a popular drama by German dramatist August Friedrich Ferdinand Kotzebue (1761–1819).

(*See also* the note on another notable playwright of this era, Hannah Cowley on page 134.)

The following extract is from *A School for Scandal* by Richard Brinsley Sheridan; the denouement of the play indicates its wit and craft.

VICTORIAN THEATRE

Queen Victoria came to the throne in 1837, and in keeping with the changing mood of the times the theatrical styles also began to shift subtly. What emerged was the continuation and development of what had gone before, and with it the founding of one particular genre: melodrama.

Enter LADY SNEERWELL.

SIR PETER. So another French milliner! Egad, he has one in every room in the house, I suppose.

LADY SNEERWELL. Ungrateful Charles! Well may you be surprised, and feel for the indelicate situation which your perfidy has forced me into.

CHARLES. Pray, Uncle, is that another plot of yours? For, as I have life, I don't understand it.

JOSEPH. I believe, sir, there is but the evidence of one person more necessary to make it extremely clear.

SIR PETER. And that person, I imagine, is Mr Snake. Rowley, you were perfectly right to bring him with us, and pray let him appear.

ROWLEY. Walk in, Mr Snake.

Enter SNAKE.

I thought his testimony might be wanted; however, it happens unluckily, that he comes to confront Lady Sneerwell, not to support her.

LADY SNEERWELL. Villain! Treacherous to me at last! (*Aside.*) Speak, fellow, have you too conspired against me?

SNAKE. I beg your ladyship ten thousand pardons. You paid me extremely liberally for the lie in question; but I unfortunately have been offered double to speak the truth.

SIR PETER. Plot and counterplot, egad!

LADY SNEERWELL. The torments of shame and disappointment on you all!

LADY TEAZLE. Hold, Lady Sneerwell. Before you go, let me thank you for the trouble you and the gentleman have taken in writing letters from me to Charles, and answering them yourself. And let me also request you to make my respects to the scandalous college of which you are president, and inform them, that Lady Teazle, licentiate, begs leave to return the diploma they game her, as she leaves off practice and kills characters no longer.

LADY SNEERWELL. You too, madam! Provoking insolent! May your husband live these fifty years.

Exit

SIR PETER. Oons! What a Fury!

LADY TEAZLE. What a malicious creature it is!

SIR PETER. Hey! Not for her last wish?

LADY TEAZLE. Oh, no!

THE SCHOOL FOR SCANDAL

SIR OLIVER. Well, sir, and what have you to say now?

JOSEPH. Sir, I am so confounded to find that Lady Sneerwell could be guilty of suborning Mr Snake in this manner, to impose on us all that I know not what so say. However, lest her revengeful spirit should prompt her to injure my brother I had certainly better follow her directly.

Exit

SIR PETER. Moral to the last drop!

SIR OLIVER. Aye, and marry her, Joseph, if you can. Oil and vinegar, egad! You'll do very well together.

ROWLEY. I believe we have no more occasion for Mr Snake at present.

SNAKE. Before I go, I beg your pardon once for all for whatever uneasiness I have been the humble instrument of causing to the parties present.

SIR PETER. Well, well, you have made atonement by a good deed at last.

SNAKE. But I must request of the company that it shall never be known.

SIR PETER. Hey! What the plague! Are you ashamed of having done a right thing once in your life?

SNAKE. Ah, sir, consider. I live by the badness of my character. I have nothing but my infamy to depend on, and, if it were once known that I had been betrayed into an honest action, I should lose every friend I have in the world.

SIR OLIVER. Well, well, we'll not traduce you by saying anything in your praise, never fear.

Exit SNAKE

SIR PETER. There's a precious rogue!

LADY TEAZLE. See, Sir Oliver. There needs no persuasion now to reconcile our nephew and Maria.

CHARLES *and* MARIA *apart.*

SIR OLIVER. Aye, aye, that's as it should be, and, egad, we'll have the wedding tomorrow morning.

CHARLES. Thank you, dear Uncle.

SIR PETER. What, you rogue, don't you ask the girl's consent first?

CHARLES. Oh, I have done that a long time – above a minute ago – and she has looked *yes.*

MARIA. For shame, Charles! I protest, Sir Peter, there has not been a word.

SIR OLIVER. Well then, the fewer the better. May your love for each other never know abatement!

SIR PETER. And may you live as happily together as Lady Teazle and I intend to do!

CHARLES. Rowley, my old friend, I am sure you congratulate me; and I suspect that I owe you much.

SIR OLIVER. You do, indeed, Charles.

ROWLEY. If my efforts to serve you had not succeeded, you would have been in my debt for the attempt; but deserve to be happy and you overpay me.

SIR PETER. Aye, honest Rowley always said you would reform.

CHARLES. Why, as to reforming, Sir Peter, I'll make no promises, and that I take to be a proof that I intend to set about it. But here shall be my monitor, my gentle guide. Ah, can I leave the virtuous path those eye illumine?

Though thou, dear maid, shouldst waive they beauty's sway.
Thou still must rule, because I will obey
An humbled fugitive from folly view,
No sanctuary near but love and you.
(*To the audience*.) You can, indeed, each anxious fear remove,
For even Scandal dies, if you approve!

Melodrama is perhaps an obvious child of the sentimental drama that had preceded it. It combined the overly theatrical style of acting with the development of ever-convincing painted scenery, and the desire for spectacle and excitement characteristic of the ever-expanding Victorian ego. The ingenuity of stage machinery also allowed great spectacular events to be included in stage presentations – horse races, earthquakes, railway crashes, sea battles and the like. Moving painted dioramas were used, stage traps, elaborate flying scenery, pyrotechnics, and a lot of water. Sadler's Wells became particularly known for its aquatic events, having a large tank of 30m (90ft) in length and 1.5m (5ft) deep that could be raised mechanically on to the stage.

The popularity of theatre and the ever-growing population made it increasingly urgent that the rules regarding the need for a royal patent to open a theatre were eased and simplified: thus the Regulation of Theatres Act was passed in 1843, allowing a greater freedom in this area. By 1850 there were twenty theatres in London, and by 1900 more than sixty. Alongside theatres staging dramatic works existed other venues for the performing of popular light entertainment, mostly comedy and song: the music halls – by 1900 there were over forty of these in London alone.

New and refurbished, theatres grew in size once more, the biggest being Covent Garden, which expanded to a stage 12.8m (42ft) wide by 20.7m

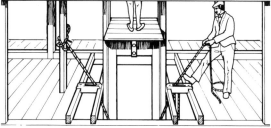

(68ft) deep and an auditorium that held 3,000. After a fire, Drury Lane was rebuilt with a stage 10m (33ft) wide by 29.2m (96ft) deep, and also accommodating an audience of over 3,000. It was so big and cavernous that actress Sarah Siddons described it derisively as 'the tomb of the drama'.

Gaslight was introduced in 1817, and grandiose special effects attempted – a letter published in the paper *John Bull* described Macready's *King Lear* as follows:

> ... forked lightnings now vividly illume the broad horizon, now faintly coruscating in small and serpent folds, and play in the distance; the sheeted elements sweep over the foreground and leave it in pitch darkness.[1]

Victorian stage machinery: a 'star' trap.

BELOW. *The Victorian stage.*

Limelight came about around 1850, and was a particular favourite of Charles Kean (qv). It combined with inventive use of gauzes, coloured light and other effects to create great spectacles.

The need for such large stages, and yet the need also to achieve a large audience, combined with the desire to make increasingly believable and brilliant stage pictures, and meant that eventually the stage apron disappeared, leaving the more formal proscenium, or the 'picture frame' stage. Ironically, of course, the need to create illusion in this way also served to separate the actors from the audience, and encouraged histrionic performance.

Victorian Melodrama

Of all the theatre produced during the Victorian era one genre grew, and then stayed forever locked in the period: the Victorian melodrama. It derived from similar works in France and Germany, and seemed to suit the mood for both spectacle and mass entertainment. It was a genre that was then ambushed and successfully kidnapped by the exciting development of the motion picture – but even here, it did not survive long.

Melodrama was a fantastical drama that suited the 'picture frame' of stage or screen, but was fundamentally flawed in its unrealistic and naïve nature. Certainly with hindsight it seems a genre that had to give way to a desire for greater intellectual value and deeper characterization within dramatic art.

A strong indication as to why this genre's existence should be so brief can be gathered from the formulaic and simplistic nature of the plays. Good is threatened by evil. Horror and mystery prevail. Heart-rending adventures are undertaken that put heroes and heroines in great and improbable peril. Success is finally plucked – but only at the last moment – from the jaws of defeat. Good triumphs over evil. Evil barons are barred from the door, heroines untied from railway tracks. Michael R. Booth in his book *English Melodrama*[ii] describes this genre as giving 'glittering illusion, wild sensation and comforting morality to millions of spectators'. In his book he divides melodrama into the following categories: Gothic and Eastern; military and nautical; domestic; sensation.

Victorian dramatists took their lead in melodrama from the continent. The following are fine examples of such works: *Götz von Berlichingen* (1773), by Goethe (qv); *Die Räuber* (1782), by Schiller (qv); and *Coelina, ou l'Enfant de Mystère* (1800), by French dramatist Guilbert de Pixérécourt.

Early examples of English melodrama include the following pieces:

A Tale of Mystery (1802) by Thomas Holcroft, based on the de Pixérécourt piece mentioned above; this was the first play in England to be called a melodrama.

Jonathan Bradford; or, The Murder at the Roadside Inn (1823), by Edward Fitzball.

The Flying Dutchman (1827), by Edward Fitzball.

Fifteen Years of a Drunkard's Life (1828), by Douglas Jerrold.

Black-ey'd Susan (1829), by Douglas Jerrold.

Maria Martin; or, The Murder in the Red Barn (c.1830), an anonymous piece.

Melodrama in the Victorian era proper included many adaptations of novels, the most notable of these being *Uncle Tom's Cabin* (1852), *East Lynne* (1861), *Trilby* (1895), *The Prisoner of Zenda* (1896), *A Tale of Two Cities* (1899) and *The Scarlet Pimpernel* (1903).

In addition, the habit of adapting works from the continent continued, with versions of plays by, for example, Brisbarre and Nus. Other examples from the period include: *The Ticket-of-Leave Man* (1863), by Tom Taylor; *The Bells* (1871), by Leopold Lewis (*see* page 135); and *The Corsican Brothers* (1878), by Dion Boucicault (qv).

VICTORIAN ACTORS

In this period a new generation of actors and actor-managers came to the fore, and in the later part of Victoria's reign in England these were dominated by the pairing of Henry Irving and Ellen Terry.

Alongside them were other famous performers of the period, such as Sarah Bernhardt, Squire Bancroft and Herbert Beerbohm Tree. Their careers and their fame help us understand the era.

Henry Irving (1838–1905)

The theatrical profession grew to a new level of respectability when in 1895 Irving became the first actor to be knighted. Irving was born John Henry Brodribb, and his first professional appearance (he had previously acted as an amateur) was at Sunderland's The Lyceum in 1856. After touring the provinces he finally achieved success on the London stage in 1866 with the role of Doricourt in *The Belle's Stratagem* (1780) by Hannah Cowley (1743–1809).

Irving then proceeded to dominate the English stage for over thirty years, particularly in partnership (on stage) with Ellen Terry (qv). He appeared for the first time with Terry in 1867 when they played opposite each other in the title roles in *Katherine and Petruchio*, an adaptation of *The Taming of the Shrew* by David Garrick (qv); this was Irving's second 'hit'.

Irving's great roles included many at London's Lyceum Theatre, of which he also became manager in 1878. Prior to this he gave one of his most memorable performances at The Lyceum (then under the managership of American impresario Hezekiah Bateman) as the leading character in *The Bells* (1871), an adaptation by Leopold Lewis of *Le Juif Polonais* (*The Polish Jew*) by Erckmann-Chatrian. As a play it is really little more than a traditional Victorian melodrama, but with Irving's contribution it was transformed into a very powerful piece. Irving played the central character, a burgomaster trying to hold a successful career together whilst haunted by the memory of the callous murder that he had perpetrated in the past in order to set him on the road to fame and fortune; the guilt of his undiscovered past action finally destroys the central character. The simplistic psychological device used to show this happening is that Irving's character associates the moment of the murder with sleigh bells, and hears these whenever he feels guilty. In this particular production the sleigh was also seen up-stage as a ghostly presence from time to time, an effect achieved by the popular theatrical device of the time, a reveal. Semi-transparent gauze cloths could be lit in varying ways to appear

Hannah Cowley

Female playwrights remained a rare breed, so it is worth noting that, although now no longer produced, Hannah Cowley's work was very popular at this time. It included *Who's the Dupe* (1779), *A Bold Stroke for a Husband* (1783) and *The Town before You* (1794).

Sir Henry Irving – a statue in London's West End.

solid or transparent. Thus the sleigh could be located behind what appeared to be a solid wall, the central section of which, behind Irving, could then apparently dissolve, revealing the sleigh behind.

In the course of such an illustrious career Irving scored many great successes and was hailed as an actor of great style and manner. A romantic figure on stage, with beautiful diction and stance, he was

'Oh no, the bells, the bells!'

A phrase often repeated in the play *The Bells* is its title. It was done with such intensity by Irving, and had such a morbid fascination for its audience, that even today when wishing to express overly melodramatic dread it can be heard being quoted: 'Oh no, the bells, the bells!'.

Count Dracula

For the main part of his career Irving's personal manager was a certain Bram Stoker (1847–1912), later known as the author of *Dracula* (1879). Irving's 'larger-than-life' dramatic cloaked persona is thought to have been used by Stoker as a model for the appearance of the count.

The Bells – the setting of this famous production.

a man who reawakened the popular interest in the works of Shakespeare, and who brought to the stage many thought-provoking and dynamic characters. The following list of Irving's major performances serves to give a real flavour of the type of theatre that was enjoyed at this time:

Richelieu by Bulwer-Lytton; Irving's first professional stage appearance, in the role of Gaston, was at The Lyceum Theatre in Sunderland.

1864: *Hamlet*; Irving's first Shakespearean role was the title character.

1866: *The Belle's Stratagem* by Hannah Cowley, at St James's Theatre.

Katherine and Petruchio by David Garrick (qv), at The Queen's Theatre in Longacre.

1869: *Uncle Dick's Darling* by H.J. Byron.

1870: *Two Roses* by James Albery (his most famous play), at The Vaudeville Theatre.

The Pickwick Papers, adapted from Dickens' novel by James Albery for The Lyceum Theatre; it was Irving's first appearance at the theatre that would dominate his career.

The Bells, possibly Irving's most famous role, and one that saw a change in fortune for The Lyceum Theatre also.

1872: *Charles I* by Ivah Wills, at The Lyceum.

1873: *Eugene Aram* and *Richelieu*, the latter a revival of a play by Bulwer-Lytton, and both at The Lyceum.

1874: *Hamlet.* In which Irving scored a huge success.

Irving starts to manage the Lyceum, and opens with *Hamlet.* (All subsequent productions are thus undertaken for and at The Lyceum, until otherwise stated.)

1879: *The Merchant of Venice*; *The Lady of Lyon* by Bulwer-Lytton (qv).

1880: *The Corsican Brothers*, by Dion Boucicault (qv).

1881: *The Cup* by Alfred, Lord Tennyson.

Two Roses, a revival of his previous success with this play by James Albery.

1882: *Romeo and Juliet*, *Much Ado About Nothing*.

1883: Irving tours America, becoming the toast of the town in New York with *The Bells* at The Star Theater in October.

1884: *Twelfth Night.*

1887: Irving returns to tour America.

1892: *Henry VIII*; *King Lear*.

1893: *Becket* by Alfred, Lord Tennyson; the title role is considered one of Irving's great impersonations. Irving travelled to America to perform once more in this year.

1895: *King Arthur*, by Comyns Carr.

A Story of Waterloo, by Arthur Conan Doyle.

Don Quixote, by Ivah Wills.

1896: *Cymbeline.*

Madame Sans-Gêne, by Comyns Carr.

1897: *Peter the Great*, by Laurence Irving.

1899: Irving retires from The Lyceum management, and tours America again.

1901: *Coriolanus.* Another tour to America.

1902: *The Merchant of Venice*, Irving's last appearance at The Lyceum.

1904: Irving makes what will be his final tour to America, ending with a performance of *Louis XI* by Dion Boucicault in The Harlem Opera House in March.

1905: *A Story of Waterloo*, a revival of Conan Doyle's play, at Drury Lane; this was Irving's last London appearance.

Irving died shortly after leaving the stage during a tour of Tennyson's *Becket* in October 1905.

Ellen Terry (1847–1928)

Terry had a very long career, starting at the age of nine when she appeared on stage as Mamillius in Charles Kean's production of *The Winter's Tale* at The Princess Theatre. Her adult career began around 1861, when she appeared in London for the first time. She took several breaks from her career, the first of which occurred in 1864 when she married G. F. Watts, the painter. On divorcing him she returned to the stage only briefly before halting her career again to live with Edward Godwin, with whom she had two children – Edith and Edward. Terry returned to the stage properly in 1874, appearing as Phillippa in *The Wandering Heir*. In 1878 she married her second husband, Charles Kelly, but this time continued to perform.

Notable roles for Terry included Portia in *The Merchant of Venice* for the Bancrofts (qv), and the title role in *Olivia*, an adaptation by Ivah Wills of a novel by Oliver Goldsmith (qv) in 1878. From 1878 she was hired by Henry Irving (qv), and she remained his leading lady until 1902. Their work together over twenty-four years can be considered one of the great stage partnerships of all time. With Irving she undertook roles in many pieces by Shakespeare, including a very fine Lady Macbeth, as well as Cordelia, Desdemona, Olivia, Viola and Beatrice, and parts in contemporary works. She was also notable as Lady Teazle in Sheridan's play *The School for Scandal*.

From 1902 she became manager of The Imperial Theatre, and produced many fine productions including in 1903 *Much Ado About Nothing* and Ibsen's *The Vikings*, with scenery designed by her son, theatrical innovator and stage designer Edward Gordon Craig (*see* page 170) (qv).

In 1906 Terry celebrated her stage jubilee at the age of sixty-nine, in the part of Lady Cicely Waynflete, a part specially written for her by George Bernard Shaw in his play *Captain Brassbound's Conversion*.

In 1907 Terry married again, this time a young American actor called James Carew. From this time on she seldom acted, but toured America and Australia lecturing and being generally fêted. Terry was made a Dame of the British Empire in 1925. She died in 1928.

Herbert Beerbohm Tree (1858–1918)

A notable actor-manager of the period, Tree was particularly renowned for his performances as Svengali in a stage adaptation of George Du Maurier's novel *Trilby*, and Professor Higgins in Shaw's *Pygmalion*. In the latter piece Tree played opposite another acknowledged great actor of the period, Mrs Patrick Campbell. Tree's success brought him fame and fortune, enabling him to build Her Majesty's Theatre

Sir Herbert Beerbohm Tree, in the role of Hamlet.

in London's West End, and to found The Royal Academy of Dramatic Art above it, in 1904. Tree was knighted in 1909.

Squire Bancroft (1841–1926)

In partnership with his wife Marie Effie Wilton (1839–1921), Bancroft encouraged a new, higher status for the actor, and training for them, too, becoming president of RADA. He was knighted in 1897.

This was also the period in which French actress Sarah Bernhardt (1845–1923) found great

---

John Wilkes Booth

Actors become notorious for many things, but perhaps none more so than successful actor Edwin Booth, brother to John Wilkes Booth, who in 1865 became infamous for assassinating Abraham Lincoln. This happened in the Ford's Theater Washington D.C. during a performance of the play *Our American Cousin*, written by Englishman Tom Taylor.

Women Actors for Shakespearian Heroes

The tradition of women playing Shakespeare's heroes continues right up to the present day, with notable sucesses from Frances de la Tour as Hamlet in 1979, and Fiona Shaw as Richard II in 1995.

international acclaim, notably for her portrayal of great tragic roles, amongst them the title role in *Hamlet*. Bernhardt lived for the theatre, even continuing to perform after having a leg amputated in 1915!

VICTORIAN PLAYWRIGHTS

The works of Shakespeare, as performed by the première actors of their day, and melodramas were naturally not the only stage works of this period. Several notable playwrights came to the fore whose work was more strikingly original and yet still generally popular. Of these, Dion Boucicault and, in particular, Oscar Wilde are perhaps the greatest exponents. Minor playwrights of the period and their most famous works include Edward Bulwer-Lytton (1803–73) with *The Lady of Lyons*, *Richelieu* and *Money*; and James Albery (1838–89) with *Two Roses*.

Dion Boucicault (1822–1929)
Born in Dublin, Boucicault's work includes *London Assurance*, *The Corsican Brothers*, *Louis XI*, *The Octoroon*, *The Colleen Bawn* and *The Shaughraun*. Boucicault was probably the first playwright to get a royalty for his work rather than a fixed fee – a change in the law that he battled to achieve.

Oscar Wilde (1854–1900)
Like Boucicault, Wilde was born in Dublin and would be acclaimed in both England and America. His full name was Oscar Fingal O'Flahertie Wills Wilde, and he was educated firstly at Trinity College, Dublin, and then at Magdalen College, Oxford. He had some success in Ireland and abroad before setting out for London to bewitch English society with his wit, his poetry and finally his plays. He also wrote prose pieces, some of them for children, and a single novel.

Whilst still at Oxford, and under the influence of Ruskin and others, Wilde took the inward-looking philosophy of 'art for art's sake' to new heights, preaching the supremacy of beauty in all things – even his choice of dress called attention to his desire to make aestheticism his creed. Notoriety, of one sort or another, never seemed far from his name. (The aesthetic set that Wilde so keenly identified with and exemplified, was satirized by Gilbert and Sullivan in their opera *Patience* of 1881.)

The Wit of Wilde

Oscar Wilde is famous still for his epigrammatic wit, and there are enough examples to quote from even just one of his plays: here are only a few such from *The Importance of Being Earnest*:

Truth is rarely pure, and never simple.

In married life three is company and two is none.

All women become like their mothers. That is their tragedy. No man does. That's his.

The good ended happily, and the bad unhappily. That is what fiction means.

I never travel without a diary. One should always have something sensational to read in the train.

On an occasion of this kind it becomes more than a moral duty to speak one's mind. It becomes a pleasure.

In matters of grave importance, style, not sincerity, is the vital thing.

No woman should ever be quite accurate about her age. It looks so calculating.

This suspense is terrible. I hope it will last.

Wilde's collected poems were published in 1881, after which he started touring America. On returning to England he had gained a certain fame, that he built on, with tours around the country. Wilde wrote two unsuccessful plays in the early 1880s. In 1884 he married Constance Mary Lloyd, the daughter of a successful Irish barrister. He was happy in marriage for a number of years and had two sons, Cyril in 1885 and Vyvyan in 1886.

Wilde next turned to prose writing, including memorable short stories for children under the title *The Happy Prince* (1888), and then for adults in *Lord*

Arthur Savile's Crime and Other Stories (1891), which included the famous *Canterville Ghost*. After other publications, including various polemics, in 1891 Wilde wrote his only novel, *The Picture of Dorian Gray*, widely condemned as being highly immoral. In this year Wilde also returned to the work of writing plays, with *Lady Windermere's Fan*. Alongside the scandal of his personal life, which in his own time came to cast a long shadow over his professional work, Wilde is best known as a dramatist, chiefly for this play and the three major works that followed it.

Wilde remained the toast of London until 1895, when, after a scandalously high profile trial, he was imprisoned with hard labour for homosexual practices. Of his imprisonment he wrote one of his most powerful poems, *Ballad of Reading Gaol*, in 1898. After his release from incarceration, Wilde never really recovered his reputation or his health, although he did write another remarkable piece about his experiences in *De Profundis*. He died in exile in France.

Wilde's reputation as a talented dandy who flirted outrageously with society only finally to fall foul of the moral values and strictures that he had so wittily mocked, lives on still. However, his four major plays are works of such joy and delicacy, of wit and wisdom, that they are still being revisited with great pleasure on a regular basis.

PLAYS
Vera; or, the Nihilists (1882)
An early, immature work that played for one week only in New York and never reached London.

The Duchess of Padua (1883)

Lady Windermere's Fan (1892)
Wilde himself described this piece as 'one of those modern drawing-room plays with pink lampshades'. However, after the success of its first performance he said of the performers: 'I congratulate you on the success of your performance, which persuades me that you think almost as highly of the play as I do.' It remains one of the finest of drawing-room comedies.

Salomé (1893)
A one-act play written by Wilde in France and in French, this play tells the biblical story, and as such

was not allowed on the English stage – where the Lord Chamberlain forbade the appearance of biblical characters. It was, however, performed by Sarah Bernhardt, in 'rehearsal' only.

A Woman of No Importance (1893)
First performed by Beerbohm Tree's company with great success at The Haymarket Theatre.

An Ideal Husband (1895)
George Bernard Shaw, writing as a critic at the time, commented on the success of this play on opening night: 'Mr. Oscar Wilde's new play ... is a dangerous subject, because he has the property of making his critics dull ... He plays with everything: with wit, with philosophy, with drama, with actors and audience, with the whole theatre.'

The Importance of Being Earnest (1895)
This piece is considered Wilde's most brilliant play, and of its kind, one of the finest constructed in the English canon. It shows Wilde clearly at the pinnacle of his skills.

A Florentine Tragedy
Left unfinished at his death.

La Sainte Courtisane

The following (*see* box, p.140) is an extract from *The Importance of Being Earnest*. It is from Act 3, and finds Cecily very much in command as she explains to Algernon (who has been pretending to be the title character, Earnest) how she has arranged, and been thoroughly enjoying their relationship so far!

Arthur Wing Pinero (1855–1934)
Pinero was born in London. By profession he was initially a lawyer, and then an actor, but then he also turned his hand to writing, using much of his theatrical experience in his work. His first professional stage appearance was at The Theatre Royal in Edinburgh in 1874; his first play, produced at The Globe Theatre in London in 1877, was *£200 a Year*. This piece was followed by many other minor plays, and established Pinero as a popular farceur. A number of even more notable successes in comedy followed,

THE IMPORTANCE OF BEING EARNEST

ALGERNON: I don't care for anybody in the whole world but you. I love you. Cecily! you will marry me, won't you?

CECILY: You silly boy! Of course. Why, we have been engaged for the last three months.

ALGERNON: For the last three months?

CECILY: Three months all but a few days. (*Looks at diary, turns over page.*) Yes; it will be exactly three months on Thursday.

ALGERNON: I didn't know.

CECILY: Very few people nowadays ever realise the position in which they are placed. The age is, as Miss Prism oftens says, a thoughtless one.

ALGERNON: But how did we become engaged?

CECILY: Well, ever since dear Uncle Jack first confessed to us that he had a younger brother who was very wicked and bad, you of course have formed the chief topic of conversation between myself and Miss Prism. And of course a man who is much talked about is always very attractive. One feel there must be something in him, after all. I dare say it was foolish of me, but I fell in love with you, Ernest.

ALGERNON: Darling! And when was the engagement actually settled?

CECILY: On the 14th February last. Worn out by your entire ignorance of my existence, I determined to end the matter one way or the other, and after a long struggle with myself I accepted you one evening in the garden. The next day I bought this little ring in your name. You see I always wear it, Ernest, and though it shows that you are sadly extravagant, still I have long ago forgiven you for that. Here in this drawer are all the little presents I have given you from time to time, neatly numbered and labelled. This is the pearl necklace you gave me on my birthday. And this is the box in which I keep all your letters. (*Opens box and produces letters tied up with blue ribbon.*)

ALGERNON: My letters! But my own sweet Cecily, I have never written you any letters.

CECILY: You need hardly remind me of that, Ernest. I remember it only too well. I grew tired of asking the postman every morning if he had a London letter for me. My health began to give way under the strain and anxiety. So I wrote your letters for you, and had them posted to me in the village by my maid. I wrote always three times a week and sometimes oftener.

ALGERNON: Oh, do let me read them, Cecily.

CECILY: Oh, I couldn't possibly. They would make you far too conceited. The three you wrote me after I had broken off the engagement are so beautiful and so badly spelt that even now I can hardly read them without crying a little.

ALGERNON: But was our engagement ever broken off?

CECILY: Of course it was. On the 22nd of last March. You can see the entry if you like. (*Shows Diary.*) "Today I broke off my engagement with Ernest. I feel it is better to do so. The weather still continues charming."

ALGERNON: But why on earth did you break it off? What had I done? I had done nothing at all. Cecily, I am very much hurt indeed to hear you broke it off. Particularly when the weather was so charming.

CECILY: Men seem to forget very easily. I should have thought you would have remembered the violent letter you wrote to me because I danced with Lord Kelso at the county ball.

ALGERNON: But I did take it all back, Cecily, didn't I?

CECILY: Or course you did. Otherwise I wouldn't have forgiven you or accepted this little gold bangle with the turquoise and diamond heart, that you sent me the next day. (*Show bangle.*)

ALGERNON: Did I give you this, Cecily? It's very pretty, isn't it?

CECILY: Yes. You have wonderfully good taste, Ernest. I have always said that of you. It's the excuse I've always given for your leading such a bad life.

ALGERNON: My own one! So we have been engaged for three months, Cecily!

CECILY: Yes; how the time has flown, hasn't it?

ALGERNON: I don't think so. I have found the days very long and very dreary without you.

CECILY: You dear romantic boy … (*puts her fingers through his hair.*) I hope your hair curls naturally. Does it?

ALGERNON: Yes darling, with a little help from others.

CECILY: I am so glad.

ALGERNON: You'll never break off our engagement again, Cecily?

CECILY: I don't think that I could break if off now that I have actually met you. Besides, of course, there is the question of your name.

ALGERNON: Yes, of course. (*Nervously*)

CECILY: You must not laugh at me, darling, but it had always been a girlish dream of mine to love some one whose name was Ernest.

ALGERNON *rises*, CECILY *also*.

There is something in that name that seems to inspire absolute confidence. I pity any poor married woman whose husband is not called Ernest.

ALGERNON: But, my dear child, do you mean to say you could not love me if I had some other name?

CECILY: But what name?

ALGERNON: Oh, any name you like—Algernon—for instance …

CECILY: But I don't like the name of Algernon,

ALGERNON: Well, my own dear, sweet, loving little darling, I really can't see why you should object to the name of Algernon. It is not at all a bad name. In fact, it is rather an aristocratic name. Half of the chaps who get into the Bankruptcy Court are called Algernon. But seriously, Cecily— (*moving to her*)—if my name was Algy, couldn't you love me?

CECILY (*rising*): I might respect you, Ernest, I might admire your character, but I fear that I should not be able to give you my undivided attention.

ALGERNON: Ahem! Cecily! (*Picking up hat*.) Your Rector here is, I suppose, thoroughly experienced in the practice of all the rites and ceremonials of the Church?

CECILY: Oh, yes. Dr. Chasuble is a most learned man. He has never written a single book, so you can imagine how much he knows.

ALGERNON: I must see him at once on a most important christening—I mean on most important business.

CECILY: Oh!

ALGERNON: I shan't be away more than half an hour.

CECILY: Considering that we have been engaged since February the 14th, and that I only met you to-day for the first time, I think it is rather hard that you should leave me for so long a period as half an hour. Couldn't you make it twenty minutes?

ALGERNON: I'll be back in no time. (*Kisses her and rushes out*).

CECILY: What an impetuous boy he is! I like his hair so much. I must enter his proposal in my diary.

---

including *Dandy Dick* in 1887. By 1884 he had written some fifteen plays, and thereafter stopped acting. His plays in this period became popularly known as The Court Theatre Farces, and they drew regular audiences, both large and enthusiastic.

In 1889 Pinero took his work in another direction with *The Profligate*. This, and similar pieces that followed can be classed as 'problem' plays, in that farce is not the driving force behind them. In a period where farce and melodrama were predominant, Pinero's carefully thought out, humane comedies stand out as works' apart. Athough they do stay within the four-walled security of conventional staging, Pinero's social commentaries are particularly notable for the manner in which they challenge the assumptions made concerning the role of women within the period, and as such they were greatly admired and highly successful. Perhaps the most famous, and still most often produced of these pieces, are *The Second Mrs Tanqueray* (1893) and *Trelawney of the Wells*, written in 1898. Entering, as he did, the world of the 'theatre of ideas' in this manner, Pinero rose above his contemporaries and put himself at the forefront of contemporary theatre. He was knighted for his services to theatre in 1909.

PLAYS
EARLY WORKS:
£200 a Year (1877)
Pinero's first play, a farce, and a success in its first production at The Globe Theatre in London.

The Money Spinner (1881)
An example of Pinero's lesser comedies. This play was first produced at St James's Theatre in London.

THE COURT THEATRE FARCES:
The Magistrate (1885)
The first of the so-called 'Court Theatre Farces' that became much in vogue at the time, and one of the best of its kind.

The Schoolmistress (1886) Also rated as one of the greatest of English farces.

Dandy Dick (1887)
Once again thought to be one of England's best farces, and perhaps the most popular and re-visited of Pinero's early works.

Sweet Lavender (1888)
An overly sentimental play and, although possibly not one of Pinero's best, one that nevertheless served to confirm his place as the leading playwright of his generation.

The Cabinet Minister (1890)
Another farce, but perhaps not as successful as those noted above.

Lady Bountiful (1891)

The Amazons (1893)

The Weaker Sex (1894)

PROBLEM PLAYS:
The Profligate (1889)
Pinero's first serious comedy, a so-called 'problem play' and one that dared to deal with the subject of seduction.

The Second Mrs Tanqueray (1893)
In its first performance this piece benefited from having as its leading lady someone who was destined to become one of the great actors of this period: Mrs Patrick Campbell. A great success at the time, it is still a play that stands up well as a serious and thoughtful comedy of a period not so distant from our own. Mrs Patrick Campbell became famous overnight after taking the title role in Pinero's comedy. She went on to make notable appearances in, amongst other things, the works of Shaw.

The Notorious Mrs Ebbsmith (1895)
A thematic sequel to the play above, although perhaps not so successful. Bernard Shaw called it a 'bad' play, and its third-act finale, involving Bible burning, became a cause célèbre.

The Benefit of Doubt (1895)

Period poster showing Irene Vanbrugh starring in Mid-channel *by Pinero.*

Mrs Patrick Campbell in the title role of Mrs Tanqueray.

Trelawney of the Wells, *a modern production in period dress, directed by Brigid Panet.*

The Princess and the Butterfly (1897)
A comedy that challenges convention.

Trelawney of the 'Wells' (1898)
A frolicsome theatrical comedy, based in and around Sadler's Wells theatre. A piece that has been regularly revived, and that contains a central role perfect for any up-and-coming young female performer of spirit and verve.

The Gay Lord Quex (1899)
Another piece based around the theatre business itself, full of artful contrivance and energy. The third act in particular is thought to be one of the finest pieces of comic theatrical construction, and is often compared to the 'screen scene' from Sheridan's *School for Scandal* (qv).

LATER 'SERIOUS' PLAYS:
Iris (1901)
Perhaps the most successful of these later serious works. In *Iris* the lowering of the house curtains to denote the passage of time was used for the first time.

Letty (1903)

His House in Order (1906)
At the time a very popular play concerning marriage and infidelity.

The Thunderbolt (1908)

Mid-Channel (1909)

The Widow of Wasdale Head (1912)

A Cold June (1932)

Pinero's last, late work, and a long mark from his finest. In any case, by this time Pinero's type of theatre had been fast left behind.

EUROPEAN THEATRE OF THE EIGHTEENTH AND NINETEENTH CENTURIES

Pierre Carlet De Chamblain De Marivaux (1688–1763)

French author of comedies and romances, Marivaux had a sensitivity for the sentimental and the affected, both of which were also popular elsewhere in this period. His ability to create works of such a specific character resulted in his style being described as 'Marivaudage'. His works were not wholly successful in his own time, but became very popular in mid-nineteenth-century France, and are still revived. They have not translated particularly well into the English language, and are therefore not as well known outside France.

Marivaux wrote mostly for the Comédie Italienne, the company of Italian performers based in the theatre known as The Hôtel de Bourgogne, and chief rivals to the Comédie Fançaise.

PLAYS
PLAYS WRITTEN FOR, AND FIRST PRODUCED AT THE COMÉDIE ITALIENNE:
La Surprise de l'Amour (1722)

La Double Inconstance (1723)

Le Jeu de l'Amour et du Hasard (1730)

Les Fausses Confidences (1737)

L'Épreuve (1740)

PLAYS WRITTEN FOR AND FIRST PRODUCED AT THE COMÉDIE FRANÇAISE:
La Seconde Surprise de l'Amour (1727)

Le Legs (1736)

Voltaire (1694–1778)

Born François Marie Arouet in Paris, Voltaire is known chiefly as a philosopher whose political writings, among them the *Lettres Philosophiques* (1734) and the *Dictionnaire Philosophique* (1764), led to his internment in the Bastille and exile in England (1726–29). He later lived in Germany and Switzerland before returning to France shortly before his death. Voltaire's avowed dislike for dogma and institutionalism of any kind – whether political or religious – can be seen as a perfect introduction to the ideas that led to the French Revolution.

Voltaire also wrote histories and philosophical stories – the best known of these being *Candide* (1759). As a writer he was known for his wit and erudition, and his dramatic works brought him fame and fortune. His tragedies, which are thought to be superior to his comedies, are often based on historical or mythological themes. Voltaire had a life-long love and respect of English literature, being particularly enamoured and critical of the works of Shakespeare.

PLAYS
Oedipe (1718)
The play that made his name, written whilst he was imprisoned in the Bastille.

Voltaire.

Brutus (1730)

Eriphyle (1732)

Zaïre (1732)
In this work Voltaire is said to have been highly influenced by the works of Shakespeare.

Le Mort de César (1735)

Alzire (1736)
One of Voltaire's most successful tragedies.

L'Enfant Prodigue (1736)
A comedy in the sentimental style of the period.

Mahomet ou le Fanatisme (1741)
One of Voltaire's most successful tragedies.

Mérope (1743)
Also described as one of Voltaire's most successful tragedies.

Nanine (1749)
A comedy.

L'Orphelin de la Chine (1755)

Tancrède (1760)

L'Écossaise (1760)

Irène (1778)

Beaumarchais (1732–99)

Pierre-Augustin Caron De Beaumarchais was born in Paris. He entered the French court as a music teacher to the daughters of King Louis XV, and became rich and successful. As a dramatist he is best known as author of two plays, both comedies: *Le Barbier de Séville* of 1775 and its sequel *Le Mariage de Figaro* of 1784. Both of these pieces are probably better known as vehicles used by Rossini and Mozart respectively, for operas of the same name.

Beaumarchais' private life was every bit as colourful as the plots of his comic plays; his love life alone was most complicated, and he married three times.

Because of his notoriety, his plays attracted fierce criticism and often struggled to find homes. Beaumarchais left not only an indelible mark on comedy (and, by default, opera), he also founded the Société des Auteurs, which finally broke the hold on authors that theatres had previously had.

PLAYS
Eugénie (1764)
Beaumarchais' first play, written on a visit to Madrid where he had gone to save his sister from an unhappy love affair! It was first produced by the Comédie Fançaise in 1767 and was a moderate success.

Les Deux Amis (1770)
Another moderate success for Beaumarchais on its first outing.

Le Barbier de Séville (1775)
Originally meant as a play with music, the central character is a masterpiece of comic realization.

Le Mariage de Figaro (1784)
This play operates not only as a sequel to the earlier play, but also, being nearer in date to the forthcoming French Revolution, can be seen as a cutting satire on the society of the period.

Carlo Gozzi (1720–1806)

An Italian poet and playwright, Gozzi satirized Goldoni for his attempts at rebuilding the Commedia dell'Arte in his most famous play *L'amore delle tre melarance* (*The Love of Three Oranges*). Nevertheless, in his own work he also placed a great significance on improvisation, forming his own dramatic style called *Fiabe*, which also used stock characters and told tales from mythology. His work was said to particularly influence that of Goethe and Schiller in Germany.

PLAYS
L'amore delle tre melarance
(*The Love of Three Oranges*) (1761)
Later turned into an opera by Prokofiev.

Il Corvo (*The Raven*) (1761)

Il re Cervo (*King Stag*) (1761)

Turandot (1765)
Famously turned into an opera by Puccini.

Bernd Wilhelm Kleist (1777–1811)

A German author, known for his comedies, especially *The Broken Pitcher* (*Der zerbrochene Krug*) of 1808, and the tragedy *The Prince of Homburg* (*Prinz Friedrich von Homburg*) of 1810. Kleist went unappreciated in his own time, dying at his own hand at the age of only thirty-four. Other plays include *Die Hermannsschlact* (1809) and *Das Käthchen von Heilbronn* (1810).

Other European authors to note in this area are Carlo Goldoni (1709–93), an Italian playwright particularly known for his play *A Servant of Two Masters* (*see* page 57); and four German authors: Ludvig Holberg (1684–1754), Gotthold Ephraim Lessing (1729–81), poet Johann Wolfgang von Goethe (1749–1832) and Friedrich Schiller (1759–1805).

Conclusion

By the end of the nineteenth century the time had come for a revitalizing wind of change to sweep across the Western world of dramatic art. Naturally this happened, not in one place or at one time, but as a gradual progression. Ellen Terry is mentioned above as appearing in an early work of Henrick Ibsen, and his work and that of many others, as we shall see, came about because many new practitioners who looked at the theatre of their day saw an institution stuck in its ways. They had a sense that drama had become stilted and repetitious, boring and predictable, unadventurous and false to its principles – that what was in place needed to be pushed aside and replaced with a new, fresh, and more honest approach. It was from this desire that a revolution in dramatic terms began, a revolution that would finally shape and define what we know today as modern theatre.

From a modern production of Schiller's **The Robbers,** *directed by Gadi Roll.*

8 THE ORIGINS OF MODERN THEATRE: NATURALISM

The historian, essentially, wants more documents than he can really use:
the dramatist only wants more liberties than he can really take.
HENRY JAMES (from *The Aspern Papers*)

Your head is pounding, and you feel like you are going to scream. Never has a rehearsal period been like this one. Never again will you act for this crazy man Stanislavsky. Somehow you doubt whether you will ever act again. You are not sure you even know what acting is any more. The ideas behind his work and the playwright Chekhov seemed to show a new way. A way of delving deeper into the human animal, of revealing how real people are, and putting it on stage. You think the writer has written a great work, you love the play, but even he, Chekhov, seems to have lost patience with Stanislavsky, he certainly has not been at rehearsals for days now. And still they go on – how many has it been, how many rehearsals? Working late into the night, and how maddening they are. Because this man insists on doing it so differently and pushing so hard. At this rate the new century will arrive before The Seagull flies again. But you are needed again, and he is shouting for you, there seems nothing else to be done but to return to the fray, it does makes sense really, it is just so new and so hard.

INTRODUCTION

The concept of 'modern' is a mercurial one. However, in terms of this history, there is a point in time when things make a significant jump towards where we are now – towards the 'modern'. This moment hovers around the later part of the nineteenth century, and in essence allows us to date 'modern theatre' from around 1880.

OPPOSITE PAGE: **The Storm, *a modern production, directed by Nicholas Barter.***

This is a period when the traditions of a stage style that had hardly changed over the previous 150 years had finally run their course, and had begun to appear jaded and weary – a time also when several notable individuals and theatre companies saw the need for this radical change. At this point, and almost simultaneously throughout the wider definition of Europe from England to Mother Russia, an evolutionary jump was made. It was a leap forward that opened the door to an explosion in variety of expression and experience that had as yet never been seen in the history of the stage; and the first major movement to take hold was that of naturalism – or, as it is also sometimes referred to, realism, the two terms being synonymous. The practitioners described below, and in particular their work, define this idea most clearly; however, in the foreword to his play *Miss Julie* of 1888, playwright August Strindberg (qv) writes with great lucidity about the naturalistic cause.

In his essay Strindberg defends the complexity of human nature portrayed in *Miss Julie*, especially in the motivation of characters, as being essential to a naturalistic realization of life on stage. In addition he also comments that the actual way a play is staged is extremely important to the verisimilitude of the piece, calling, like Chekhov before him, for 'representational' settings and action.

Of all that follow, perhaps we should bear in mind that the greatest adherents to a philosophy of showing the 'real' lives of characters on stage are thought to be Ibsen, Strindberg – and the playwright who preceded them, Anton Chekhov. Another voice that called for a radical re-think in the portrayal of 'real life' as portrayed in fiction was novelist Émile Zola.

149

Émile Zola (1840–1902)

A concise and clear definition of the naturalist movement occurs famously in the preface to Émile Zola's novel *Thérèse Raquin* of 1867, which he dramatized in 1873. In the preface Zola talks of revealing the 'truth' on stage, of 'dissecting reality', and revealing 'real life'.[1] Thus Zola's work can be seen as the first attempt at 'slice of life' drama, often focusing on the minutiae of life, and thus also definable as being *minimalist* in nature and intention.

Zola's championing of the naturalistic cause had a great influence on the drama that followed him, in particular the work of Henri Becque and the establishing of the Théâtre Libre in Paris; its first production was a staged version of Zola's short story *Jacques Damour*. (Henri Becque (1837–99) is known for two plays in particular: *Les Corbeaux* (1882) and *La Parisienne* (1885), both naturalistic plays that found their first home in the Théâtre Libre.)

The Théâtre Libre in Paris was founded by André Antoine (1858–1943), an actor, manager and producer who championed the new naturalism. At the Théâtre-Libre, which he founded in 1887, Antoine produced the works of Ibsen (*Ghosts* in 1890), Strindberg and Becque amongst others. Antoine took over the Théâtre Menus-Plaisirs, which he renamed the Théâtre Antoine, in 1906. As well as influencing those in his own country, Antoine's work and ideas also affected thinking right across Europe. He can be said to have played a part in Jack Grein's founding of the Independent Theatre in London in 1891, and in Otto Brahms' founding of the Freie Bühne in Berlin in 1899.

Zola himself wrote few plays, and what he did write failed to grip. Few of them are now easily available in English. Zola also wrote, with more success, librettos for opera.

PLAYS

Madeleine (1866)
An early three-act play, later rewritten as a novel under the title *La Honte*, then republished as *Madeleine Ferat* in 1868.

Thérèse Raquin (1867)
A dramatized version of his novel and most often produced work, famous for its preface (*see* above).

Les Héritiers Rabourdin (1874)
A satirical comedy in three acts.

Le Bouton de Rose (1878)
A farce that, like its predecessor, received indifferent notices.

L'Assommoir (1879)
A dramatized version of a prose piece which, like *Thérèse Raquin*, fared better than the pieces Zola actually wrote for the stage. This piece was written for the stage in collaboration with William B. Busnach.

Renée (1887)
Derived from Zola's novel *La Curée* of 1872, and his last piece for the stage. A long, rambling, five-act play.

L'Enfant-Roi (1905)
Appeared posthumously; a light comedy.

NATURALISM AND THE RUSSIAN TRADITION

Perhaps in Russia more than anywhere else at this time there was a need to express the reality of human experience on stage – the same need that would later lead to a bloody and all-changing revolution. The great work of Anton Chekhov was preceded by that of several somewhat lesser playwrights, whose work nevertheless can clearly be seen to have made a vital contribution.

In his one major work, *A Month in the Country* of 1850, Ivan Sergeivich Turgenev (1818–83), a Russian novelist and writer of plays, creates one of the first true works of naturalism. In what will become typically Chekhovian in style, he deals with the internal trials and tribulations of his characters, their 'inner conflict' becoming the theme of the play rather than any external plot. Similarly in his comedy *The Government Inspector* of 1836, Nikolai Vasilievich Gogol (1809–52) uses a prescient sense of 'realism'. The satire of bureaucracy in this play originally offended the Tsar's censors, but was finally played both before and after the revolution. The play has since taken on a certain universality, being applied as a condemnation of any stiflingly heavy-handed and inhumane society.

Another Russian playwright whose work had within it a sense of the 'real' was Alexander Nikoliavich Ostrovsky (1823–86). He wrote a number of pieces, but is best known for *The Storm* of 1859. This tragedy of human intolerance contains character studies and psychological insights ahead of its time; it can be seen as a clear precursor to the work of Chekhov and other writers of the 'naturalistic' style that was to follow.

Anton Chekhov (1860–1904)

Chekhov originally studied medicine in Moscow, graduating as a medical doctor in 1884. Whilst studying he wrote articles and short stories, and continued to do so throughout his life. He also turned to the writing of dramatic works, starting with short one-act comedies, but soon moving on to more serious 'comedies'. His early works, including the *The Seagull,* found little success – in fact, it was not until the newly formed Moscow Arts Theatre undertook a revival of *The Seagull* and Chekhov's work found a company that could do it justice, that he rightly found fame and flourished.

Chekhov died at the early age of forty-four whilst very much still at the height of his powers, leaving a legacy of too few brilliantly crafted jewels of dramatic perfection.

At The Moscow Arts Theatre Chekhov's mentors were impresario Vladimir Nemirovich-Danchenko (1859–1943), and director and actor Konstantin Stanislavsky, both of whom had co-founded the company. Danchenko was instrumental in persuading Chekhov to let his 'failed' play (*The Seagull*) be revived. (Danchenko also ran the drama course of the Moscow Philharmonic Society; amongst his pupils were Vsevolod Meyerhold (qv) and Olga Knipper – the future Mrs Chekhov.) Whilst Stanislavsky came to have an enormous influence on twentieth-century drama (*see* below), it was Chekhov's plays that gave him the forum within which he could mould and develop his ideas.

In his work Chekhov rebelled against the false realism of staged 'well-made plays', striving towards a new way to bring the essence of 'real life' on to the stage. He and Stanislavsky wanted real items on stage, not false painted cloths or props. His finely wrought plays also attempt to bring the idiosyncrasies and the trivia of real people's lives into focus. Chekhov's brilliant observational characterization therefore reached new heights in sympathetic delicacy and detail. The plays remain among the most poignantly beautiful and intensely moving, and Anton Chekhov is undoubtedly one of the first great dramatic artists of modern theatre.

PLAYS
EARLY ONE-ACT PLAYS:
The Bear (1888)

The Proposal (1889)

The Wedding (1890)

FULL-LENGTH PLAYS:
Ivanov (1887)

The Wood Demon (1889)

The Seagull (1896)

Uncle Vanya (1897–8)

The Three Sisters (1901)

The Cherry Orchard (1904)
In its first performance both Chekhov's wife, Olga Knipper, and Stanislavky took parts.

Konstantin Sergeivich Stanislavsky (1863–1938)

As described above, Stanislavsky was a co-founder of The Moscow Arts Theatre (1898), and a promoter of the work of Chekhov, amongst others; he was also an actor, director, teacher and an impresario. Born into a wealthy family, the early part of his career was spent as an actor for the Society for Art and Literature, an amateur group founded in 1888. His first directorial role was also for this group, and the piece was *The Fruits of Enlightenment* by the great Russian novelist Leo Tolstoy.

Stanislavsky resolved to pursue his work professionally, and joined up with Danchenko (qv) to do so when, in 1897, and after a straight eighteen hours of conversation, they decided to form a new company together. Called The Moscow Arts Theatre, the company was set up with a stringent set of rules. Actors were not to be pandered to in any way, and any signs of idolatry or idleness were punished. Rehearsals could last up to twelve hours a day, the texts had to be revered, and all the work was highly respected.

In all, the style of this new venture was very different from the rather lackadaisical and light-hearted methods that had characterized much of the established theatre that preceded it. Admittedly experiments in a new 'realism' had occurred before: the use of realistic scenic devices by the Meiningen company had greatly influenced Stanislavsky himself, but nothing quite so puritanically rigorous as was established here. For The Moscow Arts Theatre every attempt was made to bring the real thing on to the stage, and this included the emotions of the performers. Thus the working method of The Moscow Arts Theatre was such that *Tsar Fyodor* underwent sixty-nine rehearsals and five dress rehearsals; Norwegian furniture was imported for *Hedda Gabler*; and for *Julius Caesar* the entire cast had to live in togas for several days.

Moscow First Nights

The first play performed by The Moscow Arts Theatre was *Tsar Fyodor Ivanivich* by Alexei Tolstoy. Other notable successes were *Snow Maiden* by Ostrovsky, *The Power of Darkness* by Leo Tolstoy, and the only Shakespeare play performed at this time, *Julius Caesar*.

The Stanislavsky System

Until this period acting had been looked upon as more of a mechanical conceit than anything else – an actor used technical means to convey to the audience an idea of what the character they were portraying was undergoing. Obviously different actors did this in different ways, and there is no doubt that the greatest did so most successfully. However, along with the desire to reveal real things on stage as part of a new thrust towards greater realism, the actor was now encouraged to identify with the character they were

playing and make the emotion portrayed as real as possible. Stanislavky's partner in much of this, Danchenko, talked of a 'law of inner justification', in which the actor was expected to 'live' a part, not just express it. Stanislavsky's writings were enormously influential in changing the way actors thought, worked and trained. His works were published in the West as *An Actor Prepares* (1936), *Building a Character* (1949) and *Creating a Role* (1961).

The Stanislavsky system, as it is usually referred to, was created within the real working environment of The Moscow Arts Theatre, and can be found in the writings of Stanislavsky himself. In very basic form this involves an actor considering the following things: first he must understand the 'super-objective', or over-riding idea of the play, because it is from this that all general motivation derives. And whilst the actor gains a major perspective from understanding the super-objective, the 'subtext' is also imperative, since subtext for the performer involves the 'inner life' of the character. It is the concept of the subtext that can perhaps be said to distance the Stanislavskian actor most from his predecessors: no longer is it sufficient simply to learn one's lines, know where to move, and then convey the message of the character within the play: now, actors must connect with the emotional life of the character themselves, and in so doing, be true to the role.

The 'truth' of a role only comes from an understanding of where the character is in the story, and thus it becomes important for the actor to think through the total existence of the character, and not just what we see on stage as part of the play. This is, of course, what would later become described as the 'psychology' of the character. Stanislavsky talks of not only approaching the whole play in this manner, but any given scene or stage event. Thus the actor can have ever-changing 'personal objectives' throughout a piece, but these objectives are always placed in the context of the super-objective, thereby giving the actor a 'through-line of action' to follow as the play progresses.

In order for the actor to find the inner life or reality of a character, especially emotionally, he must explore his own emotions. In reacting or dealing with any given circumstances as dictated by the story of a play, the actor relates the needs of his or her character to experiences of his own. Thus the performer can react in a way that carries a great sense of 'truth', because he reacts to the problems of the character as they themselves would react – making it real by understanding it emotionally. Stanislavsky describes this as 'the conscious stimulation of the unconscious'. In the USA the acting concept of 'The Method' as famously expounded by Lee Strasburg in his Actors Theatre of the 1950s, and involving such artists as Marlon Brando amd James Dean, derived most of its ideas from the earlier of Stanislavsky's writings (*see* page 207).

With the production of *The Seagull* in 1898 The Moscow Arts Theatre really began to make its mark, especially following the earlier unsuccessful production where the symbolism within the play had been mostly misunderstood. Stanislavsky gave the play twenty-six rehearsals, and this attention to detail was exactly what a work from the pen of a genius for observation and emotional truth really needed.

Another element that derived from this period, as well as other areas within the theatre world at this time, was the concept of a central author, or 'auteur'. Danchenko believed in the need for a production to have a single underlying motivation or spirit – and that to obtain this an individual was required to drive forward this spirit. The concept of the director, who would exert an external guiding influence on the putting together of a production, had arrived.

As we have seen, the writings and teachings of Stanislavky and The Moscow Arts Theatre became universally acclaimed, and the influence they had on the theatre that followed cannot be understated. The writings and philosophies on the nature of theatre and the role of the performer in particular shaped much that is true and good in modern theatrical practice.

Maxim Gorky (1868–1936)

After Chekhov perhaps the greatest exponent of the new 'realism' in theatre, and a great promoter of the cause of the underdog, was Maxim Gorky. He was born Alexei Maximovich Peshkov, but adopted the *nom de plume* Gorky, which translates as 'the bitter', as much of his work came from a life of harsh, often brutal experience. He came from a poor background, he had to work for his living from the age of

eight, was orphaned in childhood, and attempted suicide at nineteen. He was self-educated, and spent his early life pulling himself up from the 'lower depths' that he would later depict so vividly. During the revolutionary period, from 1917 onwards, he spent many years in exile abroad, but returned to support the Soviet government in 1923. Whilst abroad he met and became a great friend and supporter of Lenin. In 1923, on returning to his country, Gorky played a major part in the formulation of the doctrine of Socialist realism. In 1934 he was appointed President of the Union of Soviet Writers.

Although his earliest work occurs before the great Russian revolution, as a commentator on social deprivation Gorky became a mainstay of the new Soviet theatre. His work strongly championed the ideals of the Communist cause. He first found fame with his short stories around 1898, and then with his novel *Foma Gordeyev* in 1899. In all, Gorky published several novels, short stories and autobiographical pieces. Of his novels, *Foma Gordeyev* and *The Mother* (1907) were later successfully adapted for the stage by others.

Gorky was so highly respected that his birthplace, Nizhni Novgorod, was renamed Gorky in his honour. At his funeral in 1936 Stalin himself was one of the pallbearers.

PLAYS

Scenes in the House of Bersemenov (1902)
First performed at The Moscow Arts Theatre after petitioning by Chekhov to have it mounted. This play has also been seen under the title *Smug Citizens*. Its forthright criticisms of the plight of the worker caused some political scandal, even in the highly edited version that was allowed to play.

The Lower Depths (1902)
Perhaps Gorky's greatest and most revived work. This play displays the hard life of the underdog of Moscow society. The deprived poor of the city are depicted with a puritanical lack of sentimentality, many of then resorting, at times, to a horrifically violent and criminal existence. The play takes place in a typical dosshouse of the period, and its vivid sense of cold reality made it one of the great highlights of The Moscow Art Theatre's season.

The Children of the Sun (1904)
A less successful work attacking the intelligentsia.

Summerfolk (1905)
A tragi-comedy with a domestic setting, again portraying the gulf between the people and the intelligentsia.

Barbarians (1906)
A tragedy set in the world of engineers striving to deal with the less educated citizens of an isolated Russian village.

Enemies (1906)
This piece dealt with strike breakers, and was originally banned by the censors; it was not produced until 1933.

Queer Folk (1910)
Also translated as *Country People* and *Old People*, a less successful story of love and adultery.

Vassa Zheleznova (1910/11)
A melodramatic piece, but one nevertheless that has been described as an excellent example of the beginnings of the Naturalist style. The depiction of the play's social setting is paramount, and in its heroine it also serves to represent the plight of the revolutionary worker. Gorky altered and refined the piece in 1936.

Dobro Pozhalovat (1910)
A Chekhovian comedy in one act.

Deti (1912)
A play about commerce and sycophancy.

Summerfolk, *a modern production in period dress, directed by Helena Kaut-Howson.*

The Zykovs (1914)
Another play with its central argument about commerce, in this case centred around a merchant.

The False Coin (1913)
A story involving the corruption of a poor jeweller.

The Old Man
Also known as *The Judge* (1919), another piece centring around the dissolution of a central character, whose life circumstances corrupt his very being.

Yegor Bulychov and Others (1932)
The first part of a trilogy, and a play that saw a return to great success for Gorky. This play, and its sequel, depict the decline of the old Russian bourgeoisie in vivid and subtly real manner; it takes place on and around the March Revolution of 1917.

Dostigayev and Others (1933)
The sequel to the aforementioned play.

Somov and Others (1934)
This work, the final part of the trilogy, was left unfinished at Gorky's death.

NATURALISM AND ITS PRACTITIONERS IN EUROPE

Henrick Ibsen (1828–1906)
Another great practitioner of the Naturalistic movement was Henrik Ibsen – although simply to label him thus does him an enormous injustice. Ibsen is one of the quintessential writers of this era, and sits alongside Chekhov as one of the great masters of the period. However, not only does Ibsen write some of the most imaginative and genre-defining plays of the period, but in doing so he also explores within his long life more than one genre. His work starts in epic poem mode, with plays such as *Peer Gynt* and *Brand*. It then moves into the new 'naturalistic' style of Chekhov and his followers, with pieces such as *A Doll's House* and *Hedda Gabler*. Later his work expands to include deeper psychological probing and overt symbolism, such as in *Ghosts* and *The Master Builder*. Finally he moves into the abstract and pure symbolism of his final work, *When we Dead Awaken*.

No other playwright spans such a breadth of experience and idiom, and combines this with such creativity and insight into human nature. Few in this period even dared to explore his themes, let alone his styles. His plays take as their central themes, and discuss in great depth, the role of women in society and women's rights, the ravages of sin, the despair of human solitude, and that of private and public failure. Perhaps not since Shakespeare had a writer understood the human dilemma so well, and exposed and explored it so well on stage.

Ibsen was born in Skien, a small coastal town in Norway. He learned his trade working as an assistant manager in theatres in Bergen and Oslo. His first works, for the theatre in Bergen, were unsuccessful, but from *The Feast at Solhaug* in 1855 he began to make a name for himself in his native country. The early works were retellings of folk stories and myths, and led naturally to other historical works: *The Pretenders* and *Emperor and Galilean*.

After 1869 Ibsen moved to a theatre in Christiania (now Oslo) where he wrote his first contemporary piece, *Love's Comedy*. In 1863 he went touring to Italy and Germany. For a time he settled in Rome and wrote his first great epic poem drama *Brand*, which gained him his first international reputation and earned him a state pension; the latter meant that his future writing could be without the worries of making a living. His last verse play, *Peer Gynt* (1867), furthered this reputation and had incidental music written for it by Edvard Grieg. Ibsen's next works, starting with *Pillars of Society*, suggest a desire to explore further into the human psyche, and for this he turned to Naturalism.

PLAYS
EARLY WORKS:
Catiline (1850)

Lady Inger of Østråt (1854)

The Feast at Solhaug (1855)

The Vikings at Helgeland (1857)

The Pretenders (1864)

Emperor and Galilean (1869–73)

Love's Comedy (1862)

EPIC POETICAL DRAMAS:
'Brand' (1864)
Peer Gynt (1867)
A huge, rambling poetic drama.

Educating Rita

It is Ibsen's *Brand* that exercises the mind of the heroine in Willy Russell's comedy *Educating Rita*. When asked to write an essay on how she would attempt to stage this complex play, her answer is 'On the radio'. Not such a bad idea, as the play does ask for, amongst other effects, an avalanche!

Pillars of Society (1877)
An intense play concerning the manner in which the leaders of society can use and abuse their power and position.

NATURALISTIC PIECES:
A Doll's House (1879)
It was reported that such was the outrage and scandal perpetrated by Nora's actions in *A Doll's House* that when she finally left the stage at the end of the play, closing the door behind her and her former life, the slamming of the door resounded across Europe!

Ghosts (1881)

An Enemy of the People (1882)

The Wild Duck (1884)

Rosmersholm (1886)

SYMBOLIC NATURALISM:
The Lady from the Sea (1888)

Pillars of Society, *a modern production in period dress, directed by Daniela Peleanu.*

Hedda Gabler (1890)

The Master Builder (1892)
The main character in this play is an architect, a man reaching the end of his life and career who cannot come to terms with not being the young man he once was; for example, his sexual prowess is but one of the aspects of his life that is not what it was. The character is said to have more than a passing connection to Ibsen himself, and the climax of the play, in which the character climbs and falls from the steeple of a church that he designed, is overtly loaded with imagery on many levels around these themes. Perhaps not surprisingly *The Master Builder*, with its less-than-subtle sexual allusions, is quoted as being the favourite play of Sigmund Freud.

ABSURDIST/SURREAL DRAMA:
When We Dead Awaken (1899)
This strange last play of Ibsen's sees him returning to a poetic style, but one in which the plot itself no longer makes much literal sense. As such it brilliantly connects the work of this grand master of theatre to much that is to come from others. Once again the central character, an elderly artist in search of answers to the big questions of life, can be clearly seen as autobiographical in nature.

August Strindberg (1849–1912)

Another great practitioner and champion of the naturalistic movement, at least in his earlier works, was August Strindberg. Indeed the preface to his play *Miss Julie* (*see* page 149) is an important treatise on this very idea. However, like Ibsen before him, Strindberg's work develops across a number of genres, as we shall see. Ibsen, Shaw and Sean O'Casey (qv) all thought very highly of Strindberg. Ibsen kept a picture of him on his desk, and said 'There is one who will be greater than I'[ii].

Johan August Strindberg was born in Stockholm. He had a tempestuous childhood, his father being declared bankrupt in 1853, and his mother dying in 1862; the following year his father remarried, taking his housekeeper as a bride. Strindberg studied at Upsala University to become a doctor, but having failed his first exam, left academia to work in the theatre, and wrote his first play. He then returned to Upsala University to study modern languages and political science. On returning to Stockholm he made a living as a journalist and a librarian; he wrote his first major stage work, *Master Olof*, in 1872. His novels and short stories found more success however, starting with *The Red Room* in 1879. He also wrote works of history and politics, but these were vehemently opposed – so much so that he left Sweden in 1883 and toured France, Switzerland, Germany and Denmark. His stage works finally found success with *Lucky Peter's Journey* in 1883.

In the later part of his life Strindberg continued to write with varying degrees of popular success – he founded his own experimental theatre in 1889 in Copenhagen, but it failed. He had three unsuccessful marriages, and teetered on the brink of mental crisis throughout the 1890s. Finally, on reaching some mental stability, he continued to write, and found The Intimate Theatre in Stockholm for whom he wrote his chamber plays; although this also failed to attract great success. He died of stomach cancer in 1912.

The breadth and creative depth of his work guaranteed him a status of great importance in the modern era. In style and content Strindberg's naturalistic work is often compared with that of Eugene O'Neill, especially for its profound expression of autobiographical material, much of it in a naturalistic style. Nevertheless, although Strindberg wrote around fifty plays, many of them, especially the early works, are now mostly forgotten.

PLAYS
EARLY WORKS:
A Birthday Gift (1869)
Strindberg's first play.

The Freethinker (1870)
Strindberg's first published play.

In Rome (1870)
Strindberg's first produced play.

The Outlaw (1871)
A piece that earned him a royal stipend.

Hermione (1871)

Master Olof (1872)
Considered by many to be Strindberg's first really major work, but it was not performed for nine years.

The Secret of the Guild (1880)

Lucky Peter's Journey (1882)
An early work, and one that has interesting similarities with Ibsen's *Peer Gynt* (1867), this piece was used as the basis for an opera of the same name in 1969 by Malcolm Williamson for Sadler's Wells in London.

Sir Bengt's Wife (1882)

Autumn-Splash (1884)

PLAYS OF NATURALISM:
Of these works Strindberg wrote:

> They are to be intimate in form; a simple theme treated with thoroughness; few characters; vast perspectives; freely imaginative, but built on observations, experiences, carefully studied; simple, but not too simple; no huge apparatus; no superfluous minor parts; none of those old machines or five-acters.[iii]

The Father (1887)
The first of Strindberg's great works, and one that saw him embark on his experiment with naturalism. Like much of his work, this piece received only a very low-key reception in Denmark, and failed initially in Sweden altogether. Its first real success came in a production in Germany, in 1888. This play can be seen as a modern version of *Agamemnon* (qv), and adheres to the strict Aristotelian unities of time and place (*see* page 26). It is also, however, a severe drama of modern, character-driven naturalism.

The People of Hemsö (1887)
A dramatization of Strindberg's novel of the same name.

Miss Julie (1888)
Another of Strindberg's great works, but again one that failed in its first outing, performed by Strindberg's own company in Copenhagen. Of this play Strindberg wrote:

> As a play Miss Julie has gone through its ordeal by fire and shown itself to be the kind of drama demanded by the impatient man of today: thorough but brief. [iv]

Strindberg on Film

Miss Julie has been filmed on no fewer than five occasions, starting in Sweden in 1912, Germany (1922), Argentina (1947), Sweden again (1951), and last in England in 1973. The 1951 version won the coveted Grand Prix at the Cannes Film Festival of that year.

The title character, Miss Julie, is a provocative one. Her relationship with the manservant Jean is an expression of the frustrations of sexuality and class. The play runs for an intense ninety minutes, without an interval.

The Creditors (1888)
Like its predecessor, this piece failed when first performed by Strindberg's own company in Denmark, but became considered one of his great works.

Pariah (1889)

The Stranger (1890)
A short piece of one act.

Simoom (1890)

The Keys of Heaven (1892)

The Bond (1892)
Originally written in German, this is a ruthless depiction of a disintegrating marriage, written as Strindberg himself was going through his own painful divorce. Said by Myron Matlaw in his excellent *Modern World Drama* to be the last of the purely naturalistic plays of Strindberg. [v]

Debit and Credit; The First Warning (1893)

Playing with Fire (1893)
A piece also originally written in German.

Facing Death; Motherlove (1893)

HISTORICAL PLAYS:
Strindberg wrote twenty-one historical pieces, although even they were not free of autobiographical allusions. They include:

Gustavus Vasa (1899)
A fine example of Strindberg's historical dramas, and perhaps his best.

The Folkung Saga (1899)

Erik XIV (1899)
Another example of the historical writings of Strindberg, and a play considered one of his best historical works.

Gustav Adolf (1900)

Carl XII; *Engelbrekt* (1901)

Kristina; *Gustav III* (1903)

The Nightingale in Wittenberg (1904)
This piece tells the story of the philosopher Martin Luther.

The Last Knight; *The Regent*; *The Earl of Bjälbo* (1909)

PLAYS OF SYMBOLISM:
To Damascus (1898–1904)
A great work of symbolism based on Strindberg's second marriage. A mystery play, and one of several exploring the subconscious and the inner life of the human psyche. Expressionistic in parts, surreal in others, the piece was written in three parts and over a period of six years.

Advent (1898)

There Are Crimes and Crimes (1899)

Easter (1900)

Kasper's Shrove Tuesday (1901)
A very slight pantomimic piece.

Midsummer; *The Dance of Death* (1901)

The Crown-Bride; *Swanwhite*; *A Dream Play* (1902)

THE CHAMBER PLAYS, 1907:
Storm Weather or *The Storm*

The Burned House; *or, After the Fire*

The Ghost Sonata
The most important of the Chamber works. Of this play Strindberg wrote:

As far as *The Ghost Sonata* is concerned, don't ask me what it is about. Discrétion, s'il vous plaît! One enters a world of intimations where one expresses oneself in half tones and with the soft pedal, since one is ashamed to be a human being.[vi]

If *Miss Julie* and *The Father* are archetypical works of naturalism, then this piece is probably the most seminal of Strindberg's abstract works. It deals expressionistically with themes of life and death, handing the audience odd and surreal characters, dialogue and events. Symbolism looms large, and obscurity sits alongside the more naturalistically mundane. It is considered one of the masterpieces of the twentieth century.

The Pelican

Also included in this group is the later play *The Black Glove* of 1909, and a fragment of a piece called *The Isle of the Dead*, published posthumously in 1918. As with many of his works, first performances of these pieces were not well received.

LATE PLAYS:
Through Deserts to Ancestral Lands (1903)
The biblical tale of Moses.

The Lamb and the Beast (1903)
Initially written in 1903 and concerning the emperors Caligula, Nero and Claudius.

Hellas (1903)
Also known as *Socrates*.

Abu Casem's Slippers (1908)
A fairytale comedy.

The Great Highway (1909)
Strindberg's last play.

George Bernard Shaw (1856–1950)

It was an Irishman, born in Dublin, who almost single-handedly prepared the English stage for the changes that those we have already discussed in this chapter came to represent. For one thing he became a great champion of the work of Henrik Ibsen.

Shaw arrived in London in 1876, became a socialist, and proved an inspiring platform speaker. Often known simply as G.B.S., he stirred the public imagination in many guises: showman, controversialist, satirist, critic, commentator, pundit, highbrow, comic and dramatist. His outspoken opinions also evoked much criticism and some jealousy – Wilde said of him: 'He hasn't an enemy in the world, and none of his friends like him.'[vii] But throughout his long life Shaw was a great benefactor to many. And as in life, so even in death, and in his will Shaw left monies to three organizations: The National Gallery of Ireland, The British Museum and The Royal Academy of Dramatic Art. He also wished to leave monies to the Esperanto alphabet, but after his death it was deemed that a person could not leave money to a thing, and the money remained divided with those above.

George Bernard Shaw (left).

Shavian Wit

Like Wilde, Shaw is famous for his epigrammatic wit and wisdom. Here are some examples taken from his plays:

'What use are cartridges in battle? I always carry chocolate instead.' *Arms and the Man*

'We have no more right to consume happiness without producing it than to consume wealth without producing it.' *Candida*

'The British soldier can stand up to anything except the British War Office.' *The Devil's Disciple*

'When a stupid man is doing something he is ashamed of, he always declares that it is his duty.' *Caesar and Cleopatra*

'The more things a man is ashamed of, the more respectable he is.' *Man and Superman*

'What really flatters a man is that you think him worth flattering.' *John Bull's Other Island*

'He knows nothing; and he thinks he knows everything. That points clearly to a political career.' *Major Barbara*

'All professions are conspiracies against laity.' *The Doctor's Dilemma*

'Assassination is the extreme form of censorship.' *The Shewing-up of Blanco Posnet*

'All great truths begin as blasphemies.' *Annajanska*

'I never resist temptation, because I have found that things that are bad for me do not tempt me.' *The Apple Cart*

'How can what an Englishman believes be heresy? It is a contradiction in terms.' *St Joan*

As a playwright Shaw rebelled in his own way from the traditions of the well-made play. He wanted to use the stage as a vehicle for social change, and he cited the work of Ibsen as doing the same thing. Shaw's opus starts with serious and socially committed plays, such that he published them collectively as 'plays unpleasant'. He then opened up to the use of comedy to tell his stories, his 'plays pleasant'. Once established, he became one of the most prolific of writers, penning over fifty works. Within this amazing output, and in his final years, his work becomes almost overtly expressionistic, and comparable with the works of Bertolt Brecht (qv). But whatever Shaw's aims in his dramatic pieces, and in his other writings as journalist, social commentator and critic, it is the sheer exuberance and joy in life that comes through and makes his work so enduring.

In 1925 Shaw was awarded the Nobel Prize for Literature, the citation reading in part: '... for his work which is marked by both idealism and humanity, its stimulating satire often infused with a singular poetic beauty.'[viii] Moreover, not only did Shaw win the Nobel Prize, he also won an Academy award, the only person ever to have won both. His Best Screenplay Oscar was for *Caesar and Cleopatra* (1938), which was based on his play of the same name.

D.H. Lawrence (qv) was another contemporary writer who also strived for social changes; but unlike Lawrence, Shaw has remained popular, possibly because of his ability to write satisfying stories and create characters that are full of life. It is not for nothing that one of his characters, Eliza Dolittle, and the story surrounding her, has become a mainstay of popular theatre, in particular through her incarnation in *My Fair Lady*, the musical based on Shaw's play *Pygmalion*. So prevailing was Shaw in the public mind that the adjective Shavian (using the Roman v) was invented to describe his own very particular style.

PLAYS
Widowers' Houses (1892)

Arms and the Man; *The Philanderer*; *Mrs Warren's Profession* (1894)

Candida; *The Man of Destiny* (1895)

Mrs Warren's Profession *recently revived in London's West End.*

You Never Can Tell (1896)

The Devil's Disciple (1897)

Caesar and Cleopatra (1898)

Captain Brassbound's Conversion (1899)

The Admirable Bashville; or, Constancy Unrewarded (1901)

Man and Superman (1903)

John Bull's Other Island; *How He Lied to her Husband* (1904)

161

Major Barbara; Passion, Poison, and Petrifaction; or, The Fatal Gazogene (1905)

The Doctor's Dilemma (1906)

Getting Married (1908)

The Shewing-Up of Blanco Posnet; The Fascinating Foundling; Press Cuttings; The Glimpse of Reality (1909)

Misalliance; The Dark Lady of the Sonnets (1910)

Fanny's First Play (1911)

Androcles and the Lion; Overruled (1912)

Pygmalion; Great Catherine; The Music-Cure (1913)

O'Flaherty, V.C. (1915)

The Inca; or, Perusalem; Augustus does his Bit (1916)

Annajanska, The Bolshevik Empress; Heartbreak House (1917)

Back to Methuselah (1920)

Jitta's Atonement (1922)

Saint Joan (1923)

The Apple Cart (1929)

Too True to be Good (1931)

On the Rocks (1933)

Village Wooing; The Simpleton of the Unexpected Isles; The Six of Calais (1934)

The Millionairess (1935)

Cymbeline Refinished (1937)

Geneva (1938)

In Good King Charles's Golden Days (1939)

Buoyant Billions (1948)

Far Fetched Fables (1949)

Why She Would Not (unfinished) (1950)

There are other writers of this period whose work can be considered similar to the precepts that underlie much of Shaw's work: naturalistic, often highly socialist, and thus forever putting the case for the working man and woman. These include D.H. Lawrence, John Galsworthy and Harley Granville-Barker.

D.H. Lawrence (1885–1930)
The son of a Nottinghamshire collier, and best known as a novelist, Lawrence's best stage work includes *A Collier's Friday Night* (1906), *The Daughter-in-Law* (1912) and *The Widowing of Mrs Holroyd* (1914). This was work of great humanity that explored, with often brutal realism, the plight of the working class. The pieces were set in the stark landscape of the nineteenth-century mining community of the north of England that Lawrence knew so well.

John Galsworthy (1867–1933)
Best known today as the author of the novel sequence *The Forsythe Saga*, Galsworthy's plays concerned themselves with the social conscience of the society of his period. His best pieces are *The Silver Box* (1906), *Strife* (1909) and *Justice* (1910).

Harley Granville-Barker (1877–1946)
Barker wrote, acted and directed. His influence was a great one in the theatre of his time and in England where he worked. He was a great champion of the work of Shaw, and appeared as a performer chosen by Shaw in many of his premiers. His simple and energetic poetic stagings of the works of Shakespeare were innovative and highly acclaimed. Barker's own work includes *The Voysey Inheritance* (1905), *Waste* (1907) and *The Madras House* (1910). Barker was also a strong believer in the need for a subsidized British theatre, writing in his book *A National Theatre: Scheme and Estimates* (1908) of how he thought it could be achieved.

THE REPERTORY SYSTEM

In Britain the demise of the actor-manager was an inevitable corollary of the end of the old ways that the new wave of naturalism represented. Actor managers had toured the provinces with their companies, staging a stock repertoire of plays, often with themselves as the 'star turn'. With the new desire to realize a greater realism on stage came the need for a greater depth of rehearsal, and in place of the manager a 'director' was required. The director, like the orchestra's conductor, would oversee rehearsals, and it was their job to find the necessary depth of meaning in a play, and communicate this to the actors in rehearsal so that they could, in turn, eventually persuade the audience of its validity. Touring or receiving house theatres began to see an alternative way of working, by engaging a resident company, which could then strive to attain a consistent and high standard of work, as well as a coherent policy of work. This would often involve new writing, and plays relevant to the community in which the theatre was based.

The first English repertory company was founded in 1907 in The Gaiety Theatre in Manchester by Annie Horniman (1860–1937), who saw the need for subsidized local theatres, and was particularly interested in presenting the work of Shaw and Ibsen. Horniman had previously founded The Abbey Theatre in 1904 in Dublin. The initial idea of a repertory system was that a number of plays would be presented 'in rep' – the acting company would learn two or three plays, and then present them on different evenings of the same week. This system was quickly replaced by short runs of plays, where one was played during the evenings whilst another was prepared in rehearsals during the day. Certainly to preserve interest and make a good income a company could no longer look to long runs of the same play, but instead had to follow a policy of short, regular programmes of work, each play running for just two to three weeks. Thus the repertory system of the three-week rehearsal period came into existence.

By the beginning of World War I there were repertory companies in Birmingham, Bristol, Glasgow and Liverpool. The repertory system in Britain continues to this day, although financial pressures and lack of subsidy from central or local government has seen the demise of many. Today there are perhaps fifty such companies in operation throughout the country.

The main provider of money for all theatres in England is the Arts Council of Great Britain. In general, theatre in the Western world cannot exist without financial assistance: if the real cost of mounting plays was shouldered by seat prices alone, then it would mean that only the very wealthy could go to the theatre. Just as in an earlier period companies were sponsored by kings and earls, so in a more egalitarian society, theatre companies have had to look to government as a provider.

After World War II it was decided that an organization was needed to bring music and theatre to an impoverished Britain, and so the Council for the Encouragement of Music and the Arts (C.E.M.A.) was set up in 1940. This evolved into the Arts Council in 1946, with a royal charter and a remit 'to develop a greater knowledge, understanding, and practice of the Fine Arts, to increase their accessibility to the public, and to improve their standard of execution.' It is this body that provided annual subsidies to all the non-profit-making repertory theatres throughout the country, including the National Theatre and the Royal Shakespeare Company (qqv), as well as all the music-based organizations and other Fine Art institutions. In recent years many theatres have had a vital chance to rebuild or develop with money from the National Lottery.

CONCLUSION

Naturalism can be seen to have had a profound effect on modern theatre: from its origins to the present day it has affected the way that we act, dress, and generally stage productions. However, it does not stand alone as the only movement to have affected our thinking. It can be seen that eventually even some of the great adherents of naturalism, as discussed above, could not stay within the confines of the naturalistic movement – both Ibsen and Strindberg, for example, wrote works that I have described as being symbolic or surreal. There seemed to be a need in their later work to pull away from this type of theatre. One collective term for this – an opposite of naturalism, one could say – is expressionism, and it is with this that the next chapter deals.

9 MODERN THEATRE: EXPRESSIONISM AND BEYOND

In realism ... actors sit about on chairs and talk about the weather,
but in expressionism they stand on chairs and shout about the world.
J.L. STYAN [i]

You are seated amongst friends in The Nouveau Théâtre in central Paris: you have come to see a new play called Ubu Roi by that controversial man of the theatre, Alfred Jarry. You know from reading Le Figaro that a scandalous play is probably going to be acted out before you. You do not want depraved theatricals in your city, and you have come to make sure that nothing indecent is being presented. You know that the author and the producer Firmin Gémier also have many friends in the audience, as they have already cheered Jarry who, in white face make-up and wearing a clown-like baggy costume, has recited a boring and mostly pointless monologue by way of introduction. Now Gémier, who is also playing the part of Ubu, has appeared on stage. He looks fiercely towards the audience and then screams the first word of the text: 'Merde'.

Immediately the place erupts, with cheers and laughter from one side of the audience, and jeers and catcalls from the other. You, too, are on you feet, shouting that you do not expect or wish for such language at the theatre. The tension builds, the shouting reaches a crescendo, several things are thrown in anger. In all, the uproar takes a full fifteen minutes to die down. Several people have walked out. Back in your seat, your hackles well up, you await the next events in what looks likely to be far from a quiet night at the theatre.

OPPOSITE PAGE: **The Resistible Rise of Arturo Ui,** *a modern production of Brecht's play, directed by Di Trevis.*

INTRODUCTION

Expressionism can be defined as a reaction to and against the naturalistic movement, and as such it clearly abhors the naturalistic obsession with a strict observation of the real and the literal. It looks for a greater truth, and strives to reveal the inner feelings of mankind, alongside external realities. The term serves, therefore, to cover a huge variety of different approaches, any of which can choose to distort an object, an emotion or just a setting in the service of expressionism. It often deals with stereotypes rather than characters, and it often takes an overtly political stance. The movement can thus be allied to surrealism, epic drama, and the theatres of the absurd and the cruel that follow it (*see* page 189).

Expressionism is 'one of the basic modes of perceiving and representing the world around us'[ii]. Whilst this is certainly true, we must also see that its advent came at a time when not only did the domination of 'naturalism' need challenging, but also when it had other means at hand to express itself anyway. The advent of cinema (and later television) must have had the same effect on the theatre world as photography did on portraiture: thus, just as photography made painting a perfect likeness of something a pointless exercise, so the same thing occurred with the moving picture, the screen being quite capable of showing 'real life' as well as could be done on the stage. Thus the stage was literally set for a new manner in which to portray things.

165

THE FORERUNNERS
OF EXPRESSIONISM

Much of the history of theatre in the twentieth century is about finding a means to make greater use of the fact that the audience and the actors occupy the same real space – that, unlike cinema, a vigorous, visceral and extremely potent experience is more possible. Expressionism was a vital part of this exploration, and is a very real solution. And like many such historical moments, a number of notable forerunners led the way, such as, for example, Georg Büchner.

Georg Büchner (1813–37)

Büchner really belongs in the last chapter, as his dates alone would suggest, but his work, mostly fragmentary and unfinished, seems to suggest a later period. Indeed, his work only really grew to respectability in the twentieth century. Of his plays, the unclear and incomplete play *Woyzeck* has alone been produced and adapted over and over again, its themes and apparent style lending itself to endless reinterpretation.

Büchner was born in the Grand Duchy of Hesse-Darmstadt, in what is now Germany. The son of a doctor, he studied zoology and anatomy in Strasburg. Later, Büchner attended the University of Giessen, and as a student, was co-founder of the radical Society of Human Rights with Pastor Weidig. Such were his political activities that eventually, in 1835, he was forced to flee Germany to avoid arrest. He returned to Strasburg with the manuscript of *Danton's Death*, which he had written as a political work over a very intense five weeks. Büchner finished his studies and was appointed lecturer in natural sciences, later rising to the position of Doctor of Philosophy at Zurich University.

In early 1837 Büchner died of typhus at the age of only twenty-four. His work went mostly unproduced until 1904, when a brilliant performance of *Danton's Death* saw him hailed as a great undiscovered talent. His work was then taken up in his native country, with a particularly notable production in Berlin in 1927. This was followed by productions around the world, with particularly noteworthy performances in New York in 1938, and London in 1971. Alban Berg also based his opera of 1925, entitled *Wozzeck*, on Buchner's fecund fragment.

The hold that Büchner's tantalizing work has had on the practitioners of the twentieth century is one that seems to prefigure the expressionist manner and the political ideologies of the era, particularly that of Bertolt Brecht (*see page 177*) – although his fascination with the experiences of real working-class people has also seen him hailed as a precursor of naturalism. Certainly his work can be seen in both political and naturalistic lights, as it deals, as do so many plays of modern times, with the centralization of the lone, insignificant and isolated victim, and the dehumanization of the individual by the state.

Büchner wrote that 'individuals are only so much surf on the wave, greatness is the merest accident, the strength of genius is a puppet play – a child's struggle against an iron law.' He also said that drama should offer 'people of flesh and blood'. Of *Danton's Death* he comments that the play should 'place us in the life of an era, give us characters instead of characterization, and forms instead of descriptions'[iii]. In 1834 Büchner co-authored a political treatise called *The Hessian Courier*, described as one of the most brilliant works of its kind to be written in German. Büchner was also author of an unfinished novel called *Lenz*.

PLAYS

Danton's Tod (1835)
Commonly translated as *Danton's Death*. First produced in 1902, this is Büchner's only full-length tragedy. The play shows the historical character of Danton from the period of the French revolution, in a surprisingly humanistic light. Danton is shown as an embittered, disillusioned older man, who regrets the blood that has been spilled as a result of his political ambitions. Of this play Büchner commented that it should not be false storytelling, but 'come as close to history as is possible'[iv].

Lena and Leonce (1836)
A romantic comedy, and a work written for a competition, but returned unread because it missed the submission date. This play deals in fairytale format with the romance of the title characters, but also comments on the social and moral conventions of the day.

Woyzeck (1837)

The archetype for all man against society polemics. Woyzeck, the central character, is driven to a moment of sublime madness in which he kills his partner. But is he really as guilty as it would first seem? The subject of deprivational medical experiments, of the cruel depersonalization of army strictures, and of the fierce hatred for the outcast by all who meet him, Woyzeck believes he is rather relieving the one he loves from the abyss of failure that awaits all mankind. He is possibly the first real anti-hero in modern dramatic literature.

Pietro Aretino

Büchner wrote this play only for it to be destroyed after his death by his lover, who considered it an 'inappropriate' work. We will never know what this may have meant!

One of the tragic aspects of Büchner's short life is the absence of the works he did not survive long enough to write. We can only wonder what may have been.

While Büchner was not writing in a genre that had any specific connection with those around him, Frank Wedekind, however, is clearly one of the greatest of the earliest exponents of a movement that was gathering momentum, and which we can label 'expressionism'.

Frank Wedekind (1864–1918)

Perhaps alongside the later works of Strindberg, Wedekind defines the most extreme of surrealists in dramatic art, with his highly involved use of abstraction and symbolism in the creation of human drama. His work helps lead to a fuller understanding of the term 'expressionism' (although it is still more apt for those that follow him) as used in theatrical practice, and his works also see the most straightforward depiction on stage to date of the power and importance of sexuality in human nature.

Wedekind was born in Germany, although of a naturalized American/German father and a Hungarian mother. A great fan of American democracy, Wedekind's father actually gave him the Christian names Benjamin Franklin!

The family moved to Switzerland where Wedekind grew up, and his sister became a famous opera singer.

Although originally studying law in Munich, Wedekind abandoned this, and started his professional life instead as a singer, before turning to acting, and then his chosen career of writer. In fact before writing the plays that were to make him famous, Wedekind worked for a time as a journalist.

Wedekind became a great friend of Gerhart Hauptmann (1862–1946), the leading German playwright of his day, who espoused the naturalistic philosophy of the period, and is known especially for his play *The Weavers* (1892), which won him the Nobel Prize for Literature in 1912. Wedekind became estranged from his family when he decided to give up law for the stage, and this sad story was used by Hauptmann as the basis for his play *The Feast of Reconciliation* of 1890. Wedekind, however, was not so interested in the naturalistic cause, and got his own back by satirizing Hauptmann in his own play *Children and Madmen* (1891), portraying him as a poet spying on the incumbents of a girls' boarding school! Hauptmann later described the so-called 'Lulu plays' as 'pure excreta'!

Wedekind's writing has, on occasion, the same fragmented bold style that characterized the writing of Georg Büchner (qv), and prefigures the expressionist works of Ernst Toller (qv), Georg Kaiser and others (*see* page 176). His subject matter and championing of the underdog caused great offence and was much criticized. He was imprisoned briefly for ridiculing the Kaiser in one of his plays, and the explicit sexual nature of many of them led to Wedekind's work being banned, although it continued nevertheless to be highly thought of amongst certain sections of the intelligentsia. Wedekind was seen as a fervent social and political critic of his time. His chosen heroes (often prostitutes and criminals) were used by him to promote his view of bourgeois society, and he saw the common attitude to sex and sexuality as a perfect symbol of the hypocrisy he saw there.

Wedekind wrote a number of pieces, but three of them in particular seem to have had the greatest long-term influence: *Spring Awakening* of 1891, about adolescent sexual yearning and expression, and *Erdgweist* (*Earthspirit*) of 1895 and its sequel *Pandora's Box* of 1904 (*see* below).

PLAYS

Der Schnellmaler, oder Kunst und Mammon (1889)
An early work, and not as highly thought of as those that followed.

Fritz Schwigerling (1889)
Another early work, a farce. Revised and completed as *Der Liebestrank* in 1892.

Spring Awakening (1891)
The play that above all others holds Wedekind's name at the forefront of the modern movement of this period. The piece tells of the adolescent yearnings of a group of young people about to graduate from Education into Life. It is subtitled 'a tragedy of childhood', and deals with the emotions of a strict upbringing, the pressures of important exams, and awakening sexual feelings. As such, the play is sexually explicit in places, full of highly charged emotional episodes, and highly critical of the repressed status quo. Such was the notoriety and general condemnation of this play that it was not seen in Britain until 1965 in a production by the Royal Court. Within its fragmented structure Wedekind weaves the stories of a number of young people and their teachers. Notable amongst them is Melchior Gabor, who eventually blows out his brains under the strain of failing his exams, and his friend Moritz Stiefel, who alongside similar worries also has deep-seated sexual frustrations. Melchior famously appears towards the end of the play as a ghost carrying his own head.

Children and Madmen (1891)
Set in a girl's boarding school, this play again deals with sexual repression.

Earth Spirit (1895)
The first of the so-called 'Lulu plays', which takes as its central character a woman who embodies all that men desire in women – but naturally this is different for each man that Lulu meets. The central character's apparently indifferent, even animalistic, nature allows her ultimately to betray all the men that want her, finally killing the one man she wanted but could not have. Once again a sexually explicit and highly controversial play, Wedekind

came back to the central character in *Pandora's Box* (*see* below). The role of Lulu was first played by Wedekind's wife, Mathilde Newes.

The Court Singer (1897)
Also known as *The Tenor*, this is a three-scene, one-act play that Wedekind described as 'the collision between a brutal intelligence and a blind passion'. Art and love are debated as a famous singer waits to go on stage and is visited by the important people in his life.

Die Kaiserin von Neufundland (1897)
A pantomime, and a very minor piece.

The Marquis of Keith (1900)
A five-act play dealing with the hypocrisy of the middle classes. Satirical in style, its eponymous hero fools and beguiles his way through life as a modern-day Casanova and fraudster.

King Nicolo, or Such is Life (1902)
A semi-autobiographical, five-act play in which a fairytale setting is used to tell a tragi-comic story of sexuality and love. With its fantastical setting, Wedekind makes much use of symbolism throughout the play, and as such it is an important one in his canon.

Pandora's Box (1904)
The second of the two 'Lulu' plays, the other being *Earth Spirit*, and one that continues to explore the nature of desire, a woman's hold over men, her own needs, and the ways that society comments on and controls the way people behave and think. In this play Lulu moves to London, takes a lesbian lover, turns to prostitution to support them both, and finally seals her doom and that of her lover by taking as a customer a certain Jack the Ripper. Both plays have been combined to make a total work, for example in Peter Barnes' adaptation of 1970 for Nottingham Playhouse and entitled *Lulu*. They were also used by Alban Berg for his powerful opera *Lulu* in 1937.

Hidalla, or Karl Hetman, the Giant Midget (1904)
Similar to *The Maquis of Keith* (qv) in tone and setting, this five-act play was very popular in its day,

considered autobiographical, and deals symbolically with the doings of the deformed central protagonist who founds a society to breed perfect people. His idealistic ideas are adopted, and then distorted; he is himself denied a place in the new order, is imprisoned and finally commits suicide.

Death and Devil (1905)

This short play, of three scenes, is sometimes considered part of the 'Lulu' sequence, in that its themes are very similar, and it involves some of the characters from the earlier plays. It is set in a brothel and deals with Wedekind's perennial themes of prostitution, sin, sexuality and death! This was arguably Wedekind's last great play, and none of those that followed have the same stature.

Music (1908)

A morality story in four scenes.

The Censor (1908)

Largely an attack on the role of the censor in the arts, and life generally.

Rabbi Esra (1808)

A dramatization of a short story.

Oaha (1908)

A four-act comedy.

Der Stein der Weisen (1909)

Castle Witterstein (1910)

Another play set in the world of prostitution and low life generally.

Franziska (1912)

A 'modern mystery play' of Faustian theme and content, but with a female protagonist.

Simson, oder Scham und Eifersucht (1913)

A reworking of the biblical story of Samson and Delilah.

Bismarck (1916)

A patriotic historical drama.

Überfürchtenichts (1916)

Herakles (1917)

A retelling of the Heracles myth.

Arthur Schnitzler (1862–1931)

Born in Austria, Schnitzler was a playwright whose work dealt with similar themes to those of Wedekind – sexuality and death among them. His best known and most revived and adapted play is *Reigen*, which translates as *Hands Around* but is better known as *La Ronde*. This play is a series of two-handed scenes, in all of which a sexual act has just taken place, or is about to do so. In each new scene one of the protagonists from the previous scene is found with their next partner. It thus implicitly follows the progress of a sexually transmitted disease, ending with the final protagonist meeting up with the partner from the first scene – hence the sense of circularity of its title.

Popular before World War II, with the exception of *La Ronde*, Schnitzler's work has now mostly faded from view.

Other Playwrights

Lesser playwrights in a similar mould to Wedekind, writing in either naturalistic or expressionistic manner, and the plays they are best remembered for, include the following:

Arno Holz (1863–1929), German, *Die Familie Selike* (1890). An early exponent of naturalism.

Max Dreyer (1862–1946), German, *Der Probekandidat* (*On Probation*) (1899); *Die Siebzehnjährigen* (1904).

Otto Ernst (1862–1926), German, *Flaschmann als Erzieher* (*Flashman as Teacher*) (1899); *Jugend von Heute* (1900).

Ludwig Thoma (1867–1921), German, *Moral* (*Morality*) (1908)

Karel Capec (1890–1938), Czech, *Ze zivota hmyzu* (*From the Life of Insects*) (1920); *RUR* (1920). The latter contains the first known account of the humanoid robot in fiction.

Elmer Rice (1892–1967). Born Elmer Reizenstein, US playwright; *The Adding Machine* (1923), *Street Scene* (1929).

EARLY THEORISTS
OF MODERN THEATRE

Two theatre practitioners of the late nineteenth and early twentieth centuries came to have a telling and lasting effect on the way the stage was thought of in terms of dramatic performance and its setting. Although neither held great sway in their own time, their theories and writings influenced many who came after. Working independently, although finally coming to greatly admire each other's work, these two individuals prescribed and inspired much that was to follow. They are Edward Gordon Craig of England, and Adolph Appia of Switzerland.

Craig and Appia came from very different Western cultures and backgrounds, and it is notable that as they in part define the beginnings of modern Western drama, two things in particular become clear from their work: that modern drama was to become increasingly diverse, and also truly international. From this point on, whilst cultural differences naturally continue, modern means of communication and intellectual creative interest are such that dramatic public events no longer fail to influence each other. Whilst the extreme diversity of performance styles and doctrines becomes a hallmark of modern Western drama, so also does the interconnectedness of all things. Craig and Appia finally met in 1914, when Craig wrote to Appia:

> To me there is far more vivid life and drama in one of your great studies for scenes than in anything else known to me in our theatre of Europe.

Edward Gordon Craig (1872–1966)

The son of two great British theatrical giants, actress and producer Ellen Terry (qv) and theatre designer Edwin Godwin, Craig started acting when still a child, and later became a stage designer and theatre theorist. Amongst his early designs were *The Vikings* (1903) for his mother, Otway's *Venice Preserv'd* in Berlin (1905), Ibsen's *Rosmersholm* (1906) in Flo-

rence for Eleanore Duse, which he also directed, and *Hamlet* for The Moscow Arts Theatre (qv) in 1912.

In 1912 Craig started the periodical *The Mask* whilst living in Florence, and its contents had a great influence on the theatre of the day. It brought together and explored many of the controversial new ideas for theatre that abounded at this time. Craig himself was a great theorist, more so in many ways than a practitioner. His books, *The Art of the Theatre* of 1905, and *On the Art of the Theatre* of 1911, were highly influential: in them he talks of the need to 'obtain a unity in the Art of the Theatre'[v] and to 'create a place which harmonizes with the thoughts of the poet'[vi].

Craig believed in a use of stage décor that was non-naturalistic, expounding the theory that the stage setting should be at one with the artistic expression of a play, with its themes and ideas – that to merely express the setting of a play in naturalistic terms was to miss the greater opportunity that theatre had to offer. Thus Craig's designs, and drawing for designs (there were more of these, as few of his designs were actually realized, or indeed were really very practical) show abstract platforms and screens amongst and in front of which actors often look dwarfed. His profound sense and use of proportion was a key factor in how he saw the stage.

More important than how Craig's designs looked was the totality of the expression he expected on stage. The setting was not to be considered a separate part of the stage action, but integral to it, even as another character, or even the main character – in fact he even went as far as to say that perhaps actors were not necessary, that an *Über-marionette* or grand puppet could take their place and be a more divine image. However, he later claimed that this idea had been much misinterpreted, and that he had never meant to imply the exclusion of real performers. Nevertheless, alongside Appia's very similar concepts, Craig's ideas meant that the era when scenery was literally and notionally merely a backcloth to the action was clearly over. Craig wrote, 'I let my scenes grow out of not merely the play, but from broad sweeps of thought which the play has conjured up in me.'

Adolphe Appia (1862–1928)

Adolphe François Appia was born in Switzerland, and took much of his inspiration from the work of

Wagner: as such he saw theatre linked inexplicably in both form and substance with music.

He rebelled against the two-dimensional scenery of the period, promoting three-dimensional plasticity as a key to all stage expression. Like Craig, very few of his great sketches were actually realized, but his ideas caught the imagination of many.

As well as promoting the idea of a plasticity of stage design, Appia also saw the need for all the scenic arts to work in harmony: he thought the stage space and setting should be a solid three-dimensional expression, with the correct proportion regarding the actor. Actors should be considered as much a part of the setting as in their own right. Costume should not be overtly realistic, and neither should the lighting, which he considered must remain fluid and responsive to the drama of the moment.

Appia wrote his ideas down in several books: *La Mise en Scène du Drame Wagnérien* (Paris, 1895), which described the staging of the operas of Richard Wagner; *Die Musik und die Inszenierung* (Munich, 1899) made the case for the link between music and theatre; and *L'oeuvre d'Art Vivant* (Geneva, 1921) describes theatre as a 'Work of Living Art'. These works proved enormously influential in the West, and stage design and the use of stages owe much to his pioneering ideas.

Joseph Svoboda (b. 1920)

Svoboda was a stage designer in a similar mould to Craig and Appia. Born in what is now the Czech Republic, he first worked in his own country for the National Theatre and The Theatre Behind the Gate, both in Prague, and then hit the international stage at the World Theatre Season in London, and the Edinburgh Festival in 1966. He continued his work in Britain for the National Theatre at the Old Vic, designing productions of *The Three Sisters* and Ostrovosky's *The Storm*. Svoboda's work continued the ideas of Appia and Craig, with abstract and fluid sets, using multi-level stage areas and revolves. He also advanced the use of stage lighting as an integrated part of the dramatic setting, and made innovative use of projection, and intense low voltage in on-stage lighting.

More importantly, Svoboda continued the idea that stage settings were no longer to be restricted to

Lighting equipment named after Joseph Svoboda – the ADB Svoboda unit in action.

Wagner

Wagner, in his opera house at Beyreuth, staged his works with increasing innovation – for example, he was amongst the first practitioners to require the lighting on the audience to be dimmed in performance.

a narrow set of values, and especially not by rules governed by a sense of naturalism; indeed, Svoboda led the way for even such eminent Czech designers as Jarolslav Malina. Malina's later reaction against Svoboda's work saw him acclaimed in his early work for designs which involved drawing away from the large scale decorative and providing a more 'mundane' reality, albeit through the use of metaphor and mixed (often usual) materials.

Alfred Jarry (1873–1907)

Jarry was born in Laval (now Mayenne) in France, the son of a merchant. He was yet another key player in the movement away from naturalism and towards a new language of theatre. As a poet and playwright his work had a profound effect on both

A set design by Jarolslav Malina.

the surrealist movement and on the theatre of the early part of the century and thereafter. Jarry's work attacked conventions – in life as well as in literature. His key work is *Ubu Roi* (*King Ubu*), of which he wrote an early version at the age of fifteen in 1888 entitled *Les Polonais*. Unfortunately this early version, co-written with brothers Henri and Charles Morin, did not survive. *Ubu Roi* so scandalized its first audience on 10 December 1896, that a riot famously broke out in the theatre.

Ubu Roi has at its centre the character Ubu Père (Father Ubu), a grotesque, vulgar giant of a man, whose total lack of respect for all, and whose use of expletives and total disregard for the sensibilities of any around him, caused in its day a shockwave of major proportions in the theatre and society generally. The play, a parody of *Oedipus Rex* (qv), not only scandalized the audience of the day but was also revolutionary in the way that it

demanded the use of marionettes, placards, masks and the generally crude theatre styles of pantomime and burlesque. Jarry clearly opposed the conventions of the theatre of naturalism that was growing up around him.

Jarry saw Father Ubu as the essential tool with which to attack the conventions he deplored. Nearly all his works, a dozen or so, include the character of Ubu. Jarry, perpetually obsessed with this character as he was, came to live his life in similar style, and in the latter part of his life explored an amoral existence, living in squalid surroundings, drinking alcohol and ether. Such abuse slowly killed him, and he died at the age of thirty-four.

Jarry consolidated much of his thinking into the study of 'Pataphysics', defined as 'the science of imaginary solutions – the laws that govern exceptions'. Followers of this philosophy later included Vian, Ionesco and André Breton (qqv).

PLAYS

Onésime ou les Tribulations de Priou (c.1890)
An early version of *Ubu Cocu*, see below.

Les Minutes de Sable Mémoial (1894)
An early play of abstract symbolism, but also featuring Father Ubu. A work published to be read, rather than performed.

César Antéchrist (1895)
An early work – a 'symbolist play', and one that once again has Ubu as a central character, but once again was published in book form rather than staged.

Ubu Roi (1896)
Jarry's major work (*see* main text above). One of the three main Ubu works.

Les Paralipomènes d'Ubu (1896)

Ubu Cocu (*Ubu Cuckolded*) (1897/8)
Considered another of the three main Ubu works.

L'Amour en Visites (1898)

Par la Taille (c.1898)
A piece of 'comic and morals in prose and verse', also designed to be enacted by a puppet company.

Ubu Enchaîné (*Ubu Enchained*) (1899)
The third of the so-called Ubu trilogy – the three main works of Alfred Jarry.

Ubu sur la Butte (1901)
A two-act version of *Ubu Roi* with songs, and primarily meant for a marionette company.

Pantagruel (1903)
Jarry wrote the libretto for this opera version of the Rabelais story.

Le Moutardier du Pape (1907)
A three-act 'operette bouffe'.

Jarry is often described as one of the fathers of the avant-garde, yet his influence only really came to flower with the surrealist movement and its adherents and heirs, some ten or twenty years after his death. One of his great followers, and another major architect of modern theatre, was another Frenchman – Antonin Artaud.

Antonin Artaud (1896–1948)

Artaud was a quite remarkable man, a passionate zealot, of whom it can perhaps truly be said that his life was his work. Martin Esslin writes in his book on Artaud that: 'Any attempt to present or understand Artaud must ... take his life as its starting point'.[vii] Throughout his life, and ever after, Artaud has been viewed as many things, from raving lunatic to inspired genius. His legacy is a body of writing that still has the power to evoke extreme reactions, inspire intense theatrical experiences, and continue to challenge the way we mount theatrical productions even today.

Artaud was born in Marseilles of a well-to-do family. However, his childhood, like his later life, was not a happy one, and he grew to become an intense and detached individual, obsessive and in many ways unbalanced. As he grew into adulthood he began to formulate ideas concerning the things he held most important in life. Initially these were religion (originally he had had intentions to be a priest), poetry and, after exposure to the theatre world, drama.

Artaud spent his early career as a writer of articles, a poet, and as an actor. He also spent long periods in a variety of sanatoriums, and under the care of various psychoanalysts. He made some startling appearances as an actor in a number of early films: as Marat in *Napoleon* and Savonarola in *Lucrecia Borgia*, both directed by Abel Gance, and as Massieu in Dreyer's *Joan of Arc*. Whilst still at school Artaud founded and contributed to a literary review, but in 1915 he destroyed all his early works in a fit of depression. At the same time he also underwent his first internment in a mental hospital. He was only nineteen.

In the 1920s Artaud became a member of the avant-garde surrealist movement, and close friends with its founder André Breton. One of Artaud's most famous works is the screenplay for the seminal surrealist film *The Seashell and the Clergyman*, made in 1927. Prior to this, however, in 1926, he was expelled from the movement itself after refusing to join the Communist party.

Artaud's theatrical life began as an actor, a career he later came to deplore, not least of all because his passionate beliefs included a refusal to rehearse anything, believing that the repetition of an action only depleted its power. It is obvious that he was never an easy person to work with or alongside; indeed his attitudes and extreme ideas lead to his expulsion from a number of companies before he co-founded The Theatre of Alfred Jarry with Raymond Aron and Roger Vitrac. Jarry (qv) and his alter-ego Ubu were among others that inspired Artaud; alongside was the vital theatre and ceremony that he saw during visits to Japan (1922), Bali (1931) and Mexico (1936); he was also influenced by exposure to work from such varied cultures as the Jewish, the Iranian and the Hindi.

Artaud wrote a number of important documents (as well as poems, plays and journalism), many of them 'manifestos' explaining his philosophies. Among them are the several *Manifestos of the Alfred Jarry Theatre* (1926–30), the two *Manifestos of the Theatre of Cruelty* (1932 and 1933) and *The Theatre and its Double* (1934).

The *Theatre of Cruelty* put forward a total concept of theatre based on the notion of cruelty, or the idea that an audience should be so changed and challenged by a performance that it could be an almost literally visceral experience. He wrote: 'The theatre is the state, the place, the point where we can get hold of man's anatomy and through it heal and dominate life.'[viii] He also talks of the text as a great enemy to freedom on stage: he wanted to put humanity back in contact with its more primitive self, through uncluttered physical action. And in *The Theatre and its Double*, Artaud even goes as far as to compare theatre to the plague, saying that it should have the same overwhelming, life-changing effect as an all-encompassing outbreak of disease, like the plague.

In 1933, Artaud directed and acted in a notable and notorious production of a stage adaptation of Shelley's *The Cenci*, concerning one of the most controversial subjects of any play – incest. For this piece Artaud insisted on moving his actors around stage by a system of planned abstract moves and numerical groupings. The play was not a great success and closed after only seventeen performances, and this was the final straw in Artaud's struggle to work: he fell into a life-long battle with depression, and was soon once again interred in a mental hospital.

Diagnosed incurably insane in 1938, Artaud was nevertheless finally released in 1945 and wrote a new poetic philosophy of life called *Artaud le Momo*, in which he found a new spiritual answer to many issues. He then wrote a book on Vincent Van Gogh (*Van Gogh, the Man Suicided by Society*) with whom he could closely identify, and in which he attacked the world of psychiatric medicine.

Artaud appeared on stage once more to lecture in 1947, and also in the same year made several radio broadcasts for a French radio station under the mantle of the 'Theatre of Cruelty'. These consisted of improvised screaming and chanting, set alongside poems and other torrents of words. Artaud was something of a cult figure by now, especially amongst the French intelligentsia – notably André Gide, playwright Arthur Adamov, Jean-Paul Sartre, Pablo Picasso and Albert Camus. Artaud died in 1948.

Many claim to have felt the powerful influence of Artaud's life and writings; dramatists amongst them include, in Russia, Ysevold Meyerhold and Vladimir Mayakovsky; in Germany, Erwin Piscator; in England, Peter Brook and Peter Weiss; and in Spain, Fernando Arrabel. In many ways it was the extremes of Artaud's own work that allowed the possibility of so much other work from others, work that challenged the norm, and used a violent or strange stage language to communicate ideas. The many and varied theatre practitioners often grouped under the banner of the Theatre of the Absurd (qv) gained most from exploring and developing his ideas.

Luigi Pirandello (1867–1936)

Pirandello was the leading playwright of his generation in Italy. In fact he was born in Sicily, and was better known in his own country for his novels, poems and short stories. He also worked as a critic. Internationally however, especially in America, Pirandello became better known for his surreal plays, particularly *Sei Personaggi in Cerca d'Autore* written in 1921 and known in English as *Six Characters in Search of an Author*. Like many of his works, this piece explores the relationship between the individual and the group, and asks the fundamental question: 'Who and what are we?' His work contains wondrous flights of fantasy and great humour, within which he nevertheless also undertakes a profound search for the essence of the human predicament.

Pirandello was initially drawn to the Italian group of playwrights known as the Futurists – however, he went much further than this group, and his work has proved much longer lasting. In 1925 he opened his own theatre in Rome called Teatro D'Arte; he

Futurism

The Futurist movement was, ironically, rather short-lived. It was founded in 1909, and was over by 1925, and propounded a nihilistic, anarchic theatre. Its main protagonist was Filippo Tommaso Marinetti.

This Time it will be Different, *a modern production of Pirandello's play* Come prima, meglio di prima, *directed by Andrew Visnevsky.*

also undertook many successful tours to Europe and South America. In 1934 he was awarded the Nobel Prize for Literature.

Pirandello wrote more than fifty plays. His best known are listed below.

PLAYS

FIRST WORKS:
The Vice (La Morsa); *Sicilian Limes (Lumie di sicilia)* (1910)
Early one-act plays.

The Doctor's Duty (Il dovere del medico) (1912)
An early one-act play.

If not Thus (Se non Cosi) (1915)
His first full-length play.

EARLY COMEDIES:
Pirandello wrote some of these early comedies remarkably quickly: *Just think, Giacomino!* took him only three days.

Just Think, Giacomino! (Pensaci, Giacomino!); *Liolà* (1916)

Cap and Bells (Il berretto a sonagli) (1917)

Right you Are, If You Think you Are
(Cosi è – se vi pare) (1917)
More recently translated, and presented in London's West End, as *Absolutely (Perhaps).*

The Jar (La Giara); *The Pleasure of Honesty*
(Il piacere dell'onestà) (1917)

The Rules of the Game (Il giuoco delle parti); *Grafting*
(L'innesto); *The License (La Patente)* (1918)

Man, Beast, and Virtue (L'uomo, la bestia
e la virtù); *All for the Best (Tutto per Bene)* (1919)

As well as before, Better than before
(Come prima, meglio di prima) (1920)
Also translated as *This time it will be Different.*

175

Cece; Mrs Morli, One and Two (La Signora Morlì) (1920)

PLAYS IN A SICILIAN DIALECT:
A Vilanza (1917)

Cappiddazzu paga tuttu (1922)
Co-written with Nino Martoglio (1870–1921)

L'Atia del Continente (1915)
Really Martoglio's play, with Priandello assisting.

MAJOR WORKS:
Six Characters in Search of an Author (1921)
Pirandello's most famous work, and part of a trilogy. During a rehearsal the characters in a play (not the actors playing them) rebel and demand control over their own destinies.

Henry IV (Enrico IV) (1922)
Named after the Shakespearean play, but actually involving a modern character who believes himself to be Henry IV. Once again Pirandello uses characters to question the notion of self.

The Man with the Flower (L'uomo dal fiore in bocca) (1923)
The best known of Pirandello's many one-act plays.

Each in his own Way (Ciasuno a suo modo) (1924)
One of the other parts of the *Six Characters* trilogy.

Tonight we Improvise (Questa sera si recita a Soggetto) (1929)
The third part of the *Six Characters* trilogy.

Lazarus (Lazzaro) (1929)

As you Desire Me (Come tu mi voui) (1930)

When One is Somebody (Quando si è qualcuno) (1933)

The Fable of the Exchanged Son (La favola del figlio cambiato) (1934)

One does not Know How (Non si sa come); Dream – but perhaps not (Sogno – ma forse no) (1935)

The Mountain Giants (I giganti della montagna) (1937)

EXPRESSIONISM IN GERMANY

In Germany traditions were also being questioned. Whilst a forerunner of the naturalist movement can be discerned in the play *Maria Magdelena* written in 1844 by Friedrich Hebbel (1813–63), it is the instigation of the Freie Bühne, a theatre club founded in 1899 by Otto Brahms, that really sees the beginnings of this and other modern movements in Germany. Max Reinhardt then carried on a tradition of experimental theatre when he took over from Brahms in 1905. Among the great playwrights to have come from this part of the world are Gerhart Hauptmann (1862–1946), Otto Ernst and Ludwig Thoma. Of these, the former can be said to have had by far the greatest influence: but others were to follow (*see* below).

Ernst Toller (1893–1939)

At times seemingly a lone voice in the expressionist movement, German playwright Ernst Toller is perhaps best known for his play *The Machine Wreckers* of 1922, which tells of the Luddite movement in England. His work passionately exposed anti-war feeling alongside a plea for the rights of the individual in an increasingly materialistic society. After seeing action at the front, he served out the rest of World War I imprisoned as a pacifist. He was imprisoned again in 1919 for participating in the Communist uprising in Munich, and started to write whilst incarcerated. He was released in 1924. After his exile from Germany in 1933, Toller's work continued to delve deeper and deeper into the darker parts of mankind, and the beginning of the world war against the country of his birth under Adolph Hitler only served to confirm his darkest fears. Toller commited suicide in 1939, leaving behind him a number of great works.

In the introduction to his collected work of 1937, *Seven Plays*, Toller said of his plays that they 'bear witness to human suffering, and to fine yet vain struggles to vanquish this suffering.'

PLAYS
Transfiguration (Die Wandlung) (1919)
Toller's first play, written while he was under arrest

as a pacifist; it tells of the transformation of a man who experiences the horrors of war.

Masses and Man (*Masse-Mensch*) (1921)
Perhaps Toller's best work.

The Machine Wreckers (*Die maschinenstürmer*) (1922)
Toller expresses the concept of organized social rebellion; in telling the story of the Luddite movement in England, he prefigures the coming of the trade union movement.

Hinkemann also known as *Brockenbrow* (1922)

Der entfesselte Wotan (1923)
A parody of the early years of Hitler, disguised in this play as a barber with pretensions to become a national hero.

Hoppla! (*Hoppla, wir leben!*) (1927)

Bougeois bleibt Bourgeois (1929)
Co-written with Walter Hasenclever.

Draw the Fires (*Feuer aus den Kesseln*) (1930)
A naturalistic telling of the World War I naval mutiny that occurred in Kiel in 1916/17.

The Blind Goddess (*Die blinde Göttin*) (1932)
A play that deals with the unfairness of a legal system too obsessed with its own processes. Based on a true story of two lovers whose fight to clear their name of a murder charge nevertheless ruins their life.

Miracle in America (*Wunder in Amerika*) (1934)
A biographical play written with Hermann Kesten, telling the story of the founder of the Christian Science movement, Mary Baker Eddy.

No More Peace! (1937)
Written with English poet W.H. Auden.

Pastor Hall (1939)
Toller's last play, which tells the story of a clergyman keeping his faith through the intolerable times of Nazi Germany.

Bertolt Brecht (1898–1956)

Eugen Bertolt Friedrich Brecht was a remarkable man of the theatre. He lived through very troubled times, and his work and writings can be said to have had the greatest effect on the modern theatre that followed him. He was born in Augsberg, Germany, and as often seems to be the case in this history, studied an alternative trade first, in this case medicine (in Munich), before turning to the writing of plays. A staunch pacifist, Brecht nevertheless served in World War I as a hospital orderly.

Initially a critic, he soon began to write plays such as *Baal* and *In the Jungle of Cities*. His first produced play was *Trommeln in der Nacht*, which won the Kleist prize in 1922. In 1924 Brecht settled in Berlin and worked as an assistant to the great Max Reinhardt at the Deutsches Theatre. Brecht's early plays were clear exercises in expressionism, but he soon began to develop his own distinct style in marked contrast. His later work was a reaction against the ideas of symbolism, expressionism and naturalism. Brecht sought to find a theatrical language that allowed the drama to make a clear and powerful point (often political). He wanted clarity, more or less void of emotion, a theatre of ideas that engaged the minds of the audience in preference to their hearts.

In his early writings Brecht described his work as being 'epic theatre', and he wrote a comparative description between the dramatic and the epic (*see* box page 178).

Brecht's famous theory, '*verfrembungseffekt*' – usually translated as 'alienation technique' – concerned itself with the need to create these distinctions. Events on stage must not lull the audience into a comfortable acceptance of the story being

---

W.H. Auden

W.H. Auden lived for a while in Berlin under the Weimar Republic, hence his collaboration here. Later he also collaborated with Isherwood on two plays; written in a rather archaic poetic style, they are *The Dog Beneath the Skin* (1935) and *The Ascent of F6* (1936).

DRAMATIC THEATRE	EPIC THEATRE
PLOT	*NARRATIVE*
implicates the spectator in a stage situation	turns the spectator into an observer, but
wears down his capacity for action	arouses his capacity for action
provides him with sensations	forces him to take decisions
experience	picture of the world
the spectator is involved in something	he is made to face something
suggestion	argument
instinctive feelings are preserved	brought to a point of recognition
the spectator is in the thick of it,	the spectator stands outside
shares the experience	studies
the human being is taken for granted	the human being is the object of the inquiry
he is unalterable	he is alterable and able to alter
eyes on the finish	eyes on the course
one scene makes another	each scene for itself
growth	montage
linear development	in curves
evolutionary determinism	jumps
man is a fixed point	man as a process
thought determines being	social being determines thought
feeling	reason

told, and every now and then an event or device should be used to startle them back into a real and intellectual engagement with the ideas of the play. He used captions, simple masks, actors coming out of character, songs and addresses to the audience, to provide such moments of 'alienation'. His first success came in 1928 with *Die Dreigroschenoper* (*The Threepenny Opera*), an adaptation of Gay's *Beggar's Opera* (qv), the first of a number of pieces with music provided by Kurt Weill.

Brecht's work became more and more influenced by the political writings of Karl Marx, and in 1933, under the shadow of an ever-powerful Adolf Hitler, Brecht left Germany to settle in the USA. He returned to Germany in 1947, at the invitation of the East German government to found his own company: the Berliner Ensemble. With this company Brecht then had the opportunity to explore his ideas and wrote extensively about them, which he did until his death in 1956.

Brecht wrote many politically extreme plays – indeed, they were often highly communist in nature – and his best work was certainly socialist in temperament. But his writing was more than this: rather, it was humane, vivid, lyrical, and sufficiently rounded as to be open to many modern interpretations. His plays, and the ideas that he promoted, live on in much of the drama of our times.

PLAYS

EARLY WORKS:
Five early comedies, all written in 1919.

Die Kleinbürgerhochzeit
Usually translated as *The Wedding*

Der Bettler oder der tote Hund
(*The Beggars and the Dead Dog*)

Man Equals Man, *a modern production of Brecht's play, directed by Richard H. Williams.*

Er treibt einen Teufel aus (*He Drives Out a Devil*)

Der Fischzug (*The Catch*)

Lux in Tenebris

MATURE WORKS:
Baal (1922)
A dark and sombre play much influenced by Brecht's war experiences.

Trommeln in der Nacht (*Drums in the Night*) (1922)

In the Jungle of Cities (1923)

Leben Eduards des Zweiten von England
(*The Life of Edward II*) (1924)
Freely adapted from Marlowe's play and written with Feuchtwanger.

Mann ist Mann (*Man Equals Man*) (1926)

Mahagonny (1930
Later adapted by Kurt Weill into an opera and retitled
Aufstieg und Fall der Stadt Mahagonny (*The Rise and Fall
of the City of Mahagonny*).

Die Dreigroschenoper (*The Threepenny Opera*) (1928)

Happy End (1929)
Also with music by Kurt Weill.

Der Jasager (1930)
Also with music by Kurt Weill.

Die Heilige Johanna der Schlachthöfe (*c.*1930)

SHORT PLAYS:
Die Massnahme (*c.*1930)

Die Ausnahame und die Regel (*c.*1930)

WRITTEN IN EXILE:
Das Leben des Galilei (*The Life of Galileo*) (1937–39)

Der gute Mensch von Sezuan
(*The Good Woman of Setzuan*) (1938–41)

Mutter Courage und ihre Kinder
(*Mother Courage and her Children*) (1941)
Based on a story by Grimmelshausen.

Der Kaukäsische Kreidekreis

ADAPTATIONS:
Brecht's adaptations were always very thorough,
such that they really stand as plays in their own right;
they include:

Pauken und Trompeten (*Trumpets and Drums*)
Adapted from Farquhar's *The Recruiting Officer.*

Koriolan
Adapted from Shakespeare's *Coriolanus.*

LATER WORKS:
Der aufhaltsame Aufstieg des Arturo Ui
(*The Resistible Rise of Arturo Ui*)

Bertolt Brecht.

Señora Carrara's Rifles

Simone Machard

The Exception and the Rule

Schweik in the Second World War

The Caucasian Chalk Circle (1948)

Herr Puntila und sein Knecht
(*Mr Puntila and his man Matti*) (1948)

Saint Joan of the Stockyards

Turandot; or, The Whitewashers' Congress
Brecht's last play, left unfinished at his death.

The following (*see* opposite) is an extract from
Mother Courage and her Children. The opening of this
play tells a great deal about the way Brecht intro-
duces his characters and themes.

I

SPRING, 1624. IN DALARNA, THE SWEDISH COMMANDER OXENSTIERNA IS RECRUITING FOR THE CAMPAIGN IN POLAND. THE CANTEEN WOMAN ANNA FIERLING, COMMONLY KNOWN AS MOTHER COURAGE, LOSES A SON

Highway outside a Town

A sergeant and a recruiting officer stand shivering

THE RECRUITING OFFICER: How the hell can you line up a company in a place like this? You know what I keep thinking about, Sergeant? Suicide. I'm supposed to knock four platoons together by the twelfth – four platoons the Chief's asking for! And they're so friendly round here, I'm scared to go to sleep at night. Suppose I do get my hands on some character and squint at him so I don't notice he's pigeon-chested and has varicose veins. I get him drunk and relaxed, he signs on the dotted line. I pay for the drinks, he steps outside for a minute, I have a hunch I should follow him to the door, and am I right? Away he's gone like a louse from a scratch. You can't take a man's word any more, Sergeant. There's no loyalty left in the world, no trust, no faith, no sense of honour. I'm losing my confidence in mankind, Sergeant.

THE SERGEANT: What they could do with round here is a good war. What else can you expect with peace running wild all over the place? You know what the trouble with peace is? No organization. And when do you get organization? In a war. Peace is one big waste of equipment. Anything goes, no one gives a damn. See they way they eat? Cheese on pumpernickel, bacon on cheese? Disgusting! How many horses have they got in this town? How many young men? Nobody knows! They haven't bothered to count 'em! That's peace for you! I've been in places where they haven't had a war for seventy years and you know what? The people haven't even been given names! They don't know who they are! It takes a war to fix that. In a war, everyone registers, everyone's name's on a list. Their shoes are stacked, their corn's in the bag, you count it all up – cattle, men, *Et cetera* – and you take it away! That's the story: no organization, no war!

THE RECRUITING OFFICER: It's God's truth, you know.

THE SERGEANT: Of course, a war's like any good deal: hard to get going. But when it does get moving, it's a winner, and they're all scared of peace, like a dice-player who daren't stop – 'cause when peace comes they have to pay up. Of course, *until* it get going, they're just as scared of war, it's such a novelty!

THE RECRUITING OFFICER: Hey, look, here's a canteen wagon. Two women and a couple of young lads. Stop the old lady, Sergeant. And if there's nothing doing this time, you won't catch me freezing my arse in the April wind a minute longer.

A harmonica is heard. A canteen wagon rolls on, draw by two young fellows. Mother Courage is sitting on it with her dumb daughter, Kattrin.

MOTHER COURAGE: A good day to you, Sergeant!

THE SERGEANT, *barring the way*: Good day to *you*! Who d'you think *you* are?

MOTHER COURAGE: Tradespeople.

She sings:

> Here's Mother Courage and her wagon!
> Hey, Captain, let them come and buy!
> Beer by the keg! Wine by the flagon!
> Let your men drink before they die!
> Sabres and swords are hard to swallow:
> First you must give them beer to drink.
> Then they can face what is to follow –
> But let 'em swim before they sink!
>
>> Christians, awake! The winter's gone!
>> The snows depart, the dead sleep on.
>> And though you may not long survive
>> Get out of bed and look alive!
>
> Your men will march till they are dead, sir.
> But cannot fight unless they eat.
> The blood they spill for you is red, sir.
> What fires that blood is my red meat.
> For meat and soup and jam and jelly
> In this old cart of mine are found:
> So fill the hole up in your belly
> Before you fill one underground.
>
>> Christians, awake! The winter's gone!
>> The snows depart, the dead sleep on.
>> And though you may not long survive
>> Get out of bed and look alive!

THE SERGEANT: Halt! Where are you from, riff-raff?

EILIF: Second Finnish Regiment!

THE SERGEANT: Where are your papers?

MOTHER COURAGE: Papers?

SWISS CHEESE: But this is Mother Courage!

THE SERGEANT: Never heard of her. Where'd she get a name like that?

MOTHER COURAGE: They call me Mother Courage 'cause I was afraid I'd be ruined. So I drove through the bombardment of Riga like a madwoman, with fifty loaves of bread in my cart. They were going mouldy, I couldn't please myself.

THE SERGEANT: No funny business! Where are your papers?

MOTHER COURAGE *rummages amoung papers in a tin box and clambers down from her wagon*: Here, Sergeant! Here's a Bible – I got it in Altötting to wrap my cucumbers in. Here's a map of Moravia – God knows if I'll ever get there – the birds can have it if I don't. And here's a document saying my horse hasn't got foot and mouth disease – pity he died on us, he costs fifteen gilders, thank God I didn't pay it. Is that enough paper?

THE SERGEANT: Are you pulling my leg? Well, you've got another guess coming. You need a licence and you know it.

MOTHER COURAGE: Show a little respect for a lady and don't go telling these grown children of mine I'm pulling anything of yours. What would I want with you? My licence in the Second Protestant Regiment is an honest face. If *you* wouldn't know how to read it, that's not my fault, I want no rubber stamp on it anyhow.

THE RECRUITING OFFICER: Sergeant, we have a case of insubordination on our hands. Do you know what we need in the army? Discipline!

MOTHER COURAGE: I was going to say sausages.

CONCLUSION

Dramatic art makes a long and varied journey through the twentieth century, splitting into many forms and formats. Expressionism has proved, alongside naturalism, to be one of the most enduring, as I hope this chapter has demonstrated. Together the influence of both of these persuasive styles pervades much that follows.

10 CONTEMPORARY THEATRE: ABSURDISM AND THE AMERICAN TRADITION

I can take any empty space and call it a bare stage. A man walks across this space whilst someone else is watching him, and this is all that is needed for an act of theatre to be engaged.
PETER BROOK [i]

The year is 1955, and you have just witnessed the first night of a play new to England, translated from the original French by its Irish author. You are out on the cold London streets feeling somewhat dazed. A light rain is falling as you stand in the shelter, waiting for your bus home. The curtain has just come down on a play the like of which you have never seen before. For the best part of two hours, two tramps have been discussing whether to leave or stay on a lonely road in the middle of nowhere – for two hours you have been watching a play about waiting. *Waiting – what for, or who for, was never entirely clear. Very little else happened, and yet you feel something quite profound has just passed before your eyes – something that is going to affect the way you view not only all the theatre you now see, but possibly life itself. You are not sure why you think this, but nevertheless you are certain something important has just occurred. The rain continues to fall, it is getting colder, and you continue to wait.*

INTRODUCTION

The twentieth century, as we started to see in the last chapter, saw an enormous diversification of human

activity. Political, social, sexual and artistic barriers were questioned, and many broken down. Science moved forward at an ever-increasing pace, and the arts reacted accordingly. People were moved and changed by revolt, division, reunification and (so-called) progress. At the extreme there were wars, genocide and famine. At a less dramatic but no less changing level there was the ever-expanding gap between the 'haves' and the 'have-nots' across the planet. Some individuals knew a greater mobility, and faster and faster means of expression and communication, through both an explosion of mass media and new-found personal freedom. With every few steps forward, however, there were also, of course, many backward ones, history, as always, never unfolding in straight lines.

To describe the theatre of this period is to explore as many differing styles as we have already touched upon in this whole book. Luckily, however, as these styles are nearer to our experience than all the earlier ones, they also communicate more clearly to us.

Twentieth-Century Staging

Alongside the enormous expansion of theatrical genres and concepts that took place during this busy century came the need and desire to experiment also with stage shapes. Thus by the end of the century, every possible shape had seemingly been explored, and more importantly was available for consideration when staging a new production (*see* the illustration, page 186, for the main staging shapes).

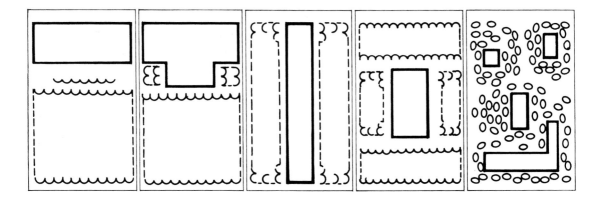

Modern staging: proscenium, apron, traverse, in-the-round.

The most extreme staging, and in many ways one deliberately at the furthest remove from the proscenium arch, is in-the-round staging. This form displays a clear link to the broad sweeping stages of Greek classical theatre (*see* page 10) and was used first in Russia by director Nikolai Pavlovich Okhlopkov (1900–67), whose company experimented with many different stage formats in the 1930s. Okhlopkov was artistic director of the Realistic Theatre Company, and among other plays premièred Gorky's play *Mother* (*see* page 153).

In the USA, the increasing interest in drama as a subject of study at university also saw a growing interest in theatre-in-the-round, especially in the 1940s. The first Department of Drama was established at Yale in 1925, and the University of Washington in Seattle became the first campus to include a purpose-built theatre in-the-round when it opened its Penthouse Theatre in 1940. Off Broadway, the Circle-in-the-Square theatre (1951) continued this trend, as did the Arena Stage in Washington D.C. built in 1961, and which opened, appropriately enough, with Brecht's play *The Caucasian Chalk Circle*.

The first UK university drama department was in Bristol in 1946. This was followed by several others, including Manchester in 1962, whose first chair was Stephen Joseph. Stephen Joseph (1921–67) had studied at the State University in Iowa before returning to his native England in 1955 as an actor and director. He believed that theatre in-the-round, which allowed the audience to feel amongst and very close to the action, gave an intimacy and an immediacy to dramatic art that no other space could afford. It is a notion that, partly due to his championing, is still widely held today.

Joseph did much of his early work in Scarborough, where he established an in-the-round space within the public library in 1955. A purpose-built theatre-in-the-round was created in the town in 1976, and was then rebuilt under the leadership of Alan Ayckbourn (*see* page 226) in 1995 and called The Stephen Joseph Theatre. (Manchester University has its own much smaller Stephen Joseph Studio in honour of the great man.)

In 1962 Joseph founded a company in Stoke-on-Trent in The Victoria Theatre, adapting it into another in-the-round space. On becoming Professor of Drama at Manchester in the same year he continued to promote his belief in the power of this particular staging shape, and his influence was sufficient that when the Manchester Royal Exchange Theatre opened in 1976, it, too, was in this style.

Nowadays many modern theatre buildings are built with wide arena spaces (like the National Theatre's Olivier Theatre) or designed to have the flexibility to adapt to many styles.

THE WELL-CRAFTED PLAY

Before we explore this period of great change and innovation further it is important to remember that the majority of theatres would actually have thrived

A modern theatre – The flexible Jerwood Vanbrugh Theatre, RADA.

on a diet fed by those playwrights who wrote with less of a burning ambition to change the world. Their work, when it was true and intelligently written, also met with success, and has also survived the test of time. Indeed, whenever one is examining the innovators who radically changed our thinking about, and use of, the stage, it is important to remember that, whilst the likes of Strindberg and Ibsen were striving towards a greater understanding of the human experience, others where simply continuing to produce well-crafted works. These pieces, often dismissed as being purely 'light entertainment', also had a role in everyday life, and usually found a larger audience.

The greatest exponents of these well-made plays also found real and vivid ways in which to touch their audience, and arguably provoked as much understanding of human nature and desire for change as their more radical counterparts. It must also be understood that their work could never be wholly uninfluenced by the preceding stylistic changes that had been made to dramatic staging, and that they owe their dues every bit as much to the naturalistic, or expressionistic movements as those writers who more obviously revelled in them.

Arthur Wing Pinero (*see* page 139) is an early exponent of the 'well made play', and amongst his successors are J.B. Priestley, Noel Coward and Terence Rattigan. They all stand as fine examples of the best in the trade of amusing, beguiling and entertaining an audience, whilst often also striving to inform and move them.

J.B. Priestley (1894–1984)

Novelist, critic and author, Priestley's reputation also rests on his finely crafted comedies of middle-class manners. His best work includes *Time and the*

Conways (1937), *When We Were Married* (1938), *An Inspector Calls* (1945) and *The Linden Tree* (1947). Indeed *An Inspector Calls* has recently come to the end of a successful ten-year run, in an imaginative production directed by Stephen Daldry, first at The Royal National Theatre and then in London's West End.

Noel Coward (1899–1973)

Hugely successful in his heyday, Coward saw his work suffer an eclipse as it came to be considered stuffy and old-fashioned. Luckily he lived long enough to see revivals reconfirm him as a superb master of stagecraft, comedy, style and wit. Coward was first known as a performer, and then author of light entertainment musical vehicles such as *Post-Mortem* (1931), *To-Night at 8.30* (1935/6) and *Set to Music* (1938). He had made his name in Britain and the USA, however, with a more serious piece, *The Vortex*, in 1924; although other attempts at serious work, such as *Sirocco* – written in 1921 but not performed until 1927 – were less successful. Coward also wrote a number of pieces of a highly patriotic flavour, a response to the times in which he lived, the best of which include *Cavalcade* (1931) and *This Happy Breed* (1942). He also wrote, directed and appeared in the patriotic, but nevertheless gritty, naval war film *In Which We Serve* in 1942.

Nowadays Coward is best known for his light-hearted stylish comedies such as *Hay Fever* (1924), *Blithe Spirit* (1941) and *Present Laughter* (1942), which portray a life-style that was evaporating fast even as he wrote. However, the best of these pieces – and Coward wrote over sixty plays – are more than just a light entertainment: somehow the truthfulness of character and situation often comes through to realize a piece that is not without human insight and true emotion. Recent revivals of *Design for Living* (1933) and *Private Lives* (1930) have stood the test of radically modern settings and interpretations.

Blithe Spirit, *a recent production for Derby Playhouse, directed by Karen Louise Hebden.*

Coward was equally famous for his music and songs, from shows such as *Bitter-Sweet* (1929) and *Sail Away* (1961), and his work spanned five decades. He was knighted for services to the theatre in 1970.

Terence Rattigan (1911–77)

Rattigan wrote a number of very successful works for the stage, although he then drifted out of favour – not unlike Noel Coward. He did not help his cause by fighting the new 'young things' of the fifties and sixties, describing himself as the playwright who wrote for 'Aunt Edna', the middle-of-the-road punter who wished for nothing more than a safe, unchallenging, yet entertaining night out in the theatre. Nevertheless many of Rattigan's well-crafted plays are still sufficiently beloved and rich in detail to be revived time and again, and like the best of Coward's, speak true testament to the dilemmas and tragedies of human nature. Rattigan first came to notice with his light comedy *French Without Tears* in 1936. Other plays followed, including notably *Love in Idleness* (1941), *The Winslow Boy* (1946) a more serious piece about a popular scandal of the day, *The Browning Version* (1948), *The Deep Blue Sea* (1952), *Separate Tables* (1954) and *Ross* (1960), the latter about the true identity of Lawrence of Arabia. His last work was *Cause Célèbre* in 1976.

Two of Rattigan's plays ran for over 1,000 performances in the West End of London, the first time this had ever been achieved. They were *French Without Tears* and *While the Sun Shines*, the latter in 1943.

Similarly popular playwrights of the early and mid-part of the twentieth century include T.S. Eliot and Christopher Fry.

T.S. Eliot (1888–1965)

Better known for his poetry, Eliot also penned a number of successful plays, the best known of which is *Murder in the Cathedral* of 1935 – a play which in telling the story of Thomas Becket's murder, interestingly and clearly displays links with the traditions of both medieval and Greek forms. Later works, many also containing a highly poetic dramatic style, include *The Family Reunion* (1939), *The Cocktail Party* (1949), *The Confidential Clerk* (1953) and *The Elder Statesman* (1958). Eliot won the Nobel Prize for Literature in 1948. Eliot's collection of poems *Old Possum's Book of Practical Cats* (1939) was the basis for Andrew Lloyd Webber's highly successful musical *Cats* of 1981 (*see* Musicals on page 204).

Christopher Fry (b. 1907)

A writer and director, Fry's poetic dramas included the comedy *A Phoenix Too Frequent* of 1946, *The Lady's Not for Burning* of 1948, the tragi-comedy *Venus Observed* of 1950, and *The Dark is Light Enough* of 1954. His work became considered generally outmoded by the new wave of dramatists led by John Osbourne (qv).

DRAMA BECOMES ABSURD

In 1962, theatre scholar Martin Esslin wrote a book that, for many, helped define a way of thinking about many of the writers of the twentieth century. A number of separate events and personalities in the world of art, and theatre in particular, were usefully categorized in the, now famous, book called *The Theatre of the Absurd*;[ii] indeed the title itself became a means of summarizing much of the great work of twentieth-century drama. Esslin saw linking themes and ideals between many of those theatre practitioners who came after those who had promoted the wave of naturalism that had swept over Europe and the theatre world generally. He uses the word 'absurd', with its dictionary definition of 'contrary to reason', 'irrational', 'incongruous'.

The 'theatre of the absurd', or 'absurdism', is a good term if we feel the need to pull together many disparate souls whose very independent work varied enormously. It speaks to a modern philosophy that sees the world as a godless one, with no rhyme or reason, a brief and often seemingly pointless struggle against many odds just to exist. At its most political it can embrace any idealism that puts the individual first. At its most personal it is perhaps best exemplified in the fine writing of philosopher Albert Camus, whose nihilistic treatise *The Myth of Sysiphus* [iii] finds a way forward in a bleak and otherwise apparently unforgiving, godless landscape. In this long essay Camus uses the Greek myth to sum up human existence: it tells of a man condemned to spend eternity rolling a rock up a hill, only to have it plunge back

Camus

Camus himself wrote several plays, the best known of which are *Le Malentendu* (1944), *Caligula* (1945), *State of Siege* (1958) and *Just Assassins* (1958).

down to the start once more, each time he nears the summit. In a world devoid of spirituality, Camus sees this myth as a suitable metaphor for life, but finds redemption in the concept that whilst life is little more than this, it is, however, the struggle that is undertaken by the individual that is important, and not any end result. Thus mankind finds dignity and meaning in the battle for survival itself.

Plays that typify the absurdist notion include Ionesco's *Rhinoceros* and Beckett's *Waiting for Godot* – although as we shall see, it is important to remember that neither Beckett, nor Ionesco, nor any others that followed, saw themselves as part of any movement, let alone one called 'absurd'. It is a useful way to help us understand the general philosophy of an era, but one that we should not feel tied to.

As an insight into the breadth of his vision it is worth noting that Esslin's book includes chapters on Beckett, Adamov, Ionesco and Genet (qqv), and that he also features the following playwrights: Jean Tardieu, Boris Vian (qv), Dino Buzzati, Ezio d'Errico, Manuel de Pedrolo, Fernando Arrabel (qv), Max Frisch (qv), Wolfgang Hildesheimer, Günter Grass (qv), Robert Pinget, Harold Pinter (qv), N.F. Simpson (qv), Edward Albee (qv), Jack Gelber, Arthur Kopit (qv), Slawomir Mrozek, Tadeusz Rózewicz and Václav Havel (qv). In addition Esslin also mentions the plays of Jean-Paul Sartre (1905–80), Jean Anouilh (1910–87) and Albert Camus (qv).

Although the playwrights listed above are all grouped together in the name of absurdism, it has to be noted that they cover quite a period of time. The first of them come from a setting of great change in the arts, and subsequent talents may well have been influenced by the literary freedom opening up around them. Certainly at the turn of the twentieth century a number of bold new ideas in art can be

seen as catalysts within all fields of creative thinking: dadaism, surrealism, cubism, impressionism, and other non-figurative movements had their adherents and counterparts in the world of dramatic art.

Interestingly, if we refer to the previous chapter we will not have to look far to see that a platform was already in existence for the staging of the plays of the absurd. They may not have intended it to be so, but designers and theorists such as Adolph Appia and Edward Gordon Craig (*see* page 170) had already almost inadvertently provided one. In their work they used the great plays of the past – *Oedipus* and *Hamlet* – to provide their models, but in fact, as well as these classic texts, the new plays of the avant-garde also came to benefit from the new freedoms of expression that their work proclaimed. In many ways the one seems to be inherently suggested by the other, as if the time was simply ripe for such artistic liberation.

Eugène Ionesco (1912–94)

Although of Romanian birth, Ionesco became one of France's greatest playwrights, and he is undoubtedly the first, and definitely one of the greatest, of the absurdists. His work challenges theatrical conventions, and strives to deal in an unreal manner with the dilemmas of existence. In his works real settings are peopled with the bizarre and imaginative. A common theme is that of the inability of man to communicate with man – and this is not altogether surprising, because Ionesco never really planned to be a writer of plays, falling into the profession almost by accident. He did not start writing until he was thirty-six years old, and most of his works were first written as short stories. It is perhaps precisely because of his understanding of

Ionesco on Show

Amongst Ionesco's short pieces are two sketches written for special occasions. *Impromptu pour la Duchesse de Windsor* was written for a party given for the exiled Duke and Duchess of Windsor in 1957. *Foursome* (*Scène à quatre*) was written for the political summit meeting at the Spoleto Festival in 1959.

the absurdity of trying to communicate ideas using such a medium, that he invented such a memorably idiosyncratic dramatic method when he did so.

Ionesco's early works are all short, and they include a set of seven sketches written in 1953, which sum up much of the 'absurdity' of his oeuvre. They include one in which a man chooses a new car, only to find out that he has really been purchasing a girl (*The Motor Show*), and another where the main character is eventually revealed to the audience to be headless (*The Leader*). One protagonist, called Berenger, a comic fool, appears in a number of plays, including his masterpiece, *Rhinoceros*, of 1960. Other plays for which Ionesco is especially renowned are *The Bald Prima Donna* and *The Chairs*.

PLAYS

EARLY SHORT PLAYS:
These were never more than a single act:

The Bald Prima Donna (*La Cantatrice Chauve*) (1950)

The Lesson (*La Leçon*) (1951)

The Chairs (*Les Chaises*) (1952)
An old married couple go about the business of preparing a room for a meeting, addressing phantom people and manipulating an ever-increasing number of real chairs.

Jack, or the Submission
(*Jacques, ou la Soumission*) (1953)

Victims of Duty (*Victimes du devoir*) (1953)

The Future is in Eggs (*L'Avenir est dans les oeufs*) (1957)
Written as a sequel to *Jack, or the Submission*.

Frenzy for Two, or More (*Délire à deux*) (1963)

The Gap (*La Lacune*) (1966)

FULL-LENGTH WORKS:
Amédée; or, How to get rid of it (*Amédée, ou Comment s'en Débarrasser*) (1954)
Ionesco's first full-length piece, featuring an ever-growing corpse and the problems of its disposal.

The New Tenant (*Le Nouveau Locataire*) (1955)
In which a simple and polite tenant is gradually buried under an increasing amount of furniture!

Improvisation, or the Shepherd's Chameleon (*L'Impromptu de l'Alma, ou le caméléon du berger*) (1956)

The Killer (*Tueur sans gages*) (1958)
The first play to feature Berenger as the main protagonist.

Rhinoceros (1960)
As described above, one of Ionesco's masterworks. Again Berenger is featured, this time becoming the only one to hold out against an ever-insistent trend to metamorphose into a rhinoceros. In general terms the play can be seen as the eternal battle of the rights of the individual against the society within which he lives.

Exit the King (*Le Roi se meurt*) (1962)
Berenger appears for a third time in this play.

A Stroll in the Air (*Le Piéton de l'air*) (1963)
Ionesco's most commercially successful play, once again featuring Berenger.

Thirst and Hunger (*La Soif et la Faim*) (1966)
In this play the character of Berenger takes centre stage once more.

Wipe-Out Games (*Jeux de Massacre*) (1970)
A play loosely based on Daniel Defoe's *A Journal of the Plague Years* of 1722.

The Mire (*Le Mire*) (1972)

The list of dramatists of the absurd provided by Martin Esslin (quoted on page 190) is by no means complete; below is more detail on some he does include, plus a few others:

Arthur Adamov (1908–70)
A Russian-born French playwright whose famous absurdist pieces include *The Parody* (1950), *Professor Taranne* (1953) and *Ping Pong* (1955). Subsequent

works turned towards the Brechtian Epic model (*see* page 177) – for instance *Paolo Paoli* of 1957.

Jean Genet (1909–86)

Genet was a French novelist who later turned to the medium of drama, and whose work startled audiences with its often bizarre absurdity. A great follower of Artaud, Genet lived much of his life outside convention, being condemned as a criminal on a number of occasions, and serving ten prison sentences. Amongst his other claims to fame Genet's criminal activities included begging, theft, forgery, drug smuggling, operating as a male prostitute, and deserting from the French Foreign Legion. His famous works include *The Maids* (1947), *The Balcony* (1956), *The Blacks* (1958) and *The Screens* (1961).

Fernando Arrabel (b. 1932)

A Spanish writer, exiled to France during Franco's reign in his native country; he was most renowned for his absurdist, blasphemous, eroticized dramatic work, in particular *Car Cemetry* (*Le Cimetière des Voitures*) of 1958. Other works include *Picnic on the Battlefield* (1959) and *The Architect and the Emperor of Assyria* (1967).

Friedrich Durrenmat (1921–90)

A Swiss dramatist whose work in German shows clear influences of Bertolt Brecht and his fellow expressionists, and yet is also clearly definable as being of the modern absurdist era. His best known play is *The Physicists* (*Die Physiker*) of 1962. Other works include *Mr Mississippi's Marriage* (1952), *The Visit* (1956) and *The Meteor* (1966).

Max Frisch (1911–91)

Swiss-born novelist and playwright who, along with Durrenmat, led the wave of absurdist drama in Germany. Best known for his plays *Biedermann and the Firebugs* of 1958, and *Andorra* of 1961. Other works include *Now they Sing Again* (1945) and *The Great Wall of China* (1946).

Günter Grass (b. 1927)

German playwright and foremost a novelist, best known as a novelist for *The Tin Drum*, and as a playwright for *The Plebians Rehearse the Up-rising* of 1966 which, whilst securely in the absurdist tradition, also has much in common with the work of Bertolt Brecht (qv).

Boris Vian (1920–59)

French novelist and playwright, and follower of Alfred Jarry (qv), most famous for his play *The Empire Builders* (*Les Bâtisseurs d'Empire*; *ou*, *le Schmürz*) of 1959. Other plays include *The General's Tea-Party* of 1967. Less notoriously than Genet above, Vian also had many strings to his bow, namely engineer, jazz musician, singer, actor, artist and pornographer.

N.F. Simpson (b. 1919)

A very English playwright, best known for his surreal comedies *A Resounding Tinkle* (1957) and *The One-Way Pendulum* (1959). Both of these works poke fun at the English Establishment and traditions, as well as taking apart the conventions of the well made play. Other plays include *The Cresta Run* (1965) and *Was He Anyone?* (1972).

Václav Havel (b. 1936)

Czech dramatist, poet and civil rights campaigner, whose satires fit neatly into the absurdist tradition and yet also suggest the political expressionism of Brecht. His early works include *The Garden Party* (1963), *The Memorandum* (1965) and *The Increased Difficulty of Concentration* (1968). These pieces deal with a number of issues that interested Havel, not the least of which was the manner in which language can debase the human spirit, particularly in a political and quasi-scientific manner. In *The Memorandum* he invents an obscure and bewildering scientific language called Ptydepe, which simply defeats the logic of all that come into contact with it.

Havel was exiled from Czechoslavakia after the Soviet invasion of 1968, writing outside his country such anti-totalitarian pieces as *Large Desolato* (1984) and *Temptation* (1985). On returning to his native land he was imprisoned for his outspoken criticisms of the government, from 1979 until 1983 and then again in 1989. However, on the fall of the Soviet regime, he was elected president in 1989, and continued to serve in this post even after the reconstitution of the country as the Czech Republic in 1993.

Samuel Beckett (1906–89)

Perhaps the greatest playwright who can clearly come under the banner of the absurd, and whose work expresses perhaps one of the farthest limits of this genre, is Samuel Beckett. In his greatest plays he abandons the conventions of characterization, plot development, and even that of action itself, and creates a truly new landscape for the idiom of theatrical performance.

Many of Beckett's plays contain brutal evocations of the pointlessness, or struggle, of living. Any positive aspects within the works have the same bleak quality as Camus' nihilistic optimism (*see* page 189). In his works, Beckett creates a barren landscape within which he places battered and worn individuals, struggling to make sense of their lives whilst often strangely accepting of their fates. At the same time the plays can evoke great humour, often rising to a macabre hilarity. The onlooker to these modern tragedies can only wonder at the depth of poetical understanding and vision. The works are abstrusely original, bizarre in many ways, and absolutely inimitable.

Amongst the plays one, *Waiting for Godot*, can rightly be described as the pinnacle of achievement in the surreal or absurd, and possibly the greatest play of the twentieth century. Certainly it goes far to describe the human condition as it seems to have been best understood for most of the later part of the century.

As his work progressed, Beckett seemed to refine his message into shorter and shorter statements – one of his last works, *Breath*, takes roughly thirty seconds to perform – see below. Samuel Beckett was awarded the Nobel Prize for Literature in 1969.

PLAYS

Waiting for Godot (1952)

Two tramps on a highway, beside a lone tree, contemplate the absurdity of life whilst waiting for the title character, in some way their superior, Mr Godot, to arrive. We learn in the play that not only will Mr Godot not arrive, he has never, on any other similar occasion, arrived, and will actually never arrive. Nevertheless it is important to wait for him. Why the tramps wait, and what for, is never made clear; they entertain themselves and observe others

– two characters Lucky and Pozzo pass by twice – violently linked to each other, and their situation only deteriorates with time. This grand and savage comedic existential metaphor brilliantly holds one's attention whilst simultaneously convincing one of the hopelessness of life's bleak travail.

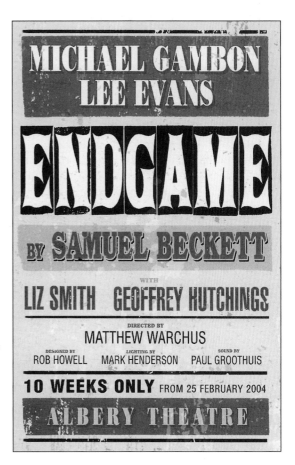

Endgame – *the poster from a recent West End production.*

Endgame (1957)

Another grand metaphor, in this case featuring an enclosed world – a bleak room with high windows, a wheelchair-bound blind man, his servant, and his two parents both confined to dustbins. As with many of his works, communication, or properly non-communication, is a central theme.

Act without Words I (1957)
This play and its sequel are short, mimed pieces with no dialogue.

Act without Words II (1959)

Krapp's Last Tape (1958)
A man sits before a tape recorder and tapes his last thoughts on life.

Happy Days (1961)
With a sublimely ironic and reflective title, this play concerns a central character, a woman, reviewing the experiences of her life and in particular her marriage. In the first act she does so whilst buried up to her waist in a mound of sand. Her husband, who does not speak, can be seen to be just out of her reach, behind her, facing away and similarly buried. The tragedy of her life continues to be revealed in the second act where we discover her now buried up to her neck. The conclusion, both physically and metaphorically, is only too obvious. Once again, and as in many of Beckett's works, the text allows plenty of scope for moments of surprising comedy, amongst an otherwise revealing tragedy of human existence.

Play (1963)

Come and Go (1966)

PLAYS FOR RADIO:
All That Fall (1957)

Embers (1959)

Words and Music (1962)

Cascando (1963)

Breath (1969)
At thirty seconds long, possibly the shortest published work. A pile of rubbish is the setting, and the play consists of a breath in, a scream and a breath out: a simple metaphor for the brevity and squalor of life.

Not I (1971)
A woman's mouth is all that we see in this piece, the rest of her remaining unlit. From the mouth cascades a torrent of words. In a tour-de-force of stream of consciousness, the woman's every immediate thought, her worries and panics – her life energy, is revealed. A dark, shadowy figure stands by and shrugs.

OTHER WORKS:
That Time (1976)

Footfalls (1976)
Like *Not I*, a monologue for the female voice.

Ghost Trio (1976)

...But the Clouds... (1977)

A Piece of Monologue (1980)

Rockaby (1980)
Another of Beckett's monologues for the female voice.

Ohio Impromptu (1981)

Quad (1982)

Catastrophe (1982)

Nacht und Träume (1983)

What, Where (1983)

Jerzy Grotowski (1933–99)
A Polish director who took as his starting point the philosophies of Antonin Artaud to create exciting experimental drama as part of the Polish Theatre Laboratory in Wroclaw during the 1960s. In some ways the most obvious heir to Artaud's work. In Grotowski the 'theatre of cruelty' found one of its most literal exponents.

Grotowski pioneered the use of non-verbal physical performance, used to assault the emotions of the audience in as visceral a manner as could be achieved. He promoted the use of bare stage settings,

Wyspiański

Stanislaw Wyspiański (1869–1907) was a Polish playwright best known for his versions of classical mythology used as allegories for Polish political issues; these included *The Legion* (1900), *The Wedding* (1901) and *Akropolis* (1903).

with very basic lighting and costume. Much of his work was concentrated on finding new and very raw physical means for the performers to convey the often brutal message of the plays. In his work the actor became the medium as well as the message, using gesture, mime, dance, abstract movement and other direct physical methods as visual metaphors. Playwrights chosen to be interpreted in this way were Calderón, Wyspiański and Shakespeare.

Grotowski toured his work throughout Europe and North America, and had a profound effect on many, including in Britain a young Peter Brook (qv) and in America the 'Living Theatre' (qv). He disbanded his company in 1976, and lived out the rest of his years in France. He published his ideas in a book *Towards a Poor Theatre* in 1968.

Peter Brook (b. 1925)

Brook also saw in Artaud an example worth exploring, and was particularly influenced by the 'Theatre Laboratory' of Jerzy Grotowski (qv). At the height of his more conventional work, within the traditional theatre system, Brook worked for the Royal Shakespeare Company (RSC) (qv), starting in 1946; he was subsequently appointed co-director with Peter Hall and Michael Saint-Denis in 1962.

For the RSC he famously directed a number of productions, finishing with his epoch-making production of Shakespeare's *A Midsummer Night's Dream* in 1970. Such was the success of this piece that it has forever after been referred to as 'Brook's Dream'. In his production Brook brilliantly reduced the essence of the piece to its simplest forms: the setting was a large white-walled space, the fairies played with simple conjuring tricks, made music by whirling plastic tubes, and everyone spoke the verse

clearly and unpretentiously. By thus cleaning away centuries of theatrical nonsense, Brook had rediscovered the strength and purity of the play itself – a play which, after all, would have been played to an audience without any tricks, on a bare stage, on an ordinary English Elizabethan afternoon.

Brook has written many pieces about his work; most famously his book *The Empty Space* (published in 1968) puts forward the argument for returning to a purer clarity in theatrical production, in which he describes theatre as being of four categories or types: Deadly, Holy, Rough and Immediate. He has written a number of other treatises, including *The Shifting Point* in 1988. Brook has also directed a number of films; most notably in 1962 he directed a version of William Golding's brutal novel *Lord of the Flies*.

In 1970 Brook was invited by the French government to set up a fully subsidized international theatre company in Paris. The International Centre for Theatre Research was thus created, and Brook has worked there ever since, continuing to expound on the ideas of Grotowski and others, and free to rehearse and develop his theatre without the constraints of having to produce something at regular intervals in order to make revenue. Nevertheless, every few years or so a new work does appear.

Notable productions directed by Brook include the following:

Dr Faustus by Marlowe

The Infernal Machine by Cocteau (*see* below)

Love's Labour's Lost for the RSC in 1946. Setting and costumes after the painter Watteau.

Jean Cocteau (1889–1963)

A French poet and novelist who started writing plays in answer to a challenge from the Russian choreographer Diaghilev. He then went on to direct and write films. His best known works are *Antigone* (1922), *Orpheus* (1926), *The Human Voice* (1930) and *The Infernal Machine* (1934).

Romeo and Juliet also for the RSC in 1947.

Salome Richard Strauss Opera for the Royal Opera, Covent Garden, in 1949, with designs by Salvador Dali.

Ring Round the Moon by Jean Anouilh; in 1950.

Measure for Measure in 1950.

Venice Preserv'd by Otway, at The Lyric Theatre in Hammersmith, London, in 1953.

The Dark is Light Enough by Christopher Fry in 1954.

The Lark by Jean Anouilh, in 1955.

Titus Andronicus in 1955.

Hamlet with Paul Scofield in the title role, in 1955.

King Lear, once more with Paul Scofield, in 1962, for the RSC.

The Marat/Sade by Peter Weiss. First directed by Peter Brook for the RSC in 1964, and taking as its underlying tenet the theatre of cruelty expounded by Artaud (qv). Set in an asylum for the insane in post-revolutionary France, it tells of the machinations of the inmates to perform for a group of honoured guests a play about the murder by Charlotte Corday of Jean-Paul Marat, the play being directed by one of the inmates – the notorious Marquis de Sade. Needless to say the ensemble treatment suggested by the piece, and taken further by Brook, produced a vividly harrowing experience.

'Marat' in Full

The full title of Peter Weiss's play, translated directly from the original German, makes it one of the longest in the English language; it is: *The Persecution and Assassination of Jean-Paul Marat as performed by the Inmates of Charenton Under the Direction of the Marquis de Sade.*

From a production of The Marat Sade *showing Marat. University Theatre, Manchester Drama Department.*

Us An experimental documentary concerning itself with the US war in Vietnam.

The Mahabharata (1989) An epic retelling of the Indian mythic cycle, lasting over nine hours.

Carmen (1989)

Hamlet (1995)

Joan Littlewood (1914–2002)

Littlewood was a British director who took many of the ideas of Brecht and utilized them to create a political drama for her own time and country. She formed her first company in Manchester in 1934 with her husband, the folksinger Ewan McColl: it was called the Theatre of Action, though later it became the Theatre Union, and then the Theatre Workshop. The company toured (including an appearance at The Moscow Arts Theatre) before moving into The Theatre Royal in Stratford East, London, in 1953 where it presented most of its famous work.

Aimed primarily at a working-class audience, Littlewood stressed the importance of improvisation and ensemble acting in her rehearsals of such plays as Jonson's *Volpone, Twelth Night* and Brecht's *Mother Courage*. She also pioneered new working-class writing in such pieces as Shelagh Delaney's *A Taste of Honey* (1958), Behan's *The Hostage* (1958) and Lionel Bart's *'Fings Ain't Wot They Used T'be'* (1959). Perhaps her most successful project was the anti-war documentary play *Oh, What a Lovely War!* (1963): this was later filmed, and the authorship credited to Joan Littlewood and the Theatre Workshop. The workshop disbanded in 1964, reappeared for a while in 1967, then finally closed in 1973.

Oh, What A lovely War *from a production directed by Richard H. Williams.*

Shelagh Delaney

Apart from *A Taste of Honey* in 1958, Shelagh Delaney (b. 1939) has written only two other stage plays: *The Lion in Love* (1960) and *The House That Jack Built* (1978).

THE ENGLISH TRADITION

The traditions of the English stage as personified by playwrights as diverse and universally talented as Shaw, Granville-Barker, Galsworthy, Coward and Rattigan (qqv) were advanced and challenged, as one would expect in this period, by those that followed. Mention has also already been made of the work of directors Peter Brook and Joan Littlewood, but naturally there were others, and particular companies that led the way.

The **Royal Shakespeare Company** (the RSC) came into existence in 1960, and has been the gauge by which all performances of Shakespeare are judged ever since. As a base it uses The Royal Shakespeare Theatre (RST), built in Stratford-upon-Avon – the birthplace of William Shakespeare. The RST started life as The Shakespeare Memorial Theatre, and was started by a local brewer, Charles Edward Flower, in 1864 to host a festival in honour of Shakespeare's 300th birthday. The first building, on the banks of the Avon, was opened in 1879, but this was burnt down in 1924 and was replaced. The new building was opened in 1932 and modified on a number of occasions, most notably by Barry Jackson in 1947, when the traditional proscenium stage of the original building was finally done away with. The open stage became home to the newly constituted Royal Shakespeare Company in 1960, under the direction of Peter Hall, later to be joined by Peter Brook (qv) and Peggy Ashcroft. Trevor Nunn took over from Peter Hall in 1968, and then in 1978 Terry Hands became co-artistic director. Since 1991 Adrian Noble has been in charge.

Whilst based in Stratford-upon-Avon the RSC has also played in various London theatres, including The Place and the Barbican Centre. Its War-

Oh, What A lovely War *from a production directed by Richard H. Williams.*

wickshire base has also expanded, with The Other Place and The Swan Theatre.

The **National Theatre**, in contrast, was a long-held pipedream of many. First thought of as early as 1848, the idea of a centre for excellence in the art of theatre was not really taken seriously until 1907 when the Shakespeare Memorial National Theatre Committee was founded. Then in 1944 a suitable site was offered on the South Bank of the Thames in London, and in 1962 a National Theatre Board was created, with Laurence Olivier as artistic director who, whilst waiting for funds to build a new theatre, took the company to a temporary home in The Old Vic Theatre. Olivier was succeeded by Peter Hall in 1975, and the company finally moved into its new building in 1977.

Posters and programmes from National Theatre and RSC productions.

It was incorporated as The Royal National Theatre in 1988, and is housed in a building containing three diverse theatre spaces: The Olivier is an open stage loosely based on the Greek theatre at Epidaurus, The Lyttelton has a more conventional proscenium space, and The Cottesloe is a large, multi-purpose studio space.

The **English Stage Company** was founded at the Royal Court Theatre in London in 1956, under the direction of George Devine (1910–66), its policy to explore and promote new dramatic writing. Thus Devine came to champion such artists as Osborne, Pinter and Bond (qqv). The Royal Court remains the home of the best of dramatic new writing in England, and serves, alongside many fringe theatres, as a promoter of the avant-garde, including, in recent years, the work of Sarah Kane, Mark Ravenhill (qqv) and many more. In addition the work done at The

Royal Court was influential in causing the end of the censorship of theatre in Britain in 1968.

Censorship Ends

In Britain in 1968 official state censorship, which had started in 1737 (*see* page 65), finally came to an end. By this date four officials worked under the Lord Chamberlain to check all new work for 'indecency, profanity, impropriety, sedition and libel'. The collapse of the notorious trial of Penguin Books for their publication of D.H. Lawrence's novel *Lady Chatterley's Lover* in 1960 had paved the way for a much more open and liberal attitude. Prior to this, several theatres, including The Royal Court, had got around the law by staging plays under the guise of a private club, for whom the law was different. Nevertheless these plays were often attended only too obviously by plain-clothes policemen checking that no other laws were broken.

The Theatres Act of 1968 did away with the notion that any work for the stage had to be inspected, and granted permission for performance before it could be attempted. After this date plays could only be prosecuted *after* they had been performed – that is, by people who thought an offence had occurred. This was very much the same as had been the case in the USA and other countries that had not had an official censor.

After 1968, plays in England came under the same legal protection as any other literature – namely the Obscene Publications Act of 1959. Obviously this did not mean that prosecutions could not occur; indeed, in 1980 Howard Brenton's play at The National Theatre, *The Romans in Britain*, became another *cause célèbre* when it was taken to court for indecency. The case centred around a scene within the play depicting male rape; it was eventually abandoned.

Inevitably as soon as the law changed, several pieces took deliberate steps to take advantage of their new freedoms. Two such to reach the West End stage, and notorious for liberal doses of full-frontal nudity, were *Hair* and *Oh Calcutta!*

Theatre in Education

Another movement of this period in Britain was the use of theatre as an educational tool. TIE originated in work by the company based at Coventry's Belgrave Theatre in 1965, and involved taking a company of actors into schools to perform work aimed at making an educational point, using theatre as an educational tool. 'Plays' on topics such as war, race, justice and bullying would be given a real context. The audience were often invited to participate, and role-playing was often a major part of this participation. Often the children would be introduced to characters without knowing that they were actors – in this way prejudices could be revealed and explored. TIE is now popular in many countries, including the UK, USA, Canada and Australia.

An example of this genre is a piece in which English junior schoolchildren (of six or seven years old) would find a native American Indian encamped in the school grounds. This character would talk to them, and engage them in some simple tasks. After the children have had a chance to befriend this character, another actor would appear as a traditional cowboy, and ask the children to help him capture the native Indian. The conflict and decision-making required of this activity, where the children have to take sides, becomes the focus of the 'performance' – which would be quite brief, and followed by discussion with the characters, and then classroom discussion with their own teachers.

THE NEW WAVE

John Osborne (1929–95)

Osborne, British dramatist and actor, is often single-handedly credited with the new era of British drama that followed the success of his play *Look Back in Anger* of 1956. The play epitomizes 'kitchen-sink drama' – plays set in everyday working-class life, and often dealing with the repressed anger of a class being subjugated by the traditions of the past. His work is also notable for its powerful speeches of bile-filled anger and bitterness, from the individual to society, and to his fellow man.

Osborne was initially a protégé of George Devine at The Royal Court, but went on to write for The National Theatre, and television. His later plays rarely compared with the strength of his work as a younger man.

PLAYS

Look Back in Anger (1956)
This play, more than any other at the time, defined a turning-point in English theatre, ushering in a new era of so-called 'kitchen sink' dramas. The play revolves around the character of Jimmy Porter and his failing attempts to get to grips with his life or relationships, and his preoccupation with what he sees as the failing society around him.

The Entertainer (1957)
This work compares the failing act of an old-fashioned music-hall comic, Archie Rice, with the withering and increasingly fading British Empire.

Epitaph for George Dillon (1958)
Originally written with Anthony Creighton in 1955.

The World of Paul Slickey (1959)
A less successful musical, written with Anthony Creighton.

Luther (1961)
A return to form, a really powerful play.

The Blood of the Bambergs (1962)
With the play below, written as *Plays for England*.

Under Plain Cover (1962)
See above.

Inadmissible Evidence (1964)

A Patriot for Me (1965)
Originally banned by the Lord Chamberlain.

A Bond Honoured (1966)

Time Present (1968)

The Hotel in Amsterdam (1968)

West of Suez (1971)

A Sense of Detachment (1973)

Watch it Come Down (1976)

Déjà Vu (1992)
A sequel to *Look back in Anger*, and Osborne's first stage work for sixteen years.

Harold Pinter (b. 1930)

Pinter is the British playwright who quickly established his reputation for tense, dramatic pieces enacted with only a small cast, pieces that revolve around the impossibilities of communication. Many of his works take apparently mundane, everyday events and characters and mould them into metaphors for the hopelessness of life's struggle. As such, his early work fits well into both the concept of absurdism and the prevalent English kitchen-sink drama of the day.

Pinter's works are also known as being imbued with an unspoken, subtle, underlying threat or menace, that can build into an intense dramatic crescendo. Part of this dramatic style is the 'Pinter Pause', where an apparently simple device, the pregnant pause, is used to create a build of tension – and ignored by directors and actors at their peril. The term 'Pinteresque' was also coined to suggest the creation of mood and atmosphere with cleverly understated and abstruse dialogue (with plenty of pauses!).

PLAYS
ONE-ACT PLAYS:
The Room (1957)
His first play.

The Dumb-Waiter (1960)
First performed with *The Room*.
A Slight Ache (1961)

Pinter on Film

Pinter has also had a successful career as a screenwriter, adapting many of his own plays as well as writing the screenplays for such successful films as *The Servant, Accident* and *The French Lieutenant's Woman.*

A Night Out (1961)

The Lover (1963)

The Dwarf (1963)

The Night (1969)

FULL-LENGTH PLAYS:
The Birthday Party (1958)
Pinter's first full-length piece.

The Caretaker (1960)

The Homecoming (1965)

Landscape & Silence (1969)
A double bill of short plays.

Tea Party (1970)
Originally written for television.

The Duchess (1970)
Originally written for television.

Old Times (1970)

No Man's Land (1974)

Betrayal (1978)

Family Voices (1980)

A Kind of Alaska (1982)

One for the Road (1984)

Mountain Language (1988)

Party Time (1991)

Moonlight (1993)

Ashes to Ashes (1996)

Celebration (2000)

The Birthday Party *from a production directed by Richard H. Williams.*

Edward Bond (b. 1934)

British playwright Edward Bond has produced uncompromising dramatic pieces concerned with a socialist didactic belief in the need to create change. As such, his work uses violent imagery and metaphor to make its point, most notably in *Saved*, where the infamous 'baby being stoned in its pram' scene was received uproariously when first shown to an unsuspecting Royal Court audience. Like many a playwright, Bond's work is perhaps not always consistent in its creative strength, but at its best its willingness to face hard truths and to pull no punches has produced some unique and powerful plays.

PLAYS
The Pope's Wedding (1962)

Saved (1965)

Early Morning (1968)

Narrow Road to the Deep North (1968)

Lear (1971)

The Sea (1973)

Bingo (1973)

The Fool (1975)

The Woman (1978)

The Bundle (1978)

ABOVE: **Early Morning** *from a production directed by John Adams.*

RIGHT: **The Sea** *from a production directed by David Sulkin.*

The Worlds (1979)

Restoration (1981)

Summer (1982)

In the Company of Men (1989)

September (1990)

Coffee (1994)

THE AMERICAN TRADITION AWAKES

Dramatic theatre of real consequence took a while to emerge in the USA because as a new country it took time to shake off the artistic influence of the 'mother country' and find its true voice. Dramatists of any real weight only came about in the USA in the middle and later part of the twentieth century, with artists of the stature of Eugene O'Neill, Arthur Miller and Tennessee Williams. However, America, too, has added one great genre of its own to the culture of the stage, and the world: the stage musical.

The Stage Musical

The intertwining of popular music and drama grew out of America's tradition of musical hall or burlesque song and dance. Starting as a form where a story was interspersed with relevant songs and dancing, it became a much more powerful vehicle when the songs clearly grew out of the drama itself, and then actually moved it on. Finally the form grew to include the 'sung-through' musical, in which no spoken dialogue occurs at all. This form, which owes some of its origins to Viennese operetta and the works of Gilbert and Sullivan, was initially always light in nature and thus originally known as 'musical comedy'. However, its growth into a more serious medium can be plotted with the

Cabaret *from a production directed by Robin Midgley.*

innovations of increasingly more rounded pieces, such as *Show Boat* (1928), *Oklahoma* (1943*)*, *West Side Story* (1957) and *Cabaret* (1966).

Today the 'musical' covers a wide range of productions and musical styles, including those of British composer Andrew Lloyd Webber (b. 1948), whose highly entertaining productions include *Jesus Christ Superstar* (1970), *Evita* (1976), *Cats* (1981), *Starlight Express* (1984) and *Phantom of the Opera* (1987). His work is in marked contrast to that of Stephen Sondheim (b. 1930), which has proved to be less popular, even though arguably more intellectually and musically challenging; Sondheim's musicals include *A Little Night Music* (1973), *Sweeney Todd* (1979), *Sunday in the Park with George* (1984), *Into the Woods* (1986), *Assassins* (1991) and *Passion* (1994).

A list of some more of the best musicals is an indication of the wealth of talent to be found in this genre:

The Black Crook (1886) Usually considered to be the very first proper 'musical'.

Show Boat (1928) By Jerome Kern.

Of Thee I Sing (1931) By George Gershwin.

Anything Goes (1934); *Kiss Me Kate* (1948) By Cole Porter.

The Boys from Syracuse (1938); *Pal Joey* (1940) By the team of Rogers and Hart.

Lady in the Dark (1941) By Kurt Weill, erstwhile partner of Bertolt Brecht (qv).

Annie Get Your Gun (1946), *Call me Madam* (1950) By Irving Berlin.

Oklahoma (1943), *Carousel* (1945), *South Pacific* (1949), *The King and I* (1951), *The Sound of Music* (1959) All by Rogers and Hammerstein.

On the Town (1944), *Wonderful Town* (1953), *West Side Story* (1957) By Leonard Bernstein.

Brigadoon (1947), *My Fair Lady* (1956), *Camelot* (1960) By the team of Lerner and Lowe.

The Boy Friend (1953) A British musical by Sandy Wilson.

Salad Days (1954) A British musical by Julian Slade.

Fings Ain't What they Used T'Be (1959), *Oliver* (1960), *Blitz* (1962) All by British composer Lionel Bart.

Funny Girl (1964) By Isobel Lennart and Jule Styne.

Fiddler on the Roof (1964) From Sholem Aleichem's stories, music by Jerry Block.

Hello Dolly (1965) An adaptation of Thornton Wilder's play *The Matchmaker* (qv) by Michael Stewart and Jerry Herman.

Mame (1966) By Lawrence and Lee, with music by Jerry Herman.

Cabaret, Chicago (1966) By the partnership of Kander and Ebb.

Hair (1967) By Galt MacDermot (*see* Censorship on page 199).

Oh Calcutta! (1969) A compilation of sketches about sex by various authors including Samuel Beckett, Tennessee Williams, and British critic Kenneth Tynan (1927–80).

A Chorus Line (1975) By Marvin Hamlisch.

Later musicals include the work of Andrew Lloyd Webber in England, and Stephen Sondheim in the USA. Other successful musicals in the same genre as Lloyd Webber included *Les Misérables* and *Martin Guerre*.

In the latter part of the twentieth century revivals became popular – and The National Theatre of Britain rediscovered and gave added respectability to *West Side Story* and *Carousel* amongst others, whilst The Donmar Theatre in London's West End continued to champion Sondheim's work under the leadership of director Sam Mendes.

In the 1990s nostalgia musicals became popular, written around the past catalogue of various pop legends; these included *Mama Mia*, based on the songs of Abba, *We Will Rock You* (2000) based on the work of rock band Queen, and *Tonight's the Night* (2003) based on that of rock legend Rod Stewart, both with books by British comedian and playwright Ben Elton. Also various films were successfully adapted for the stage, notably *The Lion King* (1999), *The Producers* (2001), *Chitty Chitty Bang Bang* (2002) and *Mary Poppins* (2004). In all, the musical remains a main crowd pleaser in most Western or Westernized capitals across the planet.

THE AMERICAN GREATS

Eugene O'Neill (1888–1953)

In straight drama the first real American star of the stage was Eugene Gladstone O'Neill. He was the son of a famous actor, James O'Neill. He flunked Princeton because he was too interested in 'wine, women and song', and became largely self-taught. He went prospecting for gold in Honduras in 1909, partly to escape a hasty marriage, and subsequently never got to know his son Eugene O'Neill Jr. He worked as a sailor, and then toured with his father James O'Neill. He worked briefly as a journalist in Connecticut, but then fell ill with tuberculosis; he wrote his first plays whilst convalescing from this illness. His work is highly influenced by his reading of the works of Ibsen and Strindberg.

James O'Neill

James O'Neill was born in Ireland, emigrating to the USA at the age of nine. His most famous role was as the hero of *The Count of Monte Cristo* (1883).

O'Neill's first full-length play *Beyond the Horizon* won great acclaim (*see* below), and in subsequent works he dealt with many large themes: racism, sexuality, human endurance and spirituality (or the lack of it). His style blends heart-wrenchingly honest naturalism with the use of persuasive symbolism. His later works became particularly autobiographical – for example, one of his greatest works, *Long Day's Journey into Night*, portrays family conflict very much based on his own. His work is not always easy, and many of his plays remained unperformed at the time of his death; but the passion evident within his works, and the manner in which they illuminate the essence of human struggle, won him the Nobel prize in 1936. At the end of his life O'Neill suffered from depression, Parkinson's disease and alcoholism.

PLAYS
EARLY PLAYS:
These short, one-act early works have been called the 'lost plays', and were written and then performed when O'Neill was a member of the Provincetown Players in Massachusetts from 1916. Many of these works tell stories written out of O'Neill's experiences at sea.

Thirst (1914)

Bound East for Cardiff; *Before Breakfast*; *Fog* (1916)

The Sniper; *In the Zone*; *Ile*; *The Long Voyage Home* (1917)

The Rope; *Where the Cross is Made*; *The Moon of the Caribbees* (1918)

The Dreamy Kid (1919)

O'Neill wrote two other works, *A Wife for Life* (c.1909) recorded as his first attempt at play writing but destroyed, and *Exorcism* (1920), an unpublished comedy based on his own attempts at suicide.

MATURE WORKS:
(The dates given are of the first performance)

Beyond the Horizon (1920)
O'Neill's first full-length play establishing him as a leading playwright and winner of the Pulitzer Prize.

The Emperor Jones (1920)
The success and failure of a negro ruler in the West Indies.

Diff'rent (1920)

Gold (1921)

The Straw (1921)
A dramatization of O'Neill's time in the sanatorium, and his illness.

The First Man (1921)

Anna Christie (1921)
One of O'Neill's most naturalistic works, and not unlike the work of Ibsen.

The Hairy Ape (1922)

Welded (1924)

The Ancient Mariner (1924)
An adaptation of Coleridge's poem and a production in which O'Neill prescribed the use of masks.

All God's Chillun Got Wings (1924)

Desire Under the Elms (1924)

The Fountain (1925)

The Great God Brown (1926)

Marco Millions (1927)

Strange Interlude (1928)
A Pulitzer Prize-winning play in which O'Neill experiments with stream-of-consciousness technique.

Lazarus Laughed (1928)

Dynamo (1929)

Mourning Becomes Electra (1931)
A fascinating and powerful adaptation of Aeschylus's Orestian trilogy (qv).

Ah, Wilderness! (1933)

Days Without End (1934)

The Iceman Cometh (1946)
One of O'Neill's greatest works.

A Moon Misbegotten (1947)

Long Day's Journey into Night (1956)
One of O'Neill's greatest works, and winner of the Pulitzer Prize.

A Touch of the Poet (1957)

More Stately Mansions (1963)

AN AMERICAN STYLE

In the post-war USA a new style of acting and directing became very influential in both stage and screen performing, known as 'the method'. It was based on the translated ideas of Stanislavky (*see* page 151), as found in his book *An Actor Prepares*; interestingly his later works, *Building a Character* and *Creating a Role*, were not to be found in the West until much later, and so in many ways 'the method' is based on only part of Stanislavsky's teachings. This may explain why 'the method' can be said to take a more extreme position than even Stanislavsky would have suggested.

Leading figures in this movement were directors Lee Strasburg (1901–82) and Elia Kazan (1909–2003), who in 1947 created the 'Actors' Studio', developing a training regime for actors that they described as based on 'the method'. The method took as its base the concept that all performance had to be totally rooted in the real experiences of the actor. Performers famous for being part of these classes were Marilyn Monroe, Karl Malden, Katherine Hunter, Eli Wallach, James Dean and Marlon Brando. Of these, the last two with their muttered, often seemingly shy performances, with underlying menace and sexuality, came to represent this movement most clearly.

Elia Kazan directed the first stage performance of *A Street Car Named Desire* as well as the film version. He also famously directed James Dean in *East of Eden*.

Tennessee Williams (1914–83)

Born in Columbus, Mississippi, and brought up in St Louis, Williams was, alongside Arthur Miller, the leading playwright of his generation. Born Thomas Lanier Williams, he adopted the name 'Tennessee' after the state in which he spent most of his youth in the early 1930s.

His works are steeped in the slow, lingering ennui of the deep south, in loneliness and despair, heavy with suggested and keenly observed sexuality, repressed emotion, and violence. His original and heavily plotted plays contain a poetic and alluring language not dissimilar to that of Federico Garcia Lorca, and with a similar use of symbolism.

Camino Real *from a production directed by Jenny Buckman.*

His best works also include brilliant descriptions of the mentally disturbed (*Glass Menagerie* and *A Street Car named Desire*). Williams' sister was herself committed to institutions, and Williams made use of his family for many other characterizations – one such being the domineering father in *Cat on a Hot Tin Roof*, partly based on his own aggressive father. Williams revealed himself to be a homosexual in his autobiographical writings, and this is clearly an underlying theme in many of his works.

PLAYS
Battle of Angels (1940)

The Glass Menagerie (1945)

A Street Car Named Desire (1947)

Summer and Smoke (1948)

The Rose Tattoo (1951)

Camino Real (1953)

Cat on a Hot Tin Roof (1955)

Orpheus Descending (1957)

Suddenly Last Summer (1958)

Sweet Bird of Youth (1959)

Period of Adjustment (1959)

The Night of the Iguana (1962)

The Milk Train Doesn't Stop Here Any More (1962)

Slapstick Tragedy (1966)

Two Character Play (1967)

In the Bar of a Tokyo Hotel (1969)

Clothes for a Summer Hotel (1980)

Arthur Miller (b. 1915–2005)

Miller's great works play to the idea of the normal man as tragic hero, and generally take as the root of the tragedy the failure of the American dream. His greatest work is *Death of a Salesman*, where Willie Loman (Low Man), the eponymous salesman, is brought to a state of desperation by an ill-fated belief in the capitalist system, with its false promise of great riches to those who simply work hard. Miller won the Pulizter Prize with this play, which, along with several others by Miller, also deals with the American family unit: its hopes, fears, failures and hypocrisies.

Miller sees in these stories of normal people confronting the stark realities of life, with its inherent charge of self discovery, the same passionate richness as in any of the great tragedies of literature. Willie Loman is his Julius Caesar, or King Lear. Loman is shown as the 'average Joe', yet Miller gives his wife the

The Crucible *from a production directed by Geoff Bullen.*

words that, even for his tragedy, 'Attention must be paid'. (This is picked up as a leitmotif by Stephen Sondheim in his musical *Assassins – see* page 205).

Miller's work is amongst the most powerful of the twentieth century, and could be said to encompass the same themes as Beckett (life's potentially destructive force), but in the naturalistic style of an Ibsen set in an all-American landscape.

PLAYS

The Man Who Had All the Luck (1944)
Miller's first play to get to Broadway, but one that closed after only four performances.

All my Sons (1947)
Miller's first real success, this play won the New York Drama Critics Award. The play tells of a family torn apart as a war veteran finds out that his father sold faulty aeroplane parts to the army during the war and inadvertently killed many men, among them his brother.

Enemy of the People (1950)
Miller's translation of Ibsen's play.

Death of a Salesman (1948)
See main biographical note above.

The Crucible (1953)
Set in 1692, Miller tells a story set in Salem during the witch-hunting years of the early part of American history. He uses the hysterically destructive force of this period as a powerful metaphor for the McCarthy anti-Communist House of Un-American Activity Committee trials of the 1950s, in which many people from the American arts scene, including Miller, were unavoidably caught up. In 1956 Miller was called to the HUAC because of his left-wing sympathies but, unlike some, he refused to name or involve anybody else in his testimony.

A View from the Bridge (1956)
Originally written as a one-act play in 1955, and dealing with the tragedy that befalls longshoreman Eddie Carbone when he finds he cannot control the lust he feels for his young niece. Another of Miller's 'tragedies of the common man'.

A Memory of Two Mondays (1955)
Originally produced alongside the shorter version of *A View from the Bridge*.

After the Fall (1964)
A patently autobiographical play, although Miller has denied this, concerned in part with his relationship with Marilyn Monroe (qv). (Arthur Miller was married to Marilyn Monroe from 1956–60. Monroe died two years after their marriage was dissolved.)

Incident at Vichy (1964)
About an incident that occurred during World War II dealing with Nazi persecution of the Jews.

The Price (1968)
A very telling piece about the legacy, both real and emotional, left to two sons by their father.

The Creation of the World and Other Business (1972)

Up from Paradise (1974)

The Archbishop's Ceiling (1977)

The American Clock (1980)

Playing for Time (1981)
A biographical play telling the story of the survival of individuals of an orchestra put together in Auschwitz from the inmates by the Nazi regime during World War II.

Danger: Memory! (1987)

The Last Yankee (1991)

The Ride Down Mt Morgan (1991, revised 1999)

Broken Glass (1994)

O'Neill, Williams and Miller represent very diverse dramatic styles, and are certainly the best writers of the period; but there were, of course, other notable American dramatists of the latter part of the twentieth century. Amongst these were **Clifford Odets** (1906–63), whose most notable play is *Waiting for*

Lefty (1935), and **Thornton Wilder** (1897–1975), whose famous works include *Our Town* (1938), *The Skin of Our Teeth* (1942), and *The Matchmaker* (1954), the last of which was the basis for the musical *Hello, Dolly!*.

Other playwrights of the USA:

Edward Albee (b. 1928)

A playwright distinctly in the absurdist mode, but with perhaps a more naturalistic bent than, say, Ionesco or Genet. His most famous works are the one-act *Zoo Story* (1959), *The Death of Bessie Smith* (1960), his masterpiece *Who's Afraid of Virginia Woolf?* (1962), and *A Delicate Balance* (1966).

His other works include *The American Dream* (1961), *The Ballad of the Sad Café* (1963), *Tiny Alice* (1964), *All Over* (1970), *Seascape* (1975), *The Lady from Dubuque* (1980), *The Man Who Had Three Arms* (1983), *Marriage Play* (1986), *Three Tall Women* (1990), *The Play about the Baby* (1996), *The Goat* (2000), and *Me, Myself and I* (2007).

Sam Shepard (b. 1943)

Actor and playwright Shepard's work includes the one-act plays *Cowboys* (1964), *Chicago* (1965) and *Icarus's Mother* (1965). His first full-length play was *La Turista* (1966), followed by *Operation Sidewinder* (1970), *The Curse of the Starving Class* (1977), *Buried Child* (1978 – this play won the Pulitzer Prize for Drama in 1978), *True West* (1980), *Fool for Love* (1983), *A Lie of the Mind* (1986), *Simpatico* (1994) and *Eyes for Consuela* (1998).

Arthur Kopit (b. 1937)

Kopit's plays include the accomplished absurd farce that made his name: *Oh Dad, Poor Dad, Mamma's Hung You In the Closet and I'm Feeling So Sad* (1960). Other works include *The Day the Whores Came Out to Play Tennis* (1964), *Indians* (1968), *Wings* (1979), *Nine* (1980), and a musical version of the *Phantom of the Opera* story called *Phantom* (1990) – not to be confused with the Andrew Lloyd Webber version.

David Mamet (b. 1947)

Plays include *Sexual Perversity in Chicago* (1974), which was filmed as *About Last Night* starring Rob Lowe and Demi Moore, and *American Buffalo* which

The Zoo Story *from a production directed by Cat Totty.*

has also been filmed (1975). Another of his plays, also filmed, was *Glengarry Glen Ross* (1983), which also won the Pulitzer Prize for 1984. Of his later works, *Oleanna* (1992) has attracted much praise. General themes running throughout Mamet's work are the failure of the American ideal, the contradictions of the sexual nature of humanity, and the inarticulate and often repressed expression of emotion, especially from the male of the species.

Other plays include *Duck Variations* (1971), *Squirrels* (1974), *A Life in the Theatre* (1976), *The Water Engine* (1977), *The Woods* (1974), *All Men are Whores* (1977), *Dark Pony* (1974), *Shoeshine* (1979), *Lakeboat* (1982), *Edmond* (1982), *The Disappearance of the Jews* (1983), *Speed-the-Plow*

(1987), *The Old Neighbourhood* (1991), *Ricky Jay and his 52 Assistants* (1994), *Death Defying Acts* (1996) and *Boston Marriage* (2000).

Conclusion

The twentieth century saw many changes in the way theatre was performed and received. For one thing, it became a part of the complex mass media that now surrounds our lives. Drama is, of course, a vital, ever-changing entity, and some would say a valuable force for change. The next chapter takes us forward into the present, and reviews those that have continued to use drama and see its continuing relevance to our lives.

11 PLAYWRIGHTS OF THE TWENTIETH CENTURY

I want to capture where we are now.
MARK RAVENHILL

INTRODUCTION

Writing about a period of time that has just passed, with a desire to treat it as fairly as any other historic period, is always problematic. The recent past seems so full of events, so much seems to have happened, that it is difficult to find a perspective from which to view it. In the following chapter I have concentrated on the main protagonists of the era, with simply a mention of those that worked alongside them. It is, of course, a purely subjective, and often personal, selection.

As we have seen throughout this history, playwrights produce their work as a result of the environment around them – they rebel against it, connive with it, and contribute to it. Commentators seek to make this work explicable by attaching labels, locating playwrights to specific periods and genres. However, whilst this is helpful in many ways, it is also always partly wishful thinking.

As we look at writers who are closer and closer to us in time, categorizing becomes almost impossible, as we are simply too close to gain any real historical perspective. In this chapter I have tried to make links, create order and summarize as best I can, but the reader must, as always, look to the work itself (the plays) for real evidence. To a greater extent than previously this chapter represents a personal selection, and I apologize if I leave out your favourite modern playwright. One thing is certainly true: that any writer worth mentioning includes, in even one work, any number of ideas and themes, and in a lifetime's work can cover a wide range.

THE POLITICAL STAGE

All dramatic art reflects the society around it, and in this context all plays can be described as political. Nevertheless some playwrights place this aspect of our existence in the foreground of their works – indeed we have already discussed one of the greatest exponents of this in Bertolt Brecht (qv). The following are dramatists of the modern era who have followed this trend, starting with three Irish playwrights. A number of Irish playwrights, including George Bernard Shaw himself, have found a dramatic cause in writing about the troubles of the Irish people, and their way of life. It is a tradition that has occupied many, and is no better illustrated than by the work of Synge, O'Casey and Behan. Their often brutally honest work can also be considered as continuing the cause of naturalism.

J.M. Synge (1871–1909)

John Millington Synge was born in Dublin and wrote poetic dramas set in the rural community of his native land. They include *In the Shadow of the Glen* (1903), *Riders to the Sea* (1904), *The Well of Saints* (1905), *The Playboy of the Western World* (1907) – his most famous and enduring work – *The Tinker's Wedding* (1908) and *Deirdre of the Sorrows* (1910).

The opening night of Synge's *Playboy of the Western World* in the famous Abbey Theatre in Dublin caused a riot, as Irish nationalists objected to the

OPPOSITE PAGE: **Installation 496 *(2004)*, *a play based on the designs of takis, celebrates the birth of Sophocles 1,500 years before.***

overly realistic portrayal of Irish life, in particular to mention of the undergarments of the women folk! Interestingly an almost identical riot was to occur nearly twenty years later for the opening night of one of the plays of our next dramatist.

Sean O'Casey (1880–1964)

O'Casey's works are saturated with the experience of living in an impoverished Dublin, and the cause of Irish nationalism. Most of his major works were produced initially at The Abbey Theatre in Dublin, and it was here on the first night of his work *The Plough and the Stars* in 1926 that a riot occurred.

Setting for Peter Oyston's** **Playboy of the Western World.

The play is set during the anti-British Easter uprising of 1916, and nationalists were outraged at the way O'Casey included the realistic themes of whoring and looting in the play: they felt that a great cause had been sullied. After The Abbey refused his next play, on artistic grounds, O'Casey moved to England, seldom returning to his native land. O'Casey's later works can be seen as explorations into a more expressionistic (qv) realm.

PLAYS
The Shadow of a Gunman (1923)

Juno and the Paycock (1924)

The Plough and the Stars (1926)

The Silver Tassie (1928)

Within the Gates (1934)

The Star Turns Red (1940)

Purple Dust (1940)

Oak Leaves and Lavender (1947)

Red Roses for Me (1946)

Cock-a-Doodle Dandy (1958)

The Bishop's Bonfire (1961)

Brendan Behan (1923–64)

A quintessentially Irish dramatist who used his experiences as a member of the IRA to furnish his plays. He was twice gaoled, and died an alcoholic. He wrote only a few pieces in an obviously busy life, but they proved very telling. They were *The Quare Fellow* (1954), *The Big House*, a play for television (1957), *The Hostage* (1958) and *Richard's Cork Leg* (1964), which was left unfinished at his death.

Dario Fo (b. 1926)

Fo is an Italian playwright and actor whose work has combined a comic genius with a strong political didactic. Along with his wife, the highly regarded performer France Rame, Fo's political cabaret style developed slowly into increasingly dramatic form. His work attacks Fascism, organized religion and other institutions that infringe personal liberties. His plays create brilliant, sparkling, slapstick comedy based on the individual's struggle against the status quo. The plays are peopled with corrupt policemen, politicians and priests, all conniving to undo the good of the common man. These universal themes have seen his plays performed with great success internationally. Fo was awarded the Nobel Prize for Literature in 1997.

MAJOR WORKS
Archangels Don't Play the Pin-Tables (1959)

Seventh: Thou Shalt Steal a Little Less (1964)

Mister Buffo (1969)

Accidental Death of an Anarchist (1970)

Can't Pay, Won't Pay (1974)

Trumpets and Raspberries (1982)

The Open Couple (1987)

Brian Friel (b. 1929)

An Irish dramatist and author, born in Omagh in Northern Ireland, Friel's work deals with the country of his birth, its people and their identity within the British Isles. The 'Irish Problem' features in many of his plays, the political English/Irish relationship being central to many. Others deal exclusively with the way of life of his native country, its people and its history. Friel has also translated works by Turgenev and Chekhov, and the influence of these writers is obvious in the gentle comedy of manners that many of his plays contain.

PLAYS
This Doubtful Paradise (1959)

Philadelphia Here I Come! (1964)

The Loves of Cass McGuire (1966)

Lovers (1967)

Crystal and Fox (1968)

The Gentle Island (1971)

The Freedom of the City (1973)

Volunteers (1975)

Living Quarters (1976)

Aristocrats (1979)

Faith Healer (1979)

Translations (1980)

The Communication Chord (1983)

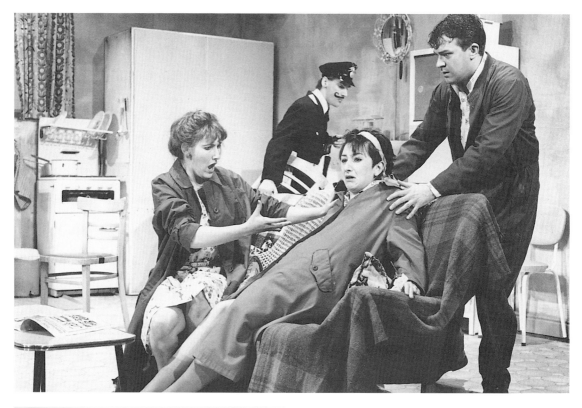

ABOVE: **Can't Pay, Won't Pay** *from a production directed by Richard H. Williams.*

LEFT: **Accidental Death of an Anarchist,** *directed by Peter Fieldson.*

Making History (1988)

Dancing at Lughnasa (1990)

Wonderful Tennessee (1993)

Molly Sweeney (1995)

Give Me Your Answer Do (1998)

John Arden (b. 1930)

Arden is a British playwright and novelist whose work came to the fore with The Royal Court Theatre in the 1950s. His work has a distinctly Brechtian feel to it: for example, in perhaps his most famous piece

Serjeant Musgrave's Dance of 1959. Arden also worked for the RSC. He has written many pieces for radio, and has written several pieces with his wife, the Irish dramatist Margaretta D'Arcy, developing an ever-strengthening belief in the need for revolution in the Irish situation. In his life and works Arden has displayed and followed strong beliefs in Marxist drama, and in promoting this has, to all intents and purposes, retired from mainstream public life, preferring to work with amateur groups.

PLAYS

All Fall Down (1955)
Performed as an amateur play in Edinburgh by students. Arden was studying architecture at the Edinburgh College of Art at the time.

The Life of Man (1956)
A play written for radio.

The Waters of Babylon (1957)
Arden's first professionally staged play.

Live like Pigs (1958)

Serjeant Musgrave's Dance (1959)

The Happy Haven (1960)
Written with Margaretta D'Arcy.

The Workhouse Donkey (1963)

Armstrong's Last Goodnight (1964)

Left-handed Liberty (1965)

The Hero Rises Up (1968)

The Island of the Mighty (1972)
Written with Margaretta D'Arcy.

The Ballygombeen Bequest (1972)

The Non-Stop Connolly Show (1975)

Vandaleur's Folly (1980)

Howard Brenton (b. 1942)

A British playwright whose often brutal portrayal of life's extremes, and overtly political themes, have been considered controversial as well as highly effective. He was resident playwright at the Royal Court (qv) from 1972–73, and wrote his first successful plays for this institution. Brenton has co-written several works with David Hare, and several satirical pieces with the journalist Tariq Ali. He has also translated works by Brecht and Brüchner.

PLAYS

Ladder of Fools; *Winter, Daddykins* (1965)

It's My Criminal (1966)

A Sky-Blue Life (1967)
Adapted from stories by Gorky.

Gargantua (1969)
Adapted from the novel by Rabelais.

Gum and Goo; *Christie in Love*; *Revenge*; *Heads and the Education of Skinny Spew* (1969)

Fruit; *Wesley* (1970)

Scott of the Antarctic; or, What God Didn't See; *Hitler Dances*; *How Beautiful with Badges* (1971)

Measure for Measure (1972)
Adapted from the work by Shakespeare.

A Fart for Europe (1973)
Written with David Edgar.

Magnificence; *Mug* (1973)

Brassneck (1973)
Written with David Hare (qv).

The Churchill Play (1974)

The Saliva Milkshake (1975)
An adaptation of the novel *Under the Western Sky* by Conrad.

Government Property (1975)

Weapons of Happiness (1976)

Epsom Downs (1977)

The Romans in Britain (1980)

The Genius (1983)

Sleeping Policemen (1983)
Written with Tunde Ikoli.

Bloody Poetry (1984)

Pravda (1985)
Written with David Hare (qv).

Greenland (1988)

Iranian Nights (1989)
Written with Tariq Ali.

H.I.D. (Hess is Dead) (1989)

Moscow Gold (1990)
Written with Tariq Ali.

Berlin Bertie (1992)

Kit's Play (2000)
Commissioned for the Royal Academy of Dramatic
Art to open their new Jerwood Vanbrugh Theatre
after a substantial refurbishment and rebuilding
programme; the play features a contemporary
story running parallel with a story concerning
Christopher Marlowe.

David Hare (b. 1947)
A writer whose work has overtly political themes
inclining strongly to the left wing of the British political spectrum. Hare's beliefs were particularly to the
fore in work he wrote whilst the Conservative government were in power under Margaret Thatcher. He
summed up much of what he thought about the state
of the nation in his trilogy focusing on the great institutions: *Racing Demon*, about the Church of England,

Murmuring Judges concerned itself with the British
legal system, and *The Absence of War* about the failings
of the Labour Party. The fourth estate – journalism –
was also dealt with in his play *Pravda*.

Hare also directs, and has directed, plays by
Brenton, with whom he has also co-authored.
David Hare was knighted for his services to the
theatre in 1998.

PLAYS
Slag (1970)

Brassneck (1973)
Written with Howard Brenton (qv).

Knuckle (1974)

Fanshen (1975)

Teeth 'n' Smiles (1975)

Plenty (1978)

A Map of the World (1982)

Pravda (1985)
Written with Howard Brenton (qv).

The Secret Rapture (1988)

Racing Demon (1990)

Murmuring Judges (1991)

The Absence of War (1993)

Skylight (1995)

Amy's View (1997)

The Blue Room (1998)

Via Dolorosa (1998)

My Zinc Bed (2000)

The Permanent Way (2003)

From **The Secret Rapture** *by David Hare.*

Other writers in this genre include David Edgar (b. 1948), whose work includes *Dick Deterred* (1973), *Destiny* (1976) and *Entertaining Strangers* (1985), although perhaps his best known work is the adaptation of *Nicholas Nickelby* (1980) written for, and memorably staged by, the RSC.

SOCIAL COMMENTARY

Obviously the many plays mentioned above often include a great deal of social comment, rather than overt political polemic. Often the playwright's desire is to inform about the human conflicts within a social setting by detailing the lives of the people caught in their particular circumstances. The following group of writers does just this.

Federico Garcia Lorca (1898–1936)

An important playwright and poet who, like many discussed above, also produced work of a lasting nature during the first half of the twentieth century, but this time from the civil-war torn country of Spain. Lorca's plays are deeply rooted to his country and its people. The works are hugely realistic, and yet also contain superb earthy and lyrical dialogue and settings, and powerful symbolism.

Lorca is best known internationally for three powerful tragedies: *Blood Wedding* (1933), *Yerma* (1934) and *The House of Bernarda Alba* (1936). In all these works Lorca deals with the oppression of the individual by tradition, and the narrowness of a life led with blind obedience to custom. The role of women is central to these works, like many of Ibsen's greatest plays, and they also contain a similar sense of the desire to rebel in order to realize the

219

Dona Rosita, the Spinster *from a production directed by Alby James.*

richness and joy of life. Powerful appetites and desires are never far beneath the surface.

The last of these plays was completed shortly before Lorca was murdered in mysterious circumstances by Spanish nationalist sympathizers, and the world lost a unique and powerful voice.

Other plays written by Lorca include:

The Butterfly's Curse (1920)
Lorca's first play.

The Billy-Club Puppets (c.1924)

Mariana Pineda (1927)
Lorca's first commercial success.

The Love of Don Perlimplín and Belisa in the Garden (1928)

The Shoemaker's Amazing Wife (1930)

Dona Rosita, the Spinster (1935)

Arnold Wesker (b. 1932)

A British playwright whose Jewish upbringing has led him to deal specifically in his work with the life of the Jewish community within the British culture. Many of his plays have an autobiographical flavour, and are set in the East End of London where he was brought up. His masterpiece begins the trilogy that first gained him critical success in 1958: *Chicken Soup with Barley*. Wesker's reputation rests on his first five plays, and as such his success has faded in later years, as he has gone somewhat out of fashion. He writes with a certain anger in his essays *Fears of Fragmentation* of 1970, about the manner in which his later work has failed to receive any acclaim from the critics. Nevertheless his plays are still performed, and *The Kitchen* was recently restaged at The Royal Court in London, to great acclaim.

PLAYS
The Kitchen (1957)

Chicken Soup with Barley (1958)
First part of a trilogy telling the story of a particular Jewish family in England between the years 1936 and 1959.

Roots (1959)
The second part of the trilogy, started with the play above.

I'm Talking About Jerusalem (1960)
The third part of the trilogy, started with *Chicken Soup with Barley*.

Chips with Everything (1962)

The Four Seasons (1965)

Their Very Own and Golden City (1966)

The Old Ones (1970)

The Friends (1970)

The Journalists (1972)

The Wedding Feast (1974)

The Merchant (1976)
Now retitled *Shylock*.

Love Letters on Blue Paper (1976)
Adapted from his own short stories.

One More Ride on the Merry Go Round (1978)

Fatlips (1980)
A play adapted from his own book for young people.

Caritas (1980)

Sullied Hand (1981)
A one-act play.

Mothers (1982)

Annie Wobbler (1983)
A full-length play that is part of Wesker's 'One Woman' cycle of plays that also includes one-acters: *Four Portraits – of Mothers, Yardsale, Whatever Happened to Betty Lemon* (1986) and *The Mistress* (1988).

Cinders (1983)
Based on the story of Madam Cynthia Payne.

When God wanted a Son (1986)

Badenheim 1939 (1987)
Adapted from Aharon Appelfeld's novel of the same name.

Lady Othello (1987)
Originally written as a film script.

Beorhtel's Hill (1988)
A community play.

Three Women Talking (1990)

Letter to a Daughter (1990)

Blood Libel (1991)

Wild Spring (1992)

Break My Heart (1997)

Denial (1997)

Longitude (2002)
Adaptation of the best-selling book by Dava Sobel.

David Storey (b. 1933)

British playwright and another 'child' of The Royal Court, indeed Storey's first play *The Restoration of Arnold Middleton* received its first production at the Court. Storey's works have since appeared in the West End, at The National Theatre and on Broadway. Generally speaking, his plays delve into the psyche of ordinary people in fairly ordinary situations. They are set at social events such as a wedding (*The Contractor*), or within institutions like a mental home (*Home*) or a Rugby club (*The Changing Room*). In particular his works look at the male of the species in varying degrees of social and mental isolation.

Storey is also famous as a novelist, and in particular for *This Sporting Life* (1960) which, like *The Changing Room*, builds on his experience as a professional Rugby League footballer. His other novels include *Saville*, which won the prestigious Booker prize in 1976.

PLAYS
The Restoration of Arnold Middleton (1967)

In Celebration (1969)

The Contractor (1970)

Home (1970)

The Changing Room (1971)

Cromwell (1973)

Life Class (1974)

Mother's Day (1976)

Sisters (1978)

Early Days (1980)

Phoenix (1984)

The March on Russia (1989)

Stages (1992)

THE INTELLECTUAL STAGE

Some writers, whilst not lacking in political knowledge and motivation, embrace a wider range of issues in their work. They tackle not only the inner life of their subjects, but the whole vast subject of *being*. The following could therefore perhaps be described as philosophers as well as playwrights.

Robert Bolt (1924–95)
British playwright whose subject matter was often historical, as with his best known piece *A Man for All*

Seasons, about the conflict between Sir Thomas Moore and King Henry VIII. It was successfully filmed starring Paul Scofield.

PLAYS
Flowering Cherry (1957)

A Man for all Seasons (1960)

The Tiger and the Horse (1960)

Gentle Jack (1963)

The Thwarting of Baron Bolligrew (1965)
A play for children.

Vivat! Vivat Regina! (1970)
A play about the relationship and conflict between Queen Elizabeth I and Mary Queen of Scots.

State of Revolution (1977)
A play that looks at the Russian revolution through the characters of Lenin and Trotsky.

The Lion in Winter

On similar historical lines to certain works of this genre is James Goldman's brilliant play dealing with the Christmas of 1183 in the life of Henry II, *The Lion in Winter*.

Peter Shaffer (b. 1926)
Like Robert Bolt, Shaffer often takes historical characters and settings for his plays; his most famous work is *Amadeus*, about Mozart. This play, and several others, have been made into powerful and effective films. Shaffer's work has also encompassed intense psychological thrillers (*Equus*) and high comedies (*Lettice and Lovage*). He was knighted for his services to theatre in 2001.

PLAYS
Five Finger Exercise (1958)

Anthony Shaffer

Peter Shaffer's twin brother Anthony Shaffer (1926–2004) also wrote plays; he is most known for his thriller *Sleuth* (1970) that was filmed starring Laurence Olivier and Michael Caine.

The Private Ear with *The Public Eye* (both 1962)
Two one-act plays staged as a double bill.

The Merry Roosters Panto (1963)
A piece written for Joan Littlewood's theatre workshop (qv).

The Royal Hunt for the Sun (1964)
A historical drama set in the land of the Aztecs at the time of the conquistadorial conquest by Pizarro of Spain.

Black Comedy (1965)
A one-act comedy where the protagonists suffer an electrical black-out, the trick of the play being to reverse the situation, so that the lights come on when they fuse so that the audience can enjoy the dilemma unfolding before them.

The Warning Game (1967)
Another one-act comedy.

White Lies (1967)
A one-act play.

The Battle of Shrivings (1970)
The first full-length piece from Shaffer since 1964 was met with a mixed reception, and has been seldom revived.

Equus (1973)
A deeply psychological study of a boy in great trauma. Fascinatingly staged with humans playing the roles of the horses necessary to the story. Filmed in more naturalistic mode with Richard Burton in the role of the psychologist.

Amadeus (1979)
See general biographical note.

Lettice and Lovage (1988)
A light comedy.

The Gift of the Gorgon (1992)

Tom Stoppard (b. 1937)

British playwright born in Zlin, Czechoslovakia, with the name Tom Straussler, Stoppard is perhaps the most profound of the so-called intellectual writers in this section. His first plays were immediately acclaimed and identified as clearly in the absurdist tradition. Throughout his career his love of games, both verbal and mental, has involved him in writing plays that ask quite profound questions and deal with many of the great and fundamental issues, including the very nature of the cosmos. Such conceits are usually deeply entwined within light but beautifully constructed comedies that often take their fun from a robust analysis of the theatrical conventions within which they are steeped.

Stoppard has also been responsible for a number of very effective screenplays, some of them adaptations. They include *Empire of the Sun* and *Shakespeare in Love*. He was knighted for his services to drama in 1997.

PLAYS
Rosencrantz and Guildenstern are Dead (1966)
A sparkling comedy based on two of the minor characters from Shakespeare's *Hamlet*, and dealing brilliantly with the art and artifice of the world of the stage play and existence itself.

Enter a Free Man (1968)
Originally written in 1964 and seen on television as *A Walk on Water* in that year, this play was produced later under the new title, following the success of *Rosencrantz and Guildenstern* above.

The Real Inspector Hound (1968)
A one-act comedy in which two critics become fatally involved with the play which they have come to review.

223

Neutral Gound (1968)
Written for television.

After Magritte (1970)
A masterpiece of the absurd.

Jumpers (1972)
A study of intellectual profundity and philosophy set within the conventions of a murder mystery.

Travesties (1974)
A play that lays bare the philosophies of such great thinkers as Lenin, Tristan Tzara and James Joyce.

Dirty Linen (1976)

New Found Land (1976)

Every Good Boy Deserves Favour (1977)
A musical play that deals with serious issues within a Soviet mental hospital. The play is written for a company of actors and a full classical orchestra.

Professional Foul (1977)
A play written for television.

Night and Day (1978)

Dogg's Hamlet (1979)

Cahoot's Macbeth (1979)

Undiscovered Country (1979)
A play adapted from a play by Austrian playwright Arthur Schnitzler (qv), *Das Wiete Land*.

On the Razzle (1981)
An adaptation of a comedy (*Einen Jux will er sich machen*) by the master of Austrian farce Johann Nepomuk Nestroy (1801–62).

The Real Thing (1982)
A study of marital disharmony.

The Dog it was that Died (1982)
A play written for radio.

Dalliance (1986)
Another play adapted from a work by Schnitzler (qv): *Liebelei*.

Hapgood (1988)
A wonderful 'take' on the spy story.

Arcadia (1993)

Indian Ink (1995)

The Invention of Love (1997)
A play about the poet A.E. Housman.

The Coast of Utopia (2002)
A trilogy of plays: *Voyage*, *Shipwreck* and *Salvage*. Premièred at The Royal National Theatre

Christopher Hampton (b. 1946)

British playwright, and another whose work was first developed at The Royal Court Theatre in London, where he was resident dramatist from 1968–70. His plays cover a diverse number of subjects, but in them, Hampton generally combines comedy with insightful characterization and dramatic situations to reveal the absurdities and nuances of human existence. His most famous work is the adaptation of Laclos' novel *Les Liaisons Dangereuses*, which has been staged several times and successfully filmed. Hampton is also a prolific translator of other work, including plays by Chekhov, Ibsen, Molière, Horvath and Yasmina Reza (qqv). He also wrote the book and lyrics, alongside Don Black, for Andrew Lloyd Webber's musical *Sunset Boulevard* of 1993.

PLAYS
When Did You Last See My Mother? (1966)
His first professionally staged play, performed at The Royal Court.

Total Eclipse (1968)

The Philanthropist (1970)

Savages (1973)

Treats (1976)

After Mercer (1980)

Tales from Hollywood (1982)

Les Liaisons Dangereuses (1986)

White Chameleon (1991)

Stephen Poliakoff (b. 1952)

A British playwright who writes powerful plays on serious political issues, and the human dilemmas involved in them. He was 'writer in residence' at The National Theatre when he wrote *Strawberry Fields* in 1977, and has since gone on to write and direct for television and film.

PLAYS
Hitting Town (1970)

The Carnation Gang (1973)

Heroes (1974)

City Sugar (1975)

Strawberry Fields (1977)

Shouting Across the River (1978)

Favourite Nights (1981)

Breaking the Silence (1984)

Coming in to Land (1987)

Playing with Trains (1989)

Sienna Red (1992)

Blinded by the Sun (1996)

Talk of the City (1998)

Michael Frayn (b. 1933)

A British playwright born in London, Frayn read philosophy at Cambridge University, and the sense of inquiry that this suggests pervades his works, as does a keen sense of humour. He worked initially as a journalist before publishing novels, and then plays. As well as his own works he has also translated a number of Russian classics by Chekhov and Tolstoy.

PLAYS
Alphabetical Order (1975)
His first play, set in a newspaper office.

Clouds (1976)

Donkey's Years (1977)

Make or Break (1980)

Noises Off (1982)
A brilliant farce that shows a play being performed both in front and behind the scenes, going from rehearsal in Act 1, behind the scenes in Act 2, and a disastrous performance in Act 3. One of the most commercially successful plays of modern times.

Benefactors (1984)

Look, Look (1990)
A less than successful comedy in which an audience is invited to watch an audience who is watching an unseen play.

And Here (1993)
Another comedy, and also not a great success. A play entirely in the present tense.

Copenhagen (1998)
Based on the 1941 meeting between German physicist Werner Heisenberg and his Danish counterpart Niels Bohr.

Democracy (2003)
Based on documented fact, this play is set in the Germany of Willy Brandt, and involves his relationship with his personal assistant, who was also a spy.

MODERN COMEDY

Many of the previous playwrights, Shaffer, Stoppard and Frayn amongst them, have used comedy rather than tragedy to get their points across, and a number of other writers have used comedy as the means to communicate with an audience, Neil Simon in the USA, and in the UK, Alan Ayckbourn are the most prominent.

Alan Ayckbourn (b. 1939)

A British playwright and an enormously prolific writer of successful comedies. His comedy derives from the machinations of the English working classes, and is often said to reveal the underlying stresses and hopelessness of this existence. Despite the seriousness of this intent, however, the works are also often undeniably hilarious, and a sense of farce is never far away. Ayckbourn also enjoys setting himself complex and technically difficult tasks to pull off: *The Norman Conquests* trilogy, for example, sees the same story from three different settings within the same house, whereas *House and Garden* takes this even further, being two separate plays that can be staged simultaneously, with characters moving from one to the other in the same plot.

Ayckbourn's popularity reached a crescendo in 1975 when he had five plays running simultaneously in London's West End! Since 1970 he has had his own theatre to play with, as artistic director of The Stephen Joseph Theatre in Scarborough. He was knighted for his services to theatre in 1997.

PLAYS
The Square Cat; Love After All (both 1959)

Dad's Tale (1960)

Standing Room Only (1961)

Christmas V Mastermind (1962)

Mr Whatnot (1963)

Relatively Speaking (1965)
Originally entitled *Meet my Father.*

Relatively Speaking *from a production directed by Michael Simpkins.*

The Sparrow (1967)

How the Other Half Loves (1969)

The Story so far... (1970)
Retitled twice as *Me times Me Times Me* and then *Family Circles.*

Time and Time Again (1971)

Absurd Person Singular (1972)

The Norman Conquests
A trilogy made up of *Table Manners* (1971), *Living Together* (1973), *Round and Round the Garden* (1973).

Absent Friends; *Confusions* (both 1974)

Jeeves (1975)
Rewritten in 1975 as *By Jeeves.*

Bedroom Farce (1975)

Just Between Ourselves (1976)

Ten Times Table (1977)

Joking Apart (1978)

Sisterly Feelings; *Taking Steps* (both 1979)

Suburban Strains; *Season's Greetings* (both 1980)

Way Upstream; *Making Tracks* (both 1981)

Intimate Exchanges (1982)
A set of eight plays.

It Could be Anyone of Us (1983)

A Chorus of Disapproval (1984)

Woman in Mind (1985)

A Small Family Business; *Henceforward...* (both 1987)

Man of the Moment (1988)

Mr A's Amazing Maze Plays
A work written for a young audience.

The Revenger's Comedies; *Invisible Friends* (both 1989)

Body Language; *This is Where I came in* (both 1990)

Callisto 5 (1990)
Rewritten in 1999 as *Callisto 7.*

Wildest Dreams; *My Very Own Story* (both 1991)

Time of my Life; *Dreams from a Summer House* (1992)

Communicating Doors; *Haunting Julia*; *The Musical Jigsaw Play* (all 1994)

A Word from our Sponsor (1995)

The Champion of Paribanou (1996)

Things we do for Love (1997)

Comic Potential; *The Boy who fell into a Book* (both 1998)

House and Garden (1999)
A duo of plays: *House* and *Garden* that can be played simultaneously; they have even been played in two adjoining auditoriums.

Virtual Reality; *Whenever* (both 2000)

Damsels in Distress (trilogy) (2001)
The trilogy is made up of *Gameplan*, *Flatspin* and *Roleplay.*

Snake in the Grass; *The Jollies* (both 2002)

Orvin – Champion of Champions; *Sugar Daddies*; *My Sister Sadie* (all 2003)

Willy Russell (b. 1947)

A British playwright whose comedies derive from, and are often set in, his native working-class background in Liverpool. He has also had great success with musicals.

227

PLAYS

John, Paul, George, Ringo... And Bert (1974)
A musical about The Beatles.

One for the Road (1980)

Stags and Hens (1978)
A comedy set in the male and female toilets of a night club.

Educating Rita (1980)
A brilliant comedy dealing with the often strained relationship between a fading university tutor and his working-class mature student, Rita. A play that transferred most successfully on to film, starring Michael Caine and Julie Walters.

Blood Brothers (1983)
A stage musical, still running in London's West End.

Shirley Valentine (1986)
A full-length play for one woman, and also successfully filmed starring Pauline Collins.

Dancing through the Dark (1989)

Mike Leigh (b. 1943)

Leigh is a British playwright who has developed his own style for creating works of dramatic art. Born from the improvisational techniques that came to the fore in the 1960s, partly from the 'method' work of the 'Actors' Studio' under Lee Strasberg (qv), Leigh's work involves the entire cast being rehearsed in character and required to improvise within certain situations. If the piece is about couples meeting, then Leigh will work intensively with the actors playing the couples, often in different locations, in order to fully develop their relationships, before introducing them to the other characters. Since the late 1980s Leigh has worked mostly on film.

Abigail's Party *from a production directed by Peter Fieldson.*

STAGE PLAYS:
Bleak Moments (1970)

Wholesome Glory (1973)

Babies Grow Old (1974)

Abigail's Party (1977)

Goose-Pimples; *Greek Tragedy* (both 1981)

It's a Great Big Shame (1993)

John Godber (b. 1956)

Godber is a British writer who founded the Hull Truck Theatre Company in 1984, and also writes for television. His bold ensemble northern comedies have found great favour and are often revived.

PLAYS
Up 'n' Under (1984)

Bouncers (1986)

Teachers (1987)

On the Piste (1993)

Weekend Breaks (1997)

Yasmina Reza (b. 1960)

Reza is a French playwright, director and actor. Her philosophical comedies have found international success, winning many awards.

PLAYS
Conversations After a Burial
(*Conversations après un enterrement*) (1987)

ART (1994)

An Unexpected Man (*L'Homme du hasard*) (1997)

Life x 3 (*Trois Versions de la Vie*) (2000)

THE FEMALE VOICE

In this history it has been noticeable that few women dramatists seem to have been held in high esteem. Even within the categories above, only Yasmina Reza has been found. However, during the later part of the last one hundred years the female of the species has been able to strike out independently in many fields, and drama is one of them. I have put them together for no other reason than to make clear their existence; their work covers many areas.

Pam Gems (b. 1925)

A British playwright whose work clearly embraces the feminist cause, before tackling other issues. Much of her work is biographical in nature.

PLAYS
My Warren (1973)

After Birthday (1973)

The Amiable Courtship of Ms Venus and Wild Bill (1975)

Dusa, Fish, Stas, and Vi (1975)
An overtly feminist piece, with strong female characters sharing a London flat, and Gems' first commercial success.

My Name is Rosa Luxemburg (1976)
A biography of its title character.

Queen Christina (1977)
An epic biographical play, first staged by the RSC.

Piaf (1978)
A vivid biography of the French *chanteuse*.

Camille (1984)
Also written for the RSC.

Loving Women (1984)

The Danton Affair (1986)
Also written for the RSC.

Stanley (1995)
A play based on the life and work of painter Stanley Spencer.

Marlene (1997)
A biographical play about Marlene Dietrich.

Caryl Churchill (b. 1938)

A British playwright whose work combines a serious attention to the political nature of life in her native country with a strong feminist integrity. The first seven of her works below are all strongly concerned with the plight of women, often in a historical context. Churchill has also experimented with various theatrical devices – for example in *Cloud Nine* she cross-casts the two sexes, with men playing women's roles and vice versa, whereas *Serious Money* is written in bold rhyming verse. Her early work was with two of the UK's leading touring theatre companies: Monstrous Regiment, and the Joint Stock Theatre Company.

PLAYS
Owners (1972)

Objections to Sex And Violence (1974)

Vinegar Tom; *Light Shining in Buckinghamshire* (both 1976)

Cloud Nine (1978)

Top Girls (1982)

Fen (1983)

Softcops (1984)

Serious Money (1987)

Mad Forest (1990)

Lives of the Great Poisoners (1991)

The Skier (1994)

Blue Heart (1997)

Far Away (2000)

Timberlake Wertenbaker (born *c.*1955)

A British playwright, although born in the USA and brought up in France, Wertenbaker has also been promoted through the good services of The Royal Court Theatre in the UK, for whom she was 'writer in residence' from 1984–85. She has also written for the RSC (*The Love of the Nightingale*). Alongside her many original works she has also adapted novels (*The Playmaker*) and reworked versions of many Greek legends. She has also been responsible for many fine translations of works by Sophocles, Euripides, Marivaux and Anouilh.

PLAYS
The Grace of Mary Travers (1985)

Our Country's Good (1988)

The Playmaker (1988)
An award-winning play adapted from the novel by Thomas Keneally.

The Love of the Nightingale (1988)
Written for the RSC, and based on the Greek legend of Philomel.

Three Birds Alighting on a Field (1991)

Credible Witness (2001)

Other Women Writers

Less prolific but equally powerful women writers of this period include: Shelagh Delaney (b. 1939), whose works include *A Taste of Honey* (1958), *The Lion in Love* (1960) and *The House That Jack Built* (1978); Nell Dunn, best known for her play *Steaming* (1981); Sheena MacDonald (b. 1960), whose best known work is *When I was a girl I used to Scream and Shout*; and Charlotte Keatley (b. 1960) with her wonderful play *My Mother Said I Never Should*.

Screen Writers

As noted above, many writers of stage plays also produced work for radio, television and film. This study does not have the space to deal with all of those that work in these media alone, but several are worthy of note, and they include Dylan Thomas, Dennis Potter and Alan Bleasdale (b. 1946). Thomas is best known for his beautifully poetic play *Under Milkwood*; Potter for his wonderfully original television scripts, although he did also write for the stage; and Bleasdale is known for his hard-hitting political television works such as *The Boys from the Blackstuff* and *GBH*, and whose stage plays include *No More Sitting on the Old School Bench*, *Having A Ball* (1981), *Are You Lonesome Tonight?* (1985), and *On the Ledge* (1993). There is also the work of Alan Plater, Peter Flannery and Donna Francheschild.

SEXUAL POLITICS

The sexual revolution of the twentieth century also put this most intimate form of human communication on the agenda. Here, then, are a few writers whose main interest was often in displaying the best and the worst excesses of this aspect of human nature.

Joe Orton (1933–67)

A very British writer of comedies, and one who sought to expose the hypocrisy of his times, and test the limits of what was allowable on stage. Yet Orton was also a writer who kept very much in touch with the common spirit of British humour – the spirit of the saucy postcard, or the *Carry On* movies. Orton's homosexuality, at a time when this was still considered unacceptable, was one of the driving forces behind his work. Another such force was his relationship with his lover Kenneth Halliwell, a man who started as his champion and respected elder, and ended as his nemesis. Halliwell, in despair at what he perceived as the failing relationship with his lover, and undoubtedly jealous of Orton's rising star,

Orton's character Inspector Truscott from Loot *interrogates Kenneth Halliwell in Peter Fieldson's play* Black and Blue *about their fatal relationship.*

brutally murdered Orton, before taking his own life. What would have become of Orton's undoubtedly burgeoning talent will never be known.

PLAYS
Entertaining Mr Sloane (1964)

Loot (1966)

The Erpingham Camp; *Ruffian on the Stair* (both 1967)

What the Butler Saw (1969)
Produced posthumously.

For all his outrageousness, Orton's homosexuality remained reasonably well hidden under the veneer of his cleverly constructed plot lines. Later writers, in an increasingly liberal Western society, were able to be bolder, and as a result of this, many plays and their composers could be described under many diverse categories: thus plays have been produced under banners that announce them as gay, lesbian, feminist, black, Asian, and so on. But whatever classification is given them, either by the writers themselves or others, one thing is certain: the work when it is good, touches us all.

Sarah Kane (1971–99)

A writer of viscerally powerful works, Kane's plays shocked even the virtually unshockable audience of the première home of new and avant-garde writing, The Royal Court Theatre (qv) in London. Nearly all her works contain images of rape, torture and wild brutality of all kinds – although her last work, *Crave*, is a gentler piece about the search for love. Sarah Kane committed suicide in 1999. She said of despair and hope: 'To create something beautiful about despair, or out of a feeling of despair, is for me the most hopeful, life-affirming thing a person can do.'

PLAYS
Blasted (1995)

Phaedra's Love (1996)

Cleansed (1998)

Crave (1998)

4:48 Pyschosis (2000)
A play posthumously produced at The Royal Court in London.

Mark Ravenhill (b. 1966)

Another success of the new writing policy of The Royal Court Theatre, Ravenhill's work has attracted controversy and awards in equal measure. Many of his works deal truthfully with the often brutal world of sex and its consequences.

PLAYS
Shopping and Fucking (1996)

Faust is Dead (1997)

Handbag (1998)

Some Explicit Polaroids (1999)

Mother Clap's Molly House (2001)

CONCLUSION

As I write, the theatre of our today will only too quickly become the theatre of our yesterday. A single volume cannot possibly hope to be fully inclusive or totally international, nor can it ever be fully up to date. This last chapter has simply attempted to give a flavour of the dramatic work closest to us in time.

In this book I have attempted to give an overview of the important figures in the history of dramatic art; however, I know there are more plays and more playwrights that I have not included in this one volume, than those I have. My advice to those really interested in this work is to go and see it. Drama is about being in a theatre *watching* a performance, not reading about it: there is no substitute for this, and no other art form or experience quite like it. Go out and enjoy.

NOTES

CHAPTER 2: MEDIEVAL THEATRE

i   Glynne Wickham, *A History of Theatre*, page 80.
ii Glynne Wickham, *Stage and Drama Till 1660*, from Sphere *History of Literature in the English Language*, Vol 3, ed. C. Ricks, page 29.
iii Quoted from *Mediaeval Drama*, A.M. Kinghorn, page 117.
iv *Tudor Interludes*, ed. Peter Happé, *see* Bibliography.
v   NB. This text is also collected in Happé's book, *see* Bibliography.
vi Ibid.
vii Ibid.

CHAPTER 3: THE RENAISSANCE STAGE AND EUROPEAN THEATRE

i   Glynne Wickham, *A History of Theatre*, page 100.
ii Nash, *The Unfortunate Traveller*.
iii Milton, *Areopagitica*.

CHAPTER 4: THE ELIZABETHAN STAGE

i   Philip Stubbes, *The Anatomie of Abuses*, 1583.
ii Brian Morris, *Elizabethan and Jacobean Drama*, page 74 – from *Sphere History of Literature in the English Language*, *Vol. 3, English Drama to 1710*, ed. C. Ricks, Sphere, 1971.

CHAPTER 5: SHAKESPEARE AND HIS CONTEMPORARIES

i   From *Aubrey's Brief Lives*, c.1680, page 438, ed. Oliver Lawson Dick (Penguin).
ii Ibid., page 437.

CHAPTER 6: THEATRE OF THE ENGLISH RESTORATION

i   On *The Feign Innocence of Sir Martin Marr-all*, a play by the Duke of Newcastle in collaboration with John Dryden. From the *Diary of Samuel Pepys*, 16 August 1667.
ii Ibid. 2 March 1667.
iii *The Wordsworth Companion to Literature in English*, ed. Ian Ousby, page 696.

CHAPTER 7: THEATRE FOR THE MASSES: 1700–1890

i   Letter in *John Bull*, 25 January 1838.
ii *English Melodrama* by M.R. Booth, Herbert Jenkins, London, 1965.

CHAPTER 8: THE ORIGINS OF MODERN THEATRE: NATURALISM

i   From preface to Thérèse Raquin by Émile Zola.
ii Letter to Adolf Paul, 6 January 1907. Quoted in *The Chamber Plays* by August Strindberg; Introduction by Evert Sprinchorn, page vii (E.P. Dutton & Co., Inc. 1962).
iii Letter to Adolf Paul, 6 January 1907. Quoted in *The Chamber Plays* by August Strindberg; Introduction by Evert Sprinchorn, page viii (E.P. Dutton & Co., Inc. 1962).
iv From the preface to *Miss Julie*, by August Strindberg.
v   *Modern World Drama, An Encyclopedia*, Myron Matlaw (Secker & Warburg, 1972), page 731.
vi Letter to Scherling, 7 April 1907. Quoted in *The Chamber Plays* by August Strindberg; Introduction by Evert Sprinchorn, page xix. (E.P. Dutton & Co., Inc. 1962).

vii Quoted in Shaw's *Sixteen self sketches*, Chapter 17.

viii The official web site of the Nobel Foundation, 2003.

CHAPTER 9: MODERN THEATRE: EXPRESSIONISM AND BEYOND

i *Modern Drama in Theory and Practice 3 – Expressionism and Epic Theatre*, J.L. Styan (Cambridge University Press, 1981) page 1.

ii Ibid, art critic Herbert Read, quoted on page 1.

iii Georg Büchner, *Semtiliche Werke und Briefe*, 4 vols (Hamburg 1967–71).

iv Ibid.

v *On the Art of the Theatre*, E.G. Craig (Heinemann, London, 1911), page 97.

vi Ibid, page 22.

vii *Artaud*, Martin Esslin (Fontana/Collins, 1976), page 13.

viii From *Aliéner l'Acteur*, May 1947.

CHAPTER 10: CONTEMPORARY THEATRE IN BRITAIN AND AMERICA

i *The Empty Space*, Peter Brook (Penguin Books, 1968), page 11.

ii *See* Bibliography for details.

iii *See* Bibliography for details.

BIBLIOGRAPHY

Andrewes, A., *The Greek Tyrants* (Hutchinson, 1956)

Aristotle, *On the Art of Poetry*, Trans T.S. Dorsch (Penguin Books, 1965)

Aubrey, John, *Brief Lives*. ed. Oliver Lawson Dick (Penguin Books, 1949)

Axton, Richard, *European Drama of the Early Middle Ages* (Hutchinson, 1974)

Barns, Philip, *A Companion to Post-War British Theatre* (Croom Helm, 1986)

Beadle, Richard, *The Cambridge Companion to Medieval English Theatre* (Cambridge University Press, 1994)

Bentley, Eric, *The Theory of the Modern Stage* (Penguin Books, 1968)

Beyer, Edvard, *Ibsen: The Man and his Work* (Souvenir Press, 1978)

Booth, Michael, *English Melodrama* (Herbert Jenkins, 1965)

Brandt, George W., *Modern Theories of Drama* (Clarendon Press, 1998)

Brecht, Bertolt, *The Development of an Aesthetic* (Methuen, 1957)

Brook, Peter, *The Empty Space* (Penguin Books, 1968)

Brook, Peter, *The Shifting Point* (Methuen, 1987)

Brook, Peter, *Threads of Time, A Memoir* (Methuen, 1999)

Brown, John Russell, *The Oxford Illustrated History of the Theatre* (Oxford University Press, 1995)

Brustein, Robert, *Who Needs Theatre* (Faber and Faber, 1987)

Camus, Albert, *The Myth of Sysyphus* (Penguin Books, 1955)

Carlson, Marvin, *Theories of the Theatre* (Cornell University Press, 1984)

Craig, Edward Gordon, *On the Art of the Theatre* (Heinemann, 1911)

Craik, T.W., *Minor Elizabethan Tragedies* (J.M. Dent & Sons Ltd, 1974)

Esslin, Martin, *Artaud* (Fontana/Collins, 1976)

Esslin, Martin, *The Theatre of the Absurd* (Penguin Books, 1961)

Ford, Boris (ed.), *The Pelican Guide to English Literature, 2 The Age of Shakespeare* (Penguin Books, 1955)

Grotowski, Jerzy, *Towards a Poor Theatre* (Methuen, 1968)

Happe, Peter (ed.), *Tudor Interludes* (Penguin Books, 1972)

Hartnoll, Phyllis (ed.), *The Concise Oxford Companion to the Theatre* (Oxford University Press, 1972)

Hartnoll, Phyllis, *The Theatre, A Concise History* (Thames & Hudson, 1968)

Harvery, Paul (ed.), *The Oxford Companion to English Literature* (The Clarendon Press, 1967)

Harwood, Ronald, *All the World's A Stage* (Secker & Warburg, 1984)

Hayman, Ronald, *Harold Pinter* (Heinemann, 1968)

Hodgson, John (ed.), *The Uses of Drama* (Eyre Methuen, 1972)

Horace: *On the Art of Poetry*, Trans T.S. Dorsch (Penguin Books, 1965)

Innes, Christopher, *Modern British Drama 1890–1990* (Cambridge University Press, 1992)

Jerome, Jerome K., *On the Stage and Off* (Alan Sutton, 1991)

Kahrl, Stanley J., *Traditions of Medieval English Drama* (Hutchinson, 1974)

Kinghorn, A.M., *Mediaeval Drama* (Evans Brothers, 1968)

Kitto, H.D.F., *Greek Tragedy* (Methuen, 1939)

Latham, Robert, *The Illustrated Pepys* (Bell & Hyman Ltd, 1978)

Law, J., Pickering, D. and Helfer, R. (eds), *The New Penguin Dictionary of the Theatre* (Penguin Books, 1988)

Longinus, *On the Sublime*, Trans T.S. Dorsch (Penguin Books, 1965)

Malone, Aubrey Dillon, *Stranger than Fiction, a book of Literary Lists* (Prion Books, 1999)

Matlaw, Myron, *Modern World Drama, an Encyclopedia* (Secker & Warburg, 1972)

May, Robin, *History of the Theatre* (WH Smith / Hamlyn, 1986)

Nagler, A.M., *A Source Book in Theatrical History* (Dover Publications, 1952)

O'Toole, John, *Theatre in Education* (Hodder & Stoughton, 1976)

Ousby, Ian (ed.), *The Wordsworth Companion to Literature in English* (Wordsworth Reference, 1994)

Palmer, Alan & Veronica, *Who's Who in Shakespeare's England* (Methuen, 2000)

Ricks, Christopher, *English Drama to 1710* (Sphere books, 1971)

Salgado, Gamini (ed.), *Four Jacobean City Comedies* (Penguin Books, 1975)

Salgado, Gamini (ed.), *Three Jacobean Tragedies* (Penguin Books, 1965)

Senelick, Laurence, *The Chekhov Theatre* (Cambridge University Press, 1997)

Stoppelman, Gabriela, *Artaud for Beginners* (Writers & Readers Publishing, 1998)

Styan, J.L., *Modern Drama in Theory and Practice 1 – Realism and Naturalism* (Cambridge University Press, 1981)

Styan, J.L., *Modern Drama in Theory and Practice 2 – Symbolism, Surrealism and the Absurd* (Cambridge University Press, 1981)

Styan, J.L., *Modern Drama in Theory and Practice 3 – Expressionism and the Epic Theatre* (Cambridge University Press, 1981)

Styan, J.L., *The English Stage* (Cambridge University Press, 1996)

Trussler, Simon, *The Cambridge Illustrated History of British Theatre* (Cambridge University Press, 1994)

Unwin, Stephen, *A Pocket Guide to 20th Century Drama* (Faber & Faber, 2001)

Wickham, Glynne, *A History of the Theatre* (Phaidon, 1985)

Zimmermann, Bernhard, *Greek Tragedy, An introduction* (The Johns Hopkins University Press, 1986)

INDEX

INDEX